"I WOULDN'T COUNT ON IT"
CONFESSIONS OF AN UNLIKELY FOLKSINGER

Also by Tom May

"Promoting Your Music-The Lovin' of the Game"
Routledge Publishers 2007

"I WOULDN'T COUNT ON IT"

CONFESSIONS OF AN UNLIKELY FOLKSINGER

TOM MAY

Blue Vignette
www.tommayfolk.com

Copyright © 2020 by Tom May

Front and back cover photos by Andy Pavuls, North Bay, Ontario, Canada
Cover and interior design by Masha Shubin | Inkwater.com

All rights reserved. No part of this book may be reproduced or transmitted in any form or by any means whatsoever, including photocopying, recording or by any information storage and retrieval system, without written permission from the publisher and/or author.

Publisher: Blue Vignette | www.tommayfolk.com

Paperback   978-1-7346819-0-1
Hardback   978-1-7346819-1-8
eBook   978-1-7346819-2-5

1 3 5 7 9 10 8 6 4 2

CONTENTS

Preface..ix
Freight Train: Omaha beginnings........................1
It Once was Mine: St. Louis...........................10
If you could read my mind: Lightfoot, learning, and
    Toronto, Canada..................................12
Gone But Not Forgotten: St. Louis.....................29
Plain and Simple Endings: Boston......................40
Vignette: St. Louis...................................52
Coming Home: Nebraska.................................65
It's Just Bessie and Me in Butte, Montana.............84
If it's all the same to you: River City Folk.........99
Open Spaces, Prairie Winds: Winterfolk...............129
Blue Northern..140
It's All for the Best: River City Folk on NPR........158
When His Lesson's Learned............................178
The River and The Road: Germany and RCF TV...........187
The Boardwalk at Skagway: The Omaha Symphony,
    Haines and Napa Valley...........................212
Cliff's Whiskers, Festival at the Fort...............234
The Weaver and the Loom..............................246
Yukon Journey, 45 Below..............................254
The Words Upon the Wire..............................291
Blue Roads, Red Wine (and a rose scented woman).....326
Thanks...355
Acknowledgments......................................367

SONG LYRICS

Vignette 48
The Ballad of the Horse Brass Pub .68
Bessie and Me 93
If it's All the Same to You 107
Blue Northern 154
Away from it All 166
The Boardwalk at Skagway 205
Yukon Journey, 45 Below 268
Rose of the Riverwalk 305
The Words Upon the Wire 322
Blue Roads, Red Wine 332
Celilo Falls 350
September 1862 360
Thanks 365

PREFACE

It was late at night, after a concert in Colorado Springs, Colorado, at the home of a thirty-something guy who had opened the show for me that evening. He had three kids, a wife, a good job, and a nice big house in the foothills of the Rockies (what Zero Mostel, of "Fiddler on the Roof" fame, once called "the whole catastrophe").

I uncorked the wine I had brought, and we all toasted to a successful show. He asked me about my life in music, the concerts, gigs, and festivals I had coming up, and about my songs and my albums. I tried to answer as humbly and honestly as possible, and a big smile came across his face.

"So that's what you have been doing all of your life – livin' the dream!"

My dear friend (and fine singer-songwriter) Chris Kennedy from Wyoming was there and had joined me on stage that night. My wife, Debbie, was also in the kitchen with us enjoying some vino after the festivities. Upon hearing that well-intentioned remark, we all looked at each other and couldn't help but crack up and try not to laugh out loud.

Also appropriate was a comment by a promoter in Alaska, who in reply to a question by traveling folksinger Bill Staines about whether there would be a good crowd at that night's show, said "I wouldn't count on it."

"I WOULDN'T COUNT ON IT" — CONFESSIONS OF AN UNLIKELY FOLKSINGER

I wish I could enumerate the times a promoter or concert presenter or bar owner said to me something like, "Lots going on in town tonight: Bert Cooties and the Klezmaniacs are doing their once a year reunion at the Pig Trough pub, and they draw big crowds," or "the Burning Stump High School football team is playing Valentine tonight, so we'll be lucky if anyone shows up."

Yes, it is many people's dream to sing and pick guitar for a living. Most of those are folks who can't imagine how difficult it is to do over the long term.

In 1972, I began a career that, like the vanished profession of the telegrapher, carriage driver, steam locomotive engineer, and so many others, is almost gone. The life of the full-time, traveling folksinger, who could somewhat support themselves with their art, did not exist at all until the mid-twentieth century and appears to me to now be fading away – but what a glorious life it has been.

This is not a memoir of great personal triumphs or "first I wrote this, and then I wrote that, then I ingested this drug, and then I got this award." I hope it portrays accurately the life of a constantly working, mostly solitary musician, plying both the big cities and back roads of North America. My purpose here is to tell a tale of some of the characters, geography, dear friends, gigs, songs, kind and tolerant women, and even a few memorable bottles of wine I have been lucky enough to experience.

BY THE TIME I came of age in the late 60's and early 70's, "folk-pop" music was still in vogue on top 40 radio stations; John Denver, Gordon Lightfoot, Cat Stevens could all be heard regularly on the airwaves across North America and beyond. Gas was cheap, rents were low, and you could still hitchhike with some degree of safety.

The drinking age had been lowered to 18 or 19 all cross the

Preface

U.S. and Canada, creating a huge new patronage for clubs and bars, many of which used music to lure young folks in the door. Colleges still featured concerts of acoustic music, and there were remnants of a coffeehouse/club circuit that had thrived in the 1960's.

Legendary venues like The Main Point in Bryn Mawr, Passim in Boston, Gerde's Folk City in New York, and the Earl of Old Town in Chicago gave young guitar players stages to aspire to, and there were also hundreds of lesser known venues that would hire a guy with a Martin guitar who could sing.

In the 1940's, Woody Guthrie and Pete Seegar had shown the way to a generation of youthful pickers, writing their own songs, playing older songs, and hoboing across the country with the purpose of singing their music, commenting on what they saw and seeing the country in an authentic style.

Before that time, this way to earn a living did not exist. There were minstrel shows and vaudeville, and there always have been folks who played and composed songs -- but like our great American troubadour Stephen Foster, many of those who tried to do music exclusively met unhappy ends or flat starved to death.

I came from a totally non-musical family. I fell in love with how the music made me feel, playing the guitar, and the joy of creating something I thought was beautiful. After 47 years of making a living with songs, I am as enamored of it as I ever was.

As a kid, my parents really never journeyed anywhere except to visit my grandfathers in Western Nebraska. Omaha, Nebraska was, and still is, a very provincial town, extremely conservative both politically and socially.

I knew I wanted to see and know more about the world, though I was unsure about how I would ever do that. Music was the magic carpet for me out of Nebraska, though I never had any idea when I was starting out how one song would lead to another. As my old friend from Texas, Alan Damron, used to say, "It was a hobby that got totally out of control." Given my background, it was indeed an unlikely destiny that I would become a wandering troubadour.

"I WOULDN'T COUNT ON IT" — CONFESSIONS OF AN UNLIKELY FOLKSINGER

Some people through the years have mentioned to me that I came along too late to be part of the real folk revival that occurred in the early 1960's, and I suppose that is true. Still, I was lucky enough to have the freest life, full of excitement, travel, and creativity, that one could ever hope for.

Though it hasn't been overly prosperous by monetary standards, I have never slept in the rain, starved or wanted for anything I really needed for my survival. Through dumb luck, perseverance, hardheadedness and belief in the inherent worth in the music I strived to present, I have been blessed beyond belief with the kind of riches that never rust or can be taken away: stimulating, fascinating friends, glorious sunsets, and often empty roads filled with momentous tales, romance and song.

Back then, we were not tethered by smart phones, the internet, computers, pagers, or even answering machines – we just lived the experience of each day. It is all I ever wanted to do, and I am grateful.

Since it has been a short period of time one could really do this for a living, I thought I would jot down some stories from my decades in this unusual profession. Some you might find funny, some odd, many of them poignant, I think – and some just plain strange anecdotes from this tiny subculture of a particularly offbeat way to make a few bucks and support one's self: as an Irish music pal once put it, negotiating this "music dodge."

At the bottom of it all was the certainty in my heart, over thousands of gigs of one kind or another, humble or grand, that this is music that truly does make a difference. You can see it on people's faces in the audiences, in their smiles and tears. I have read it in the letters of those who have taken the time to send me a note and tell me what a song has meant to them. In these tumultuous times we live in, amidst our hurried, distracted day to day, it has seemed a worthy and always-interesting way to spend a life.

My memory is still pretty good, but I will say that these stories and tales are, as John Steinbeck once prefaced in his book "Travels with Charlie"- "based on, but not restricted to, facts."

"I WOULDN'T COUNT ON IT"
CONFESSIONS OF AN UNLIKELY FOLKSINGER

FREIGHT TRAIN: OMAHA BEGINNINGS

AS I MENTIONED EARLIER, MY PARENTS WERE not musicians. Actually, there was almost no music in the house I grew up in save the AM radio in the kitchen. It was tuned to KFAB radio, which had mostly news and market reports from the Omaha stockyard and such, as well as a few of the top 40 songs of the day ("How Much is that Doggie in the Window" and other classics of that time).

My parents were not bad or abusive people: They kept a roof over my head and food on the table, but they were true Great Depression survivors, and the concept of a career in music was something that was far beyond their daily life experience or comprehension.

My mother, all of 4 feet, 10 inches, was born in a sod house and raised in an uninsulated boxcar with her father and two sisters. My father, 6 feet 4 inches, was abandoned by his mother as a child, and he kicked around with various relatives until he was able to bring in money as a Western Union messenger boy and later as

WITH MY DAD LYLE MAY, IN GRAND ISLAND, NE 1956

1

a telegraph operator. (Both Andrew Carnegie and Thomas Edison started their working lives this way.)

I remember being so in love with music from a very young age. I had one of those small plastic record turntables, a toy really, but I would listen to "The Ballad of Davy Crockett" over and over and knew all the words by heart by the age of five or six. Not exactly talent along the lines of Mozart, but I did have a real passion for most any music I got to hear, from Tennessee Ernie Ford to Jimmy Rogers, to eventually the Beatles and Chet Atkins.

When in the hospital for a minor surgical procedure at about seven or eight years old, I awoke from the ether to see a fellow with a pearl snap western shirt, boots and huge Gibson guitar at the foot of my bed. He was there as a promotional representative of Cudahy meats, which had a big packing house in Omaha, singing to kids. I was hooked – the sound of that big guitar and his voice a few feet away mesmerized me. From that day on, I knew I wanted to play music.

My mother, having lived such an uncertain, fearful life in so many ways, did all she could keep me home and under her thumb. On the other hand, they both believed in the liberating value of work since it had been hard to come by much of their lives. So, just after turning eleven, I was allowed to get a work permit and obtain a morning paper route, the necessary first step in those days to getting the cushy, more profitable evening paper route.

The morning paper route for the World Herald in Omaha was about five and a half miles long, with 50 or so subscribers and some very steep hills. I would get up before school about 4:30 AM get on my bike during decent weather (unless it was snowing too hard, in which case my dad would fire up the '56 Chevy and drive me), pick up the newspapers at the station drop-off point, and ride the bike and toss the papers on the quiet, early morning front porches.

You also had to go around later to each of those houses and collect for the cost of the papers. Some folks would pay a month in advance, but many did not – which would mean at least one extra trip to their house weekly, some evening after school or on Saturdays. I did that morning route Mondays through Saturdays for about six months until I graduated to an evening route.

Your pay was the difference between your cost of the newspapers and what the subscriber paid. On the morning route, I recall that being about $8 or $9 a week, or somewhere south of 30 cents an hour when you totaled it all up.

It was a little better on the evening route, which had about 100 subscribers over a much shorter distance and included the Sunday delivery. I remember pulling in a whopping $15 or so a week from that enterprise, though I think the hourly pay for both routes was probably similar.

However, it gave me freedom and a reason to get out of the house and away from my mother's smothering chains of overprotection. Before I began delivering papers, she was not usually amenable to even letting me go to neighborhood kids' houses – even when those houses were right next door.

So, when I began doing that paper route and had to bicycle miles to collect for the papers, I found I could steal some time for myself, too – perhaps a game of football in the street adjacent to ours with some guys I went to school with, or a stop at the gas station for a coke and a candy bar (a bad habit I would pay for later throughout my life, as I constantly fought my weight).

I went to a Roman Catholic grade school, taught by strict Ursuline nuns. We were allowed to start singing in the church choir in fifth grade. I recall the first time, as I was sitting in church listening to that choir, that I realized that part of the ensemble was singing a different note – my first appreciation of the concept of harmony.

It was a wondrous moment.

Right about that time, in one of the singing rehearsals at school a nun said to me, "You think you are a good singer, but you are not. You'll never be a good singer."

So much for encouragement.

Still, I loved using my voice and I continued to do it enthusiastically, every chance I had: in choir, on my paper route, chiming in with the tunes on the car radio, etc., generally annoying anyone within earshot.

Speaking of music in the car, my father would sometimes sing in our old '56 Chevy while we were waiting for my mom to finish shopping somewhere. He had a lovely, mellifluous voice. I recall him teaching me the chorus and singing "The Wabash Cannonball," "The Arkansas Traveler," and a few others – the first folksongs I ever heard or learned.

Those are special memories I have of my dad, though the singing episodes didn't happen very often.

I knew that somehow, I wanted to play a musical instrument, and between seventh and eighth grade I saw a way to begin. A junior high school, about a 45-minute, one transfer bus ride from my North Omaha home, was offering summer enrichment courses. One of them was beginning guitar. The cost for the four-week summer session was only $13. Of course, you had to have a guitar to play, too.

I had been diligently saving my money from my paper route, and after some heated discussion with my mother about how I should save my money and not spend it so frivolously, it was agreed I could buy, with my own funds, a guitar. I excitedly went to Hope's music in downtown Omaha and bought an inexpensive Stella guitar, about $40 with case. The door to my own life was opening.

The summer session was taught by a fellow by the name of Dean Britton. There were 30 or 40 rank beginners in that class, almost none of whom knew anything about the guitar, let alone how to tune it. The cacophony of all those dissonant instruments must have been maddening, but he seemed to take it all with good humor.

I remember him teaching all of us a few chords after we learned how to (roughly) tune our guitars. After at least some of the strings were sounding underneath our young fingers, he taught us "Tom Dooley," a hit for the Kingston Trio that had been on the radio earlier that decade, and a more challenging instrumental song, "Yellow Bird."

I practiced until my fingers bled and the paint started to wear off that cheap guitar's fingerboard, and I loved every second of it.

He was amazingly patient for someone who had worked as a professional musician. He hailed from across the Missouri River in Shenandoah, Iowa, residence of the Everly Brothers and their parents, who were also professional musicians. Dean had toured and worked with the Everlys and with other country bands, playing a big Gibson ES-355 electric guitar around Midwestern honky-tonks and dance halls.

After the month of summertime class lessons was done, Dean encouraged me to continue lessons at the same store where he worked and where I had bought the guitar. I figured I could afford a lesson or so a month on my meager paper route earnings, which was one of the best decisions I ever made.

Dean Britton was well versed in the finger style guitar playing that had been developed by first Merle Travis and refined by Chet Atkins and others, and that is what he taught his students. He also asked if you would rather learn by sheet music or by ear.

It was unusual to give kids a choice like that in those days. Learning chords by ear and showing you how to play was so much faster and more gratifying than learning from sheet music, and you immediately progressed without bring bogged down by essentially learning a foreign language.

I often have wished since then that I would have had an opportunity for a more traditional music background early on – it would have helped in many ways throughout my career. However, the excitement of actually making music so quickly on the guitar was more than worth the trade-off at the time.

Dean was a good teacher, an encouraging and inspiring presence in my young life. I learned the basics of finger style guitar – playing the bass with your thumb and the treble (melody) with your fingers, which would change my life and set me apart some from so many pickers.

I learned the basic Chet Atkins arrangements of "Freight Train," "Nine Pound Hammer," and others, which eventually would send me down the minstrel road with a performance tool most guitarists did not have. It has become even more uncommon to see guitarists play fingerstyle in recent years, and it really gave me a leg up early on.

When I would talk about becoming a professional musician someday, he warned me about the perils of that life – too much travel and too many temptations. I didn't understand or really listen to him then, though occasionally I have wished that I had heeded his words.

But I know deep down that I would not trade all of those landscapes, cities, women, books and late-night bottles of wine for a less adventurous, safer and more secure life.

My first public gig was playing at a Christmas midnight mass the year after I learned to play guitar. I was told the parish had been forced to get a special dispensation for me to play the guitar at a high mass, as having that instrument on the altar was not yet common or accepted as it soon would be.

I practiced hard. I enjoyed hanging around the Ursuline nuns' convent and rehearsing the songs for them. Even then, I had a fatal weakness for the fairer sex, though I wasn't exactly sure how their anatomy actually worked, under those voluminous black habits.

At one point they asked me to carry something downstairs for them, and I was shocked by seeing lingerie hanging from the clothesline in their basement. Of course, at that point, with my uber-sheltered Catholic background, I wasn't sure how any female anatomy actually went together.

Ironically enough, considering my opinion about electric guitars later in my life, I really wanted a better guitar, preferably an electric one, that could duplicate some of the sounds I heard Chet Atkins making on records.

Freight Train: Omaha beginnings

Our parish had a young, energetic priest, Father George Shoemaker, who also played a bit of guitar. He was effusively encouraging, which was so important to me at that point: I certainly did not have any of that at home. (One of my grandfathers lived with us at that time, and I remember him commenting, "Will that boy ever learn a complete song?")

Father Shoemaker gave me an electrified acoustic guitar, a battered looking instrument one of his parishioners was throwing away. I was thrilled by it and used it for about a year. He also loaned me a huge Vox 12-string guitar one of his parishioners had given to him. It weighed a ton, but oh, what a sound! I was hooked on 12-strings forever after that.

I worked constantly as a kid, not only doing my paper route, but also working as a janitor 40 hours a week during the summer at my grade school, shoveling snow and doing all of those odd jobs a youngster could do back then. I had saved almost enough money to purchase my heart's desire – a Gretsch Tennessean electric guitar, similar to the one that Chet Atkins used.

As I was only 14, Father Shoemaker offered to co-sign a loan for me to buy the guitar, and I could make the payments on it. After I had signed the papers at the bank, I took the check home and told my mom what I was going to do.

This kind of direct assault on her authority she just was not going to stand for, and she ranted and raved and forced me to give the check back to the bank. She then promptly called Father Shoemaker and chewed him out for usurping her tender parental role.

I felt terrible about the abuse she poured on him over the phone line, but it didn't seem to bother him much.

A few short months later I was able to buy the guitar outright without any loans at all, thank you. My mother was furious, but she could not really do anything about it since my father pointedly had told her I had worked hard for that money and I could do what I wanted with it.

The rest of my high school years were filled with my studies at the Christian Brothers all-boys school, with sports and with practicing the guitar relentlessly. I tried my hand at writing some awful songs (you have to start somewhere!) and I used the music to assuage my chronic loneliness and feeling as if I was the odd man out – typical teenage angst.

The fine musician from St. Paul, Pat Donahue, once wrote a song called "Picking in the Basement with Chet," referring to playing along and learning from Chet Atkins albums. That's what I spent much of my teen years doing.

This was decades before the internet and all of the learning aids available to musicians today. I knew no one who was trying to play fingerstyle guitar, and I pretty much taught myself and just tried to figure things out, after Dean had given me the basics.

I also performed in musical theatre productions in that high school and got a taste for being on stage and a part of presentations that required teamwork and lots of rehearsal, both skills that would serve me well later in life.

I would do my first professional gigs at a place in Omaha called The Golden Apple of Love. It was a restaurant that served crepes (very big in the 70's) with a little lounge as you walked in the front door. It was run by a dissolute looking fellow called Fred, and there was a bartender named Don who had been in that trade since his youth.

I was so excited to be performing there – and it showed. I walked in with my guitar, set up my shiny new Peavy PA system, and never wanted to take a break.

Fred, Don and the staff appreciated me and my singing and gave me a few nights a week to perform my songs. I was learning a song a day, sometimes two, and continuing to write my own songs as well. They initiated me into the service workers' custom of early morning breakfasts (sometime after midnight), plied me with various sorts of liquor, and gave me an idea of what life was like in the bar and restaurant business. It seemed pretty exciting, particularly compared to the button-down conformity all around me in Nebraska!

One night a beautiful young woman with a very short skirt sat at the bar, and after ordering a drink turned, listened intently, and carefully considered me. Turns out her profession was what was referred to at that time as a "Go-Go dancer" (where the hell did they ever get that term?).

I lost my virginity to her (thankfully), though I also got a call a few weeks later at the bar from her suggesting I should get tested for VD. Of all the luck.

I got the shots at the free clinic, bemoaning my fate and hoping it was not a precursor of my future encounters with women. Fortunately – or unfortunately, depending upon what part of my romantic misadventures I am recounting – it did not in the least put me off the gender.

Oh, and it turned out that when I got the tests back, I did not have that particular souvenir from the experience. Back then the trial of going to the free clinic and getting the test and the shots was bad enough, though: It made me think that maybe the priests and nuns might have been right about sin, lust and punishment after all – for all of about fifteen seconds.

Even with that little bump in the road, I loved that gig, and it put me on a path to all that has happened for me since. It gave me the all-important knowledge that I could move folks with my music, and that people really enjoyed hearing me sing – or at the very least, it made them want to have a drink!

IT ONCE WAS MINE: ST. LOUIS

I WENT THROUGH SOME SHORT AND VERY unsuccessful college stints in Omaha, Nebraska, and Portland, Oregon, finding out the only subjects I was really interested in exploring were guitars and girls. I then moved myself and my guitar, by that time, a Martin D-35 12-string, to St. Charles, Missouri, just outside of St. Louis. I had a couple of friends who lived there, and I bunked in a large, dilapidated house with them, determined to find a gig in a new town.

I went through the phone book and called every music club I could find listed, and amazingly I got an audition at the new Airport Marriot hotel lounge that had just been built in St. Louis. I performed for one of the Marriot brothers and the general manager and landed a month-long gig, Mondays through Fridays at cocktail hour, three hours per evening.

You can't imagine what a boost this was to me. It was good money, working in a nice hotel, learning my craft and enjoying almost all of it. It did, however, introduce me to my least favorite audience members, ones who would be an annoyance through much of my life: businessmen traveling for work, trying to impress each other and pick up women.

These guys were, and have always been, the bane of the existence of any performer unlucky enough to play for them. They are by and large loud, rude, uncouth, totally self-absorbed and obnoxious. The larger the group of them, the more unpleasant they are.

Yes, I know that is a gross generalization, but I don't care. That has been my experience.

However, that was part of the job; playing for all kinds of folks, receptive and otherwise. Particularly in those early years, I relished all of it.

At this gig I stood behind the piano bar and performed. Rarely seen today, back in those times most nice hotel lounges had one; a piano with a bar and barstools butted right up against it, so patrons could easily request their favorite songs. I knew only a few of those songs, but the Marriot brothers gave me a shot anyway.

To get the gig at the hotel, I had to be a member of the Musician's Union. My father was a committed union man, and he gave me the money to join, bless his heart.

In those days you actually had to go audition in front of a union official to demonstrate you could play an instrument adequately. (These days, all you need is the cash to join, even if all you play is the sampling machine.) I passed and became a member of St. Louis Musicians Union Local 2-197. At one time, many musician unions had been split racially, hence the "2" prefix.

St. Louis would remain part of my musical journey for years to come, as I would leave and return with regularity. I met a few life-long friends there, recorded one of my albums there, and had lots of misadventures.

My son, Dylan, was born in St. Louis – and I would write, learn a lot of songs, and have a lot of fun in the shadow of the Gateway Arch.

IF YOU COULD READ MY MIND: LIGHTFOOT, LEARNING, AND TORONTO, CANADA

How did I get to Toronto? It was a combination of impetuousness, the fervor and devil-may-care soul of youth, and sincere love for the music that had come from this charmed, still emerging and city in those years.

I was totally unafraid of taking any chance that came my way, as unlikely to lead to other things as it might appear to be.

There was an offhand remark about a possibility of helping me with gigs from Canadian icon Gordon Lightfoot when I met him at a party after one of his shows, a footloose instinct that burned to be fulfilled, and a 1967 Chevy Impala that ran pretty well most of the time (until my first wife ran into a taxicab with it, but that is another story).

In any case, the first foray across the border was made with $100 in my pocket, a PA system in the back seat, and the promise of an audition and meeting with Billy O'Conner, a well-connected agent there, and also with Al Mair, Lightfoot's business manager at the time.

I was proudly armed with a pocketful of what I remember as

If you could read my mind: Lightfoot, learning, and Toronto, Canada

pretty dreadful original songs. Somehow, however, both of those folks saw promise in me and said they would do what they could to help me find work if I moved to Toronto. I remember I played a couple of my own songs for them, plus a John Denver song, and that I had the nerve to play Lightfoot's own "Don Quixote." God knows what it was they heard in that young man's performance that prevented them from showing me the door and requesting me to never return.

Ian Tyson's first song was the memorable "Four Strong Winds. Renowned songwriter and storyteller Utah Phillips' first song was "The Telling Takes Me Home." I can earnestly assure you none of my first songs were anywhere close to being in that league.

TOM IN TORONTO 1972

At the time, I had already retired from a lackluster university sojourn and was splitting my days between St. Louis and Omaha, performing pretty regularly. (I must have been, because that was my only means of support, a preview of the rest of my wage-earning life.)

When I made the move up north, I wasn't troubled by the fact I was not a Canadian citizen. Fact of the matter was, it was much more difficult coming back into the U.S. than going into Canada.

In those days, the Canadian customs folks told me, "It is perfectly acceptable to come to Canada with your guitar, PA, etc., to audition, as long as you don't take any jobs until your work permit is in order," which required you to exit Canada and have the paperwork filed from the U.S. There of course were no computers to check up on you. Once you crossed the imaginary line, you were in and could for all practical purposes, stay for as long as you wanted or until you got caught. At that time, it was pretty unlikely that you would get caught and thrown out of Canada.

You had lots of fellow Americans as company too, north of the border. Though the draft was over in the U.S., many deserters and draft dodgers called Canada home and had no intention of leaving. Many of them could not go back in any case, particularly the deserters. I found most of them to be principled, engaging folks, with colorful stories of how they got there.

I began to give some serious thought to becoming a Canadian citizen. I had met a government official at one of my gigs who offered to give me some guidance and help me with all of the red tape. But I eventually decided against that course of action. It was very tempting though: The government benefits were generous, and the health insurance was excellent and virtually free – and still is, despite Republican propaganda to the contrary. Ask any Canadian citizen.

Plus, the inclusive philosophy of the country, the prohibition against handguns, the civility and open heartedness of almost everyone I ever met there all combined to present a more livable country, in many ways, than the U.S.

On the other hand, almost every Canadian professional musician I knew who was trying to "make it" was trying to figure out how they could do just the opposite: get a permanent work visa for the United States. At that time, Canada's population was roughly ten percent of the United States', about 20 million people. There were just a lot more venues, record companies, and general opportunities south of the border.

So, I decided to not be too hasty in changing my flag. I still do believe the average Canadians have a better quality of life than their counterparts in the U.S. – safer cities, better health care, and a superior retirement system. If I had not eventually felt I needed to leave Canada because of romantic entanglements, I don't doubt I would have become a Canuck.

In Ontario, the drinking age was 18, and the bars and clubs

were packed with young folks trying out their new right to drink legally in a public place. Add to this Ontario's odd regulations requiring bars in smaller communities to be located in hotels, the "Ladies and Escorts" additions to many clubs that had previous been men only, and the fact that even colleges had student pubs that now everyone at that institution could frequent.

This created literally hundreds of new venues with thousands of young patrons, many of them looking for entertainment to draw people in and keep them there.

I immediately had offers of work from Billy O'Conner's agency. I can't clearly remember, but I think one of the first places I performed in Canada was either the Chateau Hotel in Cobourg or the Wellington Hotel in Guelph.

Most of the gigs O'Conner got me were way out (and I mean way out) in the hinterlands.

Early on I was recruited by him to do a gig in Chapleau, Ontario, at a rough bar in that railroad town. Chapleau is at least 10 hours from Toronto, heading across the Trans-Canada Highway west, up around the Great Lakes, then a right turn north at Blind River onto a gravel road. That rocky, pot-holed ribbon of primitive beauty went 120 miles bordered on one side by a river and steep hills on the other side. There were no towns, just signposts every 20 miles or so.

When I told the locals I had come up that way, they enjoyed cluing me in that many lives were lost taking that road, either by motorists hitting moose or missing a turn and winding up in the river. The gig was supposed to last two weeks, but the bar owner had wanted all country music, not some folk crap (as she genteelly referred to it as), and I was on my way back to Toronto again after three rather intimidating weekday nights of fisherman, railroad workers, and Native Americans getting very drunk and fighting. The weekend would probably have been even more interesting.

I did drive slower on the way back to Toronto. At that time, I had no place to stay in the big city and wound up calling a girl I had met before I had left for the gig. She let me sleep on her living room hardwood floor with a blanket. There was a neon sign outside of the window of that room and no curtains. I eventually fell asleep, despite the blinking blue neon and bad dreams about rough Canadian towns.

WHAT PLACES TO learn your craft those venues were! You typically performed five to six nights a week, four to five sets per night, with an additional Saturday afternoon matinee of three hours, often performing between the strippers. You found out pretty quickly if you had what it takes to sing and play guitar for hours and days on end.

The Wellington Hotel in Guelph was owned and run by a fellow who was a Nazi concentration camp survivor.

He was difficult to deal with and never in a good mood, which I can understand looking back on it now. When you first met him, he would show you his camp identification number on his arm from those horrible years. It made problems you were going to have performing at his establishment seem insignificant. His hotel was the first where I saw an "Ontario Fire Escape" – a long, heavy rope with a hangman's knot at the end, tied to the radiator.

The idea was that in case of fire, you put the knot around you and lowered yourself the two or three stories to the ground holding on to the rope! Years later, I heard that the place had burned down. I was lucky it didn't happen while I was there, as I'm not at all sure I could have lowered myself out of that old, decrepit hotel room down the three stories to the ground, even at 19 years old.

If you wanted to move to another table in the bar, the waitress had to carry your drink there for you, as you weren't allowed to walk around the establishment with a beverage yourself. In the rougher spots, the small cocktail tables were covered by a terry-cloth topper to absorb all the spilled beer.

On Sundays, only bars that had a restaurant license were permitted to be open and serve liquor, and then only after you bought a certain amount of food. I remember the amount being $1.65. The old joke then was that there was just one cheese plate per Sunday bar that was passed around to everyone, which no one dared eat, but which you had to order to get your beer.

Drinking was pretty serious business. In downtown Toronto, you could go to the Yonge St. station, where you could only order eight-ounce glasses of lager by the *dozen*, which would set you back $2. There were raucous Newfie bars, for Newfoundlanders homesick for the Rock, and other taverns that catered to specific nationalities.

I have rarely paid for a drink in the places I performed, and as a very young man I met many bartenders who took it upon themselves to introduce me to the mysteries of various kinds of alcoholic concoctions. Like music, alcohol was nonexistent in the house I grew up in, so I was a willing, enthusiastic and ignorant (but not for long) student.

From Canadian Rye whiskey to the liqueur crazes of that time, Galliano and Amaretto, I eagerly and blithely sampled them all. I was very fortunate not to be prone to alcoholism, the demise of many fellow musicians, because it was always available – and mostly free.

My first real experience with wine was drinking the Canadian version, at that time all produced in a small area south of Toronto, close to the town of St. Catherine's. My previous knowledge of that beverage had pretty much been Boone's Farm and Almaden jugs of red wine. Canadian wines at that time were about the same quality as those – really dreadful stuff. I knew that I enjoyed wine, but looking back on those early experiences it is hard to imagine why. Most of it tasted like sugared turpentine.

However dicey some of the Canadian gigs might have been, the rewards were great. You got to meet lots of interesting, sociable, and sometimes dangerous women (all of whom I have always had a undue fascination with). You got a room at the hotel you were performing at – not a great room, by any means, but it was usually warm enough and dry – and you got a really fair amount of pay for that day and age.

Remember that this was the early 1970's. Gas was less than 50 cents a gallon, and a big meal at a cafe or restaurant was less than $2.00. Apartments rented for $150 a month in a city that later would surpass New York as the most expensive in North America.

These hotel gigs I mention paid between $300 to $450 per week – a lot of money in those days. Sometimes you had to pay an agent 10 percent commission out of that, but we are still talking about fair pay to learn your craft and practice on a generally less-than-critical audience.

If you were in Toronto proper, you had to belong to the union for most of the decent gigs. I had already joined the AF of M in St. Louis, so I was okay in that regard, though filing contracts and paying work dues was always a gigantic pain. Occasionally the owner of the establishment was not willing to pay scale, unless you kicked part of it back to him.

Regardless of whether you were starving or not, the union would prohibit you from doing the engagement unless you were paid scale, so sometimes you just lied about your fee on the contract.

For most of this period, my only guitar was my Martin D-12-35 12-string. I didn't purchase an additional guitar, a Martin six-string, until 1975 or so.

One night around my 21st birthday, I was performing at a club I worked regularly in the charming little town of Elora, Ontario. A woman who was quite a bit older than me convinced me to come to her house 10 or so miles away to join her for a nightcap. When I got there, my rush to get inside – and the forgetfulness that a few beers, plus lust, can induce – caused me to leave my beautiful guitar in the 10 degree below zero overnight. I'm not sure that evening's fun and games were worth all of the finish cracks that are on the guitar to this day, but she did write me a touching poem that I still have.

I found a place to live, my first place I had truly lived on my own, in the Broadview/Danforth area of Toronto.

I still remember the address as 57 Withrow St. It was a third-floor walk-up: two furnished rooms consisting of a bedroom and kitchen, and I shared the bathroom with the second-floor family. The kitchen chairs and table were painted chartreuse.

The rent was paid weekly, $25 total included utilities. My landlady was a younger woman who had lots of sex books on display as you walked through and up the stairs, in the bookcases and on the end tables. I always wondered about that but never had the nerve to ask.

It was a great place to call home, except for the parking. Toronto was and is a high-density city, and though many people just use public transit, there are a lot of cars. In the older section of town where I lived with Victorian clapboard homes, there were no driveways.

Coming home late at night as I almost always did from a gig, I would have to park blocks away, if I were lucky. Some nights there was just no parking even blocks away, and I would park in the school zone no-parking spot in front of my building. If I got up and moved the car before 7 AM, I could usually avoid a ticket. However, sleeping the untroubled sleep of the young, particularly after too much Canadian beer and god knows what else, I often missed that deadline, which always resulted in a $10 ticket.

I must have had a few hundred dollars in parking tickets by the time I moved out of that place, and I worried constantly about being stopped by the police, being given a one-way bus fare and the bum's rush to the U.S. border. "Illegal folksinger deported because of unpaid parking fines" would be the headline.

The famed Yorkville district where began the careers of Joni Mitchell, Gordon Lightfoot, Neil Young, and so many others was already gentrifying furiously by the time I got there in the 70's.

"I WOULDN'T COUNT ON IT" — CONFESSIONS OF AN UNLIKELY FOLKSINGER

But the famous Riverboat Coffeehouse still existed, and I got to do one opening act there before it closed later in that decade. I also performed some week-long gigs just down the street at the Red Lantern – a nice place as I recall.

I also played my first Irish bar there in Toronto, a dive called the "Wild Rover" on Bloor St. I learned the song by that title specifically for the occasion at the behest of the owner, an older Irish woman, but I was still fired after one night for not being Irish enough. No great loss there.

Though I was pretty damn green as a performer, I remember being booked much of the time. I certainly was enthusiastic and was up for playing a few songs anywhere, anytime, whether I was paid for it or not.

PETER MATHIESON

My pal Peter Mathieson, who I met in Guelph, Ontario, lived in a cupola tower of an old house that he and his wife rented for $40 a month. I spent lots of time over there, learning and trading guitar licks, learning to drink and enjoy coffee, and being introduced to the subtle joys of backgammon, which was quite the game craze in the 70's.

Peter was one of the best guitarists and songwriters I ever met, and I still perform some of his pieces. He was a profound influence on my own songs and guitar arrangements. Just learning one of his songs, like "Time for a Change" or "Simple Song" was a graduate guitar symposium unto itself.

He used a lot of partial chords with complicated fingerstyle picking patterns that would maximize their open sound. He wrote some songs in alternate guitar tunings, but his best were difficult songs in standard tuning.

All of his compositions were true arrangements, not just some words with a few random chords underneath them. He had actually given Joni Mitchell (then Joni Anderson) some of her early guitar lessons back in his hometown of Calgary, Alberta, and I picked his brain and got him to show me a lot of his tricks. Some of them I even learned to do.

In return, I taught him the card game Pinochle, which my parents had taught me. We would play with his wife, Susan, or later on with my first wife, Jennifer. Bottom line, we loved guitars, girls and games. Life was simple, beer was cheap, and many women were amenable to boys with acoustic guitars, long hair and beards.

Peter passed away in 2018. Rest in peace, dear companion. Your smile, your laugh and your songs enriched my life so much.

John Stockfish was Gordon Lightfoot's first bass player, and I was introduced to him by old friends of Gordon's. Most Canadians were familiar with his timeless bass work on Lightfoot's "Song for a Winters Night" and those early United Artist albums. He also later played on the recording of Gord's, "Sundown," which went to number one on the charts.

John was very kind to me, and I spent many afternoons at his Toronto home playing my new songs for him and talking about music. He was very intense and had a wealth of music business experience. I learned a lot from him. He and his wife, Pat, had me over for a Christmas Eve that would have been bleak and lonely without their hospitality when I had few acquaintances in that big city.

Often on nights on which I was not performing, I would hoof it over to the streetcar line and ride to the Four Seasons Hotel in downtown Toronto to hear the jazz band John played in. I usually could afford one or two Molson Stock Ales, which I would nurse in the bar while I would listen to that ensemble. They were wonderful.

John would join me during breaks, and we would talk music. I think he was glad to have the company. Sometimes Lightfoot would wander in, and the two of us would chat and listen to John. What a touch he had on that bass.

John once joined me for a concert I did at a high school in Fergus, Ontario, about 100 miles north of Toronto. It was such a great thrill to have his trademark bass style accompanying me on stage. I was quite excited after the show – no doubt far more than he was.

He would eventually move to Nashville, and we kept in touch until he passed away in 2012. I wrote an epitaph for him printed in an Oregon music magazine that was distributed widely on the internet.

I got to see quite a bit of the province of Ontario from my driver's seat as I traveled to remote gigs: North Bay, Orillia, Kingston, Thunder Bay, Chapleau, Sarnia and exotic places like those. I got a kick out of all of them, though the audiences were often kind of sketchy – and dangerous. I saw some very lethal looking bar fights on those trips.

I dodged a few personal bullets too, along the way. One weekend I played at a little out-of-the-way bar/hotel in the tiny town of Brechin, Ontario. A girl in the audience kept asking me to come over to a "party" she was having next door. She wanted me to come "play guitar for her and visit." I told her I would come over in due course, after I was done with the folks I was chatting with.

When I finally got there, she was entwined with the owner of the bar – who was much older than I – and also married. I was sociable but regretful, as it occurred to me I had lost out on a night's frolics by not immediately taking the lady up on her offer. I played a song for them as they made out, then hastened my retreat to the solace of a bottle of beer.

I heard later that the girl was only 14 (she sure looked older) and that the bar-owner had gotten her pregnant, which caused his divorce and later bankruptcy.

It could have been me. I was lucky that time around, avoiding what could have been a life-changing error.

In addition to spending a good deal of time with and having the opportunity to open for Gordon Lightfoot, I met many other inspirational artists who impacted me and my music during that Canadian sojourn. Bruce Cockburn ran what was essentially an open mic in Ottawa that I dropped in at a couple of times, and Bruce was friendly and supportive.

Dan Hill, who went on to have a couple of radio hits, was a pal who I met through my association with John Stockfish. Dan had also been mentored by John.

Raffi was living in Toronto, performing when he could, and had not yet come up with the idea that would make him rich – writing and singing children's music. I am probably one of the only people who still has his first album, consisting of original songs and covers he was doing at the time. Much of it was recorded in the tiny closet of my buddy, Peter Mathieson, on a Revox stereo tape recorder with two Shure SM-57 microphones.

Though opening concerts for a famous act like Gordon Lightfoot is great for your career resume, it is a tough gig. The people are not there to see you, and you have to attempt to win them over while being aware of your proper role in the evening, as a warm-up act. Stick strictly to your time frame, don't talk too much, and make appropriate referrals to the artist you are opening for, who will be on in just a few minutes.

Many times, the opening act does not get a sound check or gets just a cursory bit of time with the PA crew. You have to be aware that you are not the primary artist and not get testy about the lack of time to get everything set up as you like.

Lightfoot mostly used Liona Boyd and Mimi Farina as openers, and I was abundantly thankful for the occasional

"I WOULDN'T COUNT ON IT" — CONFESSIONS OF AN UNLIKELY FOLKSINGER

OPENING FOR LIGHTFOOT 1973

chance I got to play some songs before his performances.

Folks seem to be endlessly fascinated with famous people like Gordon Lightfoot. Much was made of his drinking, partying and other supposed misbehaviors – things most young people will do given the opportunity. Gord would say himself in later years, "Since 1985, I have made it a priority to make amends to all the folks I was less than kind to in the early days of my success."

For myself, I can say Gordon was almost always gracious and helpful towards me back then, and he certainly has been so in the years since. I value his friendship and appreciate him giving me advice, along with those unique opportunities.

I think there was and is a lot of jealousy in the way certain people remember and describe him. He would be the first to admit how lucky he was to get those early breaks, but he has followed those opportunities with great dedication to his craft. He has written hundreds of songs, recorded more than 25 albums of original material, and is still touring at age 80.

Thanks, Gord.

Sometime during my Toronto years, a woman who I had met in St. Charles, Missouri, came to visit me in my little Withrow St. flat. Her name was Jennifer, and I would eventually marry her at an Anglican church on Avenue Road in Toronto, in November of 1974.

It was probably (hopefully) the only time in my life I will ever wear an English morning suit with tails. No alcohol was allowed at the reception in the church – only coffee, tea, marzipan cake and ice cream. Copious amounts of alcohol would have been a better idea for that union, as it turned out.

The honeymoon was in a small room at the famous Royal

York hotel. Unfortunately, in that corridor of the floor we were on, there was a Lithuanian group who had drunk too much. All of them eventually passed out, mostly outside of their rooms in the passageway. At least the shouting in the hallway stopped at that point!

The wedding gift from the hotel was a huge, heavy glass ashtray with their logo on it. Seemingly everyone in Canada smoked in those days. I inhaled so much second-hand smoke in those bars, I felt like I could do a tobacco ad.

Jennifer had been at Webster College in St. Louis on an acting scholarship before transferring to Lindenwood College in St. Charles, where I met her. I did one concert at Lindenwood while she was still a student there – just a couple of weeks after an unknown named Billy Joel played the same small theatre.

I tried to incorporate her into my act – she sang harmony and played the tambourine. Being attractive, she also added certain feminine panache to the often-somber themes of the songs I was performing back then.

I still have some charming promotional pictures that I had taken of us, two young kids without a clue of what the world had in store. Most entertainers would agree it is not wise to mix romance and business, and that was indeed the case with our marriage.

There were some funny vignettes along our performing path together, though. We once had a two-week long gig in Kirkland Lake, Ontario, close to the Quebec border, way up north of Toronto a few hundred miles. I don't recall why, but we decided we would take the train up there rather than drive.

So, we got the PA system down to the train station, located at Toronto's Royal York Hotel. Believe it or not, they put the whole damn thing on the train in the baggage car, no extra charge. Unfortunately, there was a derailment, so we had to switch to a bus along the way—and then we, the PA system and the guitar were put on another train to continue north.

In the tiny rail junction of Swastika they transferred us for a short line, six-mile run to Kirkland Lake. The baggage car attendant on that train let us sit on the PA those last few miles.

It was late September, already very chilly that far north, and the sky seemed as if it were only 20 feet high, with the low clouds characteristic of that region. We arrived about 7 AM at the station and got a cab to the hotel/bar we would be performing at. We certainly could have walked it except for the PA system we were lugging with us.

The front of the hotel was glass, and I could see through it to a front desk that had holes punched in it, with some obscene graffiti scribbled on the wall behind it. It didn't look promising.

Even worse, the door of the hotel/bar was locked. It was in the 20's outside, and our stuff was stacked on the street outside the hotel door. The cab driver had not left, and he said he would let the police know our predicament.

In just a few minutes, an officer arrived and tried to jimmy the back door of the hotel for us. He was unsuccessful, but he went to another bar right next door. He asked the janitor who was cleaning up if we could go in there to warm up until someone came to open the front door of the establishment we were lucky enough to be booked in. We were fortunately able to camp out there for a couple hours.

Mid-morning, another janitor arrived to clean the hotel where we would be regaling patrons with sensitive music later that evening. We asked him what we should do. He suggested just dropping our gear in the bar and going upstairs and picking a room that was empty and getting some sleep. (We had been awake all night traveling at that point.)

Well, that was unlike any check-in procedure I had ever experienced in a hotel, but by that time we were so tired and cold, anything would do, so we took his suggestion. I'm pretty sure the sheets weren't even clean in that room, and the door didn't really lock, but at that point neither of us cared.

After we had slept for awhile, I went downstairs to meet the owner to tell him about what we had done and the troubles we had encountered, but he shrugged it off as if that was the typical welcome all his performers received. No big deal. We went on stage that night, and the bar, while very rough, was generally no better or worse than similar joints I had played.

One fellow came in every night to hear us, a French guy who was very friendly and seemed to enjoy our music. He would come in, drink heavily and stay until we finished performing at 1 AM. Then he would stumble back to his car to somehow drive home.

One night he invited us to join him at a Chinese restaurant in town, after hours. We sat down with him and ordered, then he asked us if we would like a drink. I answered that I would, "but after closing time." He replied, "no problem," and signaled the waiter over. He ordered a fifth of some vile-tasting Canadian rye whiskey, for which he paid $40 – a lot of money in those days. He said it was on him and not to worry about it, and I marveled that he was even able to get it, considering the strict Ontario liquor laws.

We lit into our Chinese food and whiskey, and about 10 minutes later an Ontario Provincial Policeman wandered in. I tried to surreptitiously slip the bottle under the table, until our French fan told me not to worry about it. Sure enough, the cop walked right to the cash register. The restaurant owner opened it and in plain sight handed the officer a wad of cash and another full whiskey bottle. Life was indeed interesting and somewhat sketchy up on the northern Ontario frontier.

After hours one night, that French fan of ours also wanted to drive us over to Rouen, Quebec, where the bars were open to 4 AM or so. But I decided that riding with him on a dark Canadian highway, after he had imbibed a prodigious amount of beer and whisky would be more adventurous than even I wanted to be.

The second week of our gig in colorful Kirkland Lake was cancelled, probably because I was a little too folky in my song selection. Our French friend felt sorry for us and invited us to dinner at his apartment the last evening we were in town, before our final gig there. He had touted the great steaks he had purchased to show us his appreciation for our companionship and music, and we decided to accept his kind invitation. We arrived, and he had already done severe damage to a special bottle of cognac he had bought for the occasion. Subsequent bottles he opened didn't stand a chance, either.

The steaks were fine, but his conversation was slurred and difficult to understand, and he insisted on eating the beef with his hands and fingers – like one of the bears that overpopulated that cold wilderness. Usually though, you don't have to try to communicate with and be grateful to the bear as he is eating. It was a weird scene.

Somehow, Jennifer and I became convinced that after we got paid that last night, that the hotel owner was going to break in and steal back the money from us (remember, the door to the hotel room did not lock). I no longer recall why we thought that, but we were ever so relieved to board that homebound train the next morning – particularly because it was about 10 degrees and lightly snowing as we waited on the platform for the train with that PA, my guitar and our luggage.

With romantic experiences such as that, what young woman wouldn't be enthralled by sharing the life of a musician? Eventually, I made the decision that I was better off performing solo. Jennifer would still come with me to the gigs though. There were occasional concerts, but mostly my gigs were in dive bars in places like Sarnia, Belleville and London, Ontario.

Jennifer was becoming very homesick and fell into a deep depression. I was very concerned about her – so concerned that I eventually suggested we move back to St. Louis, so she could be close to her brother, sister-in-law and other friends for support.

This was a major life decision for me, but I don't remember agonizing over it too much. I just wanted to do right by my wife, and it seemed to be the only way that the marriage might survive.

GONE BUT NOT FORGOTTEN: ST. LOUIS

SO BACK TO ST. LOUIS WE WENT, WITH NO JOBS, little money and even fewer prospects.

Though it was still an era where there was lots of music opportunities, gigs were harder to come by in St. Louis, and they paid far less than they had in Canada. I worked as a part-time school bus driver for a short time as we got settled and I looked for more places to perform. Jennifer got a job, which I thought would be settling for her, but her depressions and black moods were not eased by either the move or the work.

It got so I was performing quite a bit, though. The gigs in St. Louis were different: You tended to play a club on a certain night each week for as long as you could "hold the crowds." Some of the spots I played that I can remember were Duff's, in the Central West End; Bernard's Pub, in South St. Louis; and a loud, businessmen's bar at Westport Plaza, out in the suburbs. (I hated that place: Burnham's St. Louis Opera House.)

Some fine musicians were working in St. Louis at that time, and we enjoyed spending time and sharing a few songs together when we could. Probably the most successful and popular folkie in the area was Walt Jenkins. Walt was very handsome, in a long-haired

Clark Gable sort of way, with a big dark mustache and wide open smile. He was fine on his own, but also had some kick-ass, country-influenced guys who would play in his band. I remember Walt doing a wonderful version of the song "Spider John," written by the reclusive Texas songwriter Willis Alan Ramsey.

Walt would eventually leave behind the secular music world after he became a born-again Christian and determined he shouldn't do any music that wasn't spiritually motivated. To my way of thinking, what a waste.

Walt was always a kind, very talented and moral person from what I could see, but he chose another path, left the bar scene, and wound up moving down to the Ozarks.

Bernie McDonald was another of those guys who had grown up in St. Louis and carved out a regular performing niche for himself in area clubs. He had also traveled some, living in Washington D.C. and southern Colorado, and had developed a unique playing style. His guitar work was a blend of classical and John Renbourne/Fairport Convention fingerstyle methods. He was writing a number of his own songs, as well as doing things like "Crazy Man Michael," by Fairport Convention.

Bernie and I knew each other slightly, but we really became friends after we were double-booked at a forgettable burger/beer joint called "The Ground Round." It could have been a really uncomfortable situation if it was anyone else, but Bernie and I just decided to split the night and the pay. We would go on to share a lot of songs at his little apartment in Clayton over his strong, Melita style coffee.

A couple of years later when I returned from some wanderings, Bernie and I both lived in South St. Louis and were members of the South Side YMCA. He would teach me the game of handball – which I was never any good at. Racquetball was my game.

Bernie was a fierce handball competitor beneath his gentle, friendly surface. During one particularly vigorous match (not against me), he lost his temper and slugged the solid steel court door in frustration. The door won the fight.

The knuckles on his hand were sorely injured, but fortunately there was no permanent damage. Still, he was unable to play guitar – or handball – for a few months. He would show up regularly at my flat, and we would drink Busch beer, listen to dark, moody Celtic music, joke and generally have too good of a time.

Bernie became thoroughly fascinated and enamored of traditional Celtic music and would go on to marry a talented Irish flute player, Barbara Dayhill. He would also host a weekly Celtic music radio program on the community radio station in St. Louis and do a concert tour in Ireland accompanying the legendary traditional button accordionist, Joe Burke.

Bernie and his wife moved to the Ozarks about 20 years ago to get away from the city hustle and bustle. He was a good friend, a fine musician with a sense of humor, and I think of him often.

The kind of gigs where I met those men were thankfully punctuated by the occasional true folk concert at places like the Focal Point in Webster Groves, Charlotte's Web in Rockford, Illinois, The Quiet Knight in Chicago, and a few others. Those engagements gave me the impetus to keep writing songs and polishing some of my earlier efforts.

The move back to St. Louis didn't really help either our marriage or Jennifer's deep depression. Though I tried everything I knew of to try and lift her spirits, nothing seemed to work. It became impossible to stay and be a target of irrational verbal abuse, and I decided I needed to move out, at least for a while. Hopefully that would give her time to reflect on her demons without me in the mix. I moved into a room in a lodgings that had been a slave quarters, behind one of the grand old houses on Lafayette Square.

Unlike what I thought might happen, my moving out seemed to only exacerbate matters. Jennifer got in touch with her brother, and he was worried enough that he checked her into the Missouri State Psychiatric Hospital.

This was a place right out of the Ken Kesey book, "One Flew Over the Cuckoo's Nest." It was built in the 19 century, had bars on all the windows and locked doors to get into the units.

Though Jennifer was not diagnosed as such, she was put into a "chronic" ward because of overcrowding. Her fellow patients were truly desperate folks with a variety of delusions, paranoias and schizophrenia – many of the conditions with religious underpinnings. They were disturbing folks to talk to, and not a little frightening.

All the doctors were foreign, most with very poor English skills – which makes you wonder how they could effectively counsel and help the people in their charge. I visited her every day.

Jennifer remained there only a couple of weeks. I think she figured that regardless of whatever was terrible in her life, she wasn't as badly off as her fellow inmates at that prison-like madhouse. She was released to her brother and myself, and she and I found a little inner-city apartment to call home.

During that time, I continued on with a variety of part time jobs and music gigs. I did a stint as a painter-groundskeeper at an apartment complex in the St. Louis suburbs by day and performed as many nights as I could.

The relationship between myself and my wife continued to deteriorate, however. I think a part of me died at that time – the belief that if you loved someone enough, you could help them through whatever they were enduring; a belief in the kind of storybook endings most of us hope for in romance.

I felt I had given up Toronto and a steady performing schedule and great prospects, and that I tried to love her through it all, but that it didn't make a damn bit of difference. That was difficult to accept.

Though Jennifer's general outlook on life was a little better, it didn't seem to carry over to us getting along. I decided I needed to begin again and forge a life on my own.

Gone But Not Forgotten: St. Louis

A couple of years earlier, I had met a fellow by the name of Byron Wagner, a Nebraskan who was making his way in the music business out in Los Angeles. I called him, and he invited me to stay in his place while I checked out opportunities in a city that was a hotbed of music production at that time.

A couple of guys had given me tips about taking driveaway cars to the west coast. I knew my old vehicle probably wouldn't make it all the way out there, so I arranged to leave it a friend's house and sign a contract to drive a loaner to L.A. The arrangement was that you agreed to pick up the car and drive it to its destination in a specified number of days, and they gave you a stipend for gas and expenses.

The conveyance I drove out west was a ridiculous looking small pickup truck that had a suspension system that had been jacked up high in the air. I probably couldn't get into it today, even if I had a ladder. I must have looked pretty silly in it. It ran fine, though, and it was my very first drive across the beautiful landscape of the southwestern U.S.

I got to L.A., dropped off the truck and contacted Byron. He had some ideas for me about possibilities I could investigate while I was there. I also contacted Joni Mitchell, who I had met in Toronto, and she was very kind to me and shared some ideas and contacts, too.

Aside from making recording company contacts, the first order of business was to find a job that could bring in some regular income, preferably somehow related to the music business. A restaurant called "The Great American Food and Beverage Company" was holding auditions for singing waiters, waitresses and busboys. I figured, "What the hell, I might as well give that a shot."

I think one or two positions were available, and there were at least 30 people at the audition. The concept of this joint was that you would do your job of serving or cleaning up, then when you had a minute free you would take your guitar or banjo off of the wall, where it would be hanging, and you would play a song for the patrons in your section.

I know it sounds crazy - it sounded crazy to me at that time too – but that is how it worked, and they were evidently very successful. Also, it being located very close to L.A.'s recording studios and music offices, the hopes were someone from that world would hear you and you could get your foot in the door there.

I played my song, "Vignette," for the audition, and one or two more (which hopefully were more upbeat than that one is) and then left. I didn't hold out much hope of getting the job, since there were so many incredibly talented folks at the audition.

Surprisingly, a couple of days later I got a call at Byron's from the manager who told me I would be hired, and that I was to start as a singing busboy the following week. The jobs at that place evidently wound up paying quite well when factoring in the tips you got from playing impromptu music for the diners, particularly when you eventually were promoted to waiter status.

Before I stated, however, I was feeling overwhelming grief, sadness and guilt about leaving Jennifer behind, and I was terribly homesick for her and St. Louis. I just didn't seem to be able to lose myself in my music ambitions and songs as I had during previous relocations.

I let those emotions get the best of me, and after only being in L.A. a couple of weeks, made the decision to turn down the job I had been offered, fly back to St. Louis and try again with Jennifer. I of course called her before I made that decision, and she begged me to return and begin again with her.

I made some kind of cockamamie excuse to the manager at the restaurant, put the plane fare on my credit card, turned tail and headed back to St. Louis. I often wondered how my life would have been different had I stayed in L.A. and taken that job.

Jennifer and I had a little boost of good times when I returned, but they weren't to last for long. There had simply been too many harsh words spoken between us and too many feelings hurt.

But somehow, right about then, I got a truly plum gig at a famous St. Louis address. I did five nights a week for a month at one of the bars at the elegant Chase Park Plaza Hotel, in midtown St. Louis. I don't remember much about it, but I do remember that Jennifer's mother made me a silver-studded denim suit to wear there. Fortunately, no pictures survive of me in the outfit. A fellow folksinger called it my "Rhinestone Cow Pie" outfit.

Another amusing side story arose from that difficult time. I had encouraged Jennifer to get out, visit a girlfriend, to do something on her own to gain confidence and capture some of her old joie de vivre. She agreed, and she drove my 1967 Chevy Impala, which I had left behind in St. Louis at a pal's house during my L.A. experiment, to meet an old college pal for a night on the town.

Well, her driving ability wasn't very good that night. She ran into a taxi, damaged the cab and badly dented up our only means of transportation. (From that time on, my car always looked as if it were coming down the road sideways.)

Fortunately, no one was hurt. A couple of weeks later, however, I received a notice saying as the owner of the car, I was being sued by the taxicab company for the damages to the cab and also by the occupants of the taxi. The riders in the cab had not actually been hurt, and since we did not have any money or any possessions at all to speak of, the riders' claims went unanswered.

My car insurance had just expired before the accident.

I do not remember why I felt I had to respond to the taxi company's claim for $800 to fix the cab: Perhaps they threatened to garnish my bank account (yeah, like that was a significant threat). Whatever the reason, I called and asked them if I could take a job with them to work off the repair amount.

It seems there are never enough taxi drivers. It is a tough profession, and of course it can be dangerous, too. County Cab in St. Louis gave me a job, with the caveat that I cut my hair and chop off my beard. You rented the cab from 4 AM to 4 PM and paid for your own gas. The rest of the money from the fares and tips was yours.

I quickly paid off the $800 I owed them and began making progress on some credit card debt Jennifer and I had racked up. Many nights I played music until 1 AM in the morning, got home and went to bed about 2 AM, grabbed two or three hours of sleep, and would pick up the cab between 4 and 5 AM.

Somewhere during this stretch I realized the marriage was a goner, and I filed for divorce. At one of my gigs I had become friendly with a young attorney who had just graduated from St. Louis University law school. I had played for his wedding at the Jewel Box Conservatory in Forest Park and had not charged him anything.

He agreed to do my divorce on the same basis. It was the barter system in action – free wedding music in exchange for a divorce decree. (I always thought there was great poetic justice there.) Interestingly enough, he and his wife became devout Scientologists, and he went to jail a couple of years later for trying to extort Missouri Senator Thomas Eagleton (one-time vice-presidential candidate who ran with George McGovern) out of $100,000 for their church.

But in any case, this chapter of my life was pretty much over. Jennifer wound up marrying a close friend of mine who had kindly provided me with a room at his house to stay in after the divorce. (He had also gotten me a job in the warehouse of a drug company where he was a chemist. I did it for a month, until they offered me a permanent position, which I could not have been less interested in.) He and Jennifer have been married for more than 40 years now. They are both dear folks, and I am grateful to have had them in my life.

My old Chevy was barely limping along by this time, and I purchased an elderly Toyota station wagon from Jennifer's brother. It would get me from here to there, belching exhaust fumes and hauling my meager possessions for the next few years.

During this unsettled period of my life, I met of couple who would become lifelong friends by the name of Al and Anita Avery. They greatly enjoyed my music, and I got to know them well. Al was a finance professor at a university and Anita was a piano instructor and accomplished musician.

We became fast friends. They once even talked me into water-skiing with them on the Mississippi River. (Yes, I know how ridiculous that image seems to folks who have known me over the last 20 years. It is true, nonetheless.)

Al invited me on a business trip with him to Chicago. He was renting a small airplane for the journey, and he knew I loved flying. I had old friends in Chicago and had performed there a few times, and I thought it would be a fun adventure.

It was January, so it was awfully cold – below zero when we flew up there. This was back in the days when they still allowed small engine aircraft to operate out of O'Hare airport. It was rather intimidating to land in that little single engine Cessna amidst the jumbo jets.

I stayed with my pal, Tom Armbruster, who had helped me produce a couple of demos at Universal Recording Studio, where he worked. We had an uproarious visit, full of songs, stories, female participants and mood-enhancing substances. I recall Al even missed part of his conference because he decided to stay and party with us, rather than undergo the tedium of those academic presentations.

Everyone was back in good shape by the time we were scheduled to fly back to St. Louis on a bitterly cold evening, but there were problems from the start. First of all, the airplane would not start. We had to get it jump-started. (Never heard of such a thing? Neither had I.)

The temperature was minus 20 and felt colder on that windy, wide-open runway. After the engine coughed to life, it was my job to clamber down the wing and disconnect the charging device from the fuselage of the aircraft. With the outside temperature and the wind from the propeller, I have never been so frozen feeling in my life.

O' Hare runway at night is a jumble of confused colored lights and taxiways. Trying to negotiate it all in a small plane while listening to air traffic control is a nightmare. (Not too long after we were there, they disallowed single engine aircraft from operating out of O'Hare.) Al became disoriented and mistook a truck access road for a taxiway. He wound up running into a fence stanchion and clipping his wingtip, putting a hole in the fiberglass.

Well, this was not good news. Al was a very accomplished pilot, had lots of hours and had been a flight instructor when he was doing his master's degree at Purdue. He looked at the damage, said, " Well, I'm not supposed to fly with it like this, but I'll duct tape it up and we'll be okay." Though I was starting to become a little nervous, I still trusted him.

He found his way onto the runway, and we took off toward St. Louis. After a few minutes, however, he was concerned that his cruising airspeed was not what it should be. He decided to divert to his old airfield where he had taught flight instruction, in Lafayette, Indiana, retape the wingtip and have a buddy inspect it. (At this point, I saw the headline, "Little known folksinger dies in air crash.")

Right about this time, he realized that at least part of the reason for the reduced airspeed problem was his landing gear was still down! This was a rental plane, and he just was not familiar with it. I was beginning to get progressively more nervous. He still decided to stop in Lafayette and take a look at that wingtip.

We made our way to Lafayette, and Al said, "Where is the runway? It should be right there!" I saw only the black, frigid Midwestern night as we descended. Finally, his friend at the airport finally responded to Al's radio calls and turned on the runway lights.

We landed without incident, retaped the wingtip and flew on to St. Louis safely. I would tease Al about that journey for years to come. He and Anita remained wonderful friends to me, and they offered their home and hospitality in Virginia Beach, and later in Baltimore, as headquarters of a sort for me in those years when I would regularly tour the East Coast.

Al passed away this past year. I miss his spirit, irreverence, sense of humor and his incomparable margaritas. Rest in peace, old pal.

While I was living at my friend's house in St. Louis, I met a couple of other women who would figure into my future. One of them seduced me with ouzo (the licorice-flavored Greek liqueur) at a Central West End nightclub gig I had. The other I met at a different venue, a real hippie-type musical-poetry reading event where I played a few songs.

Diana was a nurse-anesthetist who was quite fond of me, and we kept company for awhile, though I have never had another shot of ouzo since that somewhat foggily remembered night. What a headache the next morning brought!

Mary Ann was a Catholic school elementary teacher (of religion, no less!) who also played guitar and loved folk music. We began seeing each other and got along well.

She had been contemplating a move to Boston and had been offered a job there, I had always been intrigued by Boston and had often thought of going there and checking out the folk scene. As it happened, Mary Anne had a connection to get an apartment in Brookline for $125 a month – an exceptional deal, even in 1977. We agreed to split the cost and that I would leave early to secure it, while she wrapped up some loose ends in St Louis.

PLAIN AND SIMPLE ENDINGS: BOSTON

When I arrived in Boston in the late summer of 1977, the folk music glory days of the 1960's were long over. The Club 47 in Harvard Square was gone, replaced by Passim, owned by Bob and Rae Ann Donlin.

There were few clubs left featuring anything like acoustic music. Things did not look too promising for me continuing my professional folk music dreams here.

Still, you could find vestiges of those earlier times if you looked hard enough. There was the venerable Sword in the Stone coffeehouse on Charles St., in the Beacon Hill neighborhood, the Nameless Coffeehouse in Harvard Square, a few other clubs and some longtime concert series in church basements.

The Sword in the Stone: Now that was an odd little place. It was on Charles St. in Beacon Hill, run since the early 60's by Mark Edwards, truly a survivor/throwback of the folk revival. Playing through a miserable sound system, you would perform your songs for a miniscule audience of street people who had wandered in. The owner would sit in the back in a little booth and introduce the acts – as well as cajole the performers to play "something that people knew," rather than original music.

Plain and Simple Endings: Boston

This was all set in cheesy, Camelot-like décor, with terrible coffee and even worse sandwiches. I think it was the last of the 60's folk-boom establishments to close in that area, which it did later that decade. Playing there a number of times, I was amazed it lasted as long as it did.

The owner did have some interesting stories of the characters, famous and infamous, who had performed for him in the past. The pay was "pass the hat" plus a few bucks the owner might kick in.

The Nameless Coffeehouse had also been running since the 60's, and you could sign up to do a song or two on a Friday night – gratis, of course. It did have the advantage of having a consistently full house, but you could only play there every other month or so. It continues to exist, in the same Harvard Square church, to this very day.

Of course, there was the famous Passim in Harvard Square. I attended some shows there, but never really made connections with the owner, Bob Donlin, until a couple of years later.

I had met the popular singer/songwriter Bruce Cockburn when I lived in Canada, had gotten to know him a bit, and was invited to play at a couple of his songwriter nights in Ottawa. He was friendly and accessible – and was such a talent. When Bruce played a weekend at Passim, I made a point of attending the Sunday afternoon show. There were probably fewer than 10 of us there that October afternoon.

The opening act was a red haired, wiry guy from Maine with a down east accent by the name of David Mallett. He had just recorded his first album at Paul Stookey's (of Peter, Paul and Mary) newly opened studio in Blue Hill, Maine.

Cockburn was marvelous, as always, but it was really the music of David Mallett that knocked me out that afternoon. He performed "Inches and Miles," "Phil Brown," and "Fire" – the story of his grandparents' barn burning down. To that point in my young life, it was the most affecting batch of songs I had ever heard live on stage.

David and I eventually became friends, and our paths would cross often in our musical careers. I always tried to help him out as much as I could, as I had such faith in his poetry and music. When that first album of his was released, "The Garden Song" (inch by inch, row by row) became a folk music standard, sung by hundreds of people and even taught to schoolkids in China.

♪ ♪ ♪ ♪ ♪ ♪

I PRETTY QUICKLY figured out that supporting myself in Boston with music alone was going to be impossible.

But I was there, so I figured it was worthwhile to stay and immerse myself in the vapors of the legendary scene that existed a few short years before. So I applied for a day job at an Oriental rug/carpeting/ carpet cleaning company called Able Rug.

Looking back on that couple year stretch of my life, I am so grateful that I took that job. It was hard physical labor most of the time: doing a variety of tasks from carpet cleaning with antique, filthy equipment (they discontinued that phase of the business before I left); carrying rugs hither and yon (usually balanced on your shoulder); running up and down the conveyer belt between floors (the stairs were for salespeople); cutting and binding carpets in the warehouse; and delivering rugs to customers.

Boston had an old ordinance that only required elevators for buildings over five stories. In shorter buildings, you were carrying those 30 to 100-pound rugs upstairs, most of the time by yourself, then often moving the customer's furniture to lay down the rug.

I drove the delivery truck for Able Rug during the winter of 1978, worst winter of the century in Boston.

Now that was an adventure. Anyone who has navigated Beantown's streets know how, um, unpredictable the drivers can be there. Seeing cars triple parked by the curb was not unusual. Add to the cantankerous nature of the drivers there two feet of snow and ice, and you have a really interesting situation.

Though I was terrified of sliding down Beacon Hill and other neighborhoods in a big Chevy stepvan with bald tires and no seatbelts, I somehow survived. In the decent weather, I usually drove with the driver's door slid wide open, even on the interstate – unbelievable, when I think about it now, but it never even occurred to me at the time that it might be dangerous.

When I began working at Able Rug, an old Irishman by the name of Pat Ryan initiated me into the very dirty job of cleaning the rugs with the Rube Goldberg type machine they had. You would get up on a rickety ladder in a drying room which was heated to 125 degrees and make sure the rugs were hanging properly.

Pat had been at Able Rug for decades. After a few weeks, I began to understand why he kept bottles of whisky stashed all over the store and even outside in the police call box, which a sympathetic Irish cop had given him a key to. It was a monotonous, dangerous, filthy job. A little shot of whisky took the edge off.

Pat had come from County Tipperary in Ireland and knew his way around a bottle, but he also had a mischievous smile and the Irish knack for good storytelling. He was the best part of that particular chore.

After a few months, they retired Pat, and I started doing all sorts of other things, including driving that truck. It wasn't exactly what I had planned on doing when I moved to Boston, but I gained a lot of satisfaction fromgetting into tip-top shape and feeling like I could accomplish anything. The young guys I worked with were colorful, profane, energetic fellows who I enjoyed being around, and I wasn't letting my music slide, either.

I was writing a lot of new songs and playing whatever gigs I could scrounge up, many of them in southern New Hampshire. I also had a semi-regular gig at the Cantab Lounge near Central Square in Cambridge, an establishment that still exists today.

"I WOULDN'T COUNT ON IT" — CONFESSIONS OF AN UNLIKELY FOLKSINGER

As in other times in my life when I temporarily had to fill in with something additional to make my life in music possible, it was by and large a very positive experience. It also made me fully appreciate the job of writing songs, standing on stage, and singing them. Though sometimes that can be tough too, it doesn't really compare to a lifetime of hard physical labor for low pay, doing something boring you would rather not do.

In the music business, it's by and large low pay for something you mostly want to do. As the great Dave Van Ronk said in his brilliant autobiography, "Mayor of McDougal Street," "There are any number of times in my life I would have given up this crazy business if I had anything to fall back on, but basically I am glad things turned out as they did." I kind of feel the same way.

I split up with Mary Ann and found a room to rent that was only about a mile and a half from Able Rug.

That commenced a period of intense loneliness but also a time of profound personal growth. Some weeks I would fast for three days, concentrating on getting thin (and I did get as thin as I ever have been in my adult life).

I would take long walks on Sundays from my room in Brookline, following old streets and historic landmarks down to Faneuil Hall and the North End. There I would buy six oysters and a beer at the Union Oyster House, where Daniel Webster, the great 19 century orator and legislator, had sat and done the same thing I was doing at that very spot. Now that was living history.

I also began to buy and appreciate wine during that time in Boston. I had tasted enough good wine in the company of Lightfoot, who enjoyed quality spirits and pretty much everything else, to know that there was a world of interesting vino out there.

In Boston, many of the corner stores where I would buy my meager food supplies would have displays of discounted French wines. I later found out that Boston, being a major importation point for international goods, was a liquidation town for wine wholesalers looking to unload broken cases split up by damage or partial orders. Consequently, these discount bins in neighborhood stores would often have incredible values on amazing wines and vintages.

I remember purchasing premium French Bordeaux and Rhone, from renowned vintners, for between $1 and $2 a bottle. I bought whatever looked good to me and shared them with my friend Steve Gannon, a New England native who I had met in Missouri. We became quite the youthful wine aficionados, back in the years when few Americans drank the stuff. I love the world of wine now, and I always have, ever since that low-cost tasting education in Boston.

Mary and I still were sociable, and she told me about a fellow she had dated by the name of Jeff McLaughlin, who wrote for the arts section of the Boston Globe. He had also been metro editor, shared a Pulitzer Prize and held many other positions at that prestigious newspaper.

He did not date Mary for very long, but he and I met, and Jeff became one of my closest lifetime friends.

Jeff was a true intellectual, but not in a stuffy, snobby way. He was a lover of all kinds of music, but he especially appreciated folk and roots music.

Back in the heyday of vinyl records, he had thousands of them, along with hundreds of books, all stashed in a large apartment about six blocks from Harvard Square, on Appleton Road. I would stay there intermittently the rest of the time I lived in Boston, and because of his kindness I frequently called that space home in later years, when I would tour the east coast doing concerts and shows. I also took some extra days to help him move out of that place, a few years later. Carrying all those records and books down those rickety stairs was quite the chore!

Jeff was always kind and friendly toward me and became a very good pal and confidante. His house was kind of a crash pad for many itinerant non-conformists and musicians back then, and he threw a number of memorable parties.

"I WOULDN'T COUNT ON IT" — CONFESSIONS OF AN UNLIKELY FOLKSINGER

I remember one such gathering he arranged for Maddy Prior and Steeleye Span after they performed a concert at Symphony Hall that lasted well into the next day. It was one of those after-show soirees which I was lucky enough to experience a few times in my music career, where memories the next day were short, the hangovers were long, the music continued when you woke up – and you knew you had been a part of something special.

I met Bill Morrissey, the fine songwriter who passed away a few years ago, at Jeff's house, long before Bill became well known in the folk world. Bill was in a pretty down period then, living at Jeff's after working a spell at a gas station. He was soon to make a big impact in the acoustic music world with his powerful songs such as "Birches."

Hearing Bill's songs was like experiencing a minimalist play. There was no fat or gushy sentiment, just the import of well-chosen words against a simple canvas of melody. He enjoyed McDonald's hamburgers, whisky, and poetry. His passing at age 59 was a great loss to lovers of concise, descriptive songwriting.

Jeff talked about musicians and books and introduced me to lots of folks like Bill who I was not familiar with, but who would later become friends: people like Utah Phillips, Tom Rush and many others. He also gave me ideas on authors to read, other kinds of music to listen to, poetry, and so much more. Though he graduated from Harvard University at 17, he was as down to earth, unprepossessing, and as modest of a man as I have ever known.

Jeff was a lifelong learner and inspiration and one of the most gentle and interesting people I have ever met – and I miss him. He passed away suddenly in 2006 after retiring from editing the Cape and Islands edition of the Boston Globe.

He was also an avid Red Sox baseball fan.

I have always been a St. Louis Cardinals baseball fan due to my time living there and the fact the their legendary 1960's pitcher, Bob Gibson, came from my hometown of Omaha. I had the opportunity to meet Bob there many times.

Though I was sorry the Cardinals lost the 2004 World Series in four games to Boston, I was grateful Jeff got to see one Red Sox championship in his lifetime, when they broke the dreaded "curse of the Bambino" (the hex supposedly affixed to the Red Sox after they traded Babe Ruth to the Yankees). He was so thrilled about that series victory: He phoned and needled me good-naturedly for an hour after the final out.

I was burning to make my first record during this time in Boston. I had recorded a number of demos in both Toronto and Chicago, during the early seventies, but so far no record deal had materialized. An old acquaintance and supporter, Don Fitch, offered to bankroll my first album, which wound up being recorded at the Grange Studios, just outside of Toronto, in the summer of 1978.

It was produced by my old buddy Peter Mathieson, and the arrangements of the songs were quite pop-oriented, which is difficult for me to go back and listen to now. It kind of fit the definition of being "overproduced." However, it was recorded that way for the music market of the time, and it eventually did wind up being a (failed) Capitol of Canada release. Later I would buy the rights back and release it on my own label.

I remember vividly the night before I left Boston to drive to Canada to record that album. I spent the night in Watertown with a woman I had met when I delivered her rug a month or so earlier (yes, really!). My little Toyota station wagon was parked in front of her house, with everything I owned in it.

When I got up early the next morning and hit the road for Ontario, I felt as if the sun was rising just for me. It was as good as a feeling as I would ever have in my life, heading for the northland to record my first real album in the summer of my 25th year.

As I recall, the actual recording project and mixing took about a week. It was done on a 16-track, two-inch tape machine in a well-equipped studio in Whidby, Ontario. The studio was in an old, cozy farmhouse, and I sang through their venerable Neumann U-47 microphone.

The whole process was a preview of the thousands of hours I have spent in studios since then, recording not only my own albums, but also my national radio program; producing other people's albums; and other studio work. But at the time, it was all new and exciting.

I chose the title song to be "Vignette." It was a piece inspired by a restaurant I used to walk by in Toronto when I was performing in the Yorkville area, one of those places with the menu and prices posted by the doorway. Looking at those prices, I knew it was extremely unlikely I would ever eat there. So, I imagined what it must be like inside on a cold, Canadian weekday night, with just a bartender, waiter and young woman in the cafe as closing time approached.

Lightfoot had mentioned he really liked that song, and other folks seemed to enjoy it, too, so I decided to make it the name of the album.

Vignette

Quiet and lovely she walked in
alone in the Cafe Auberge
no escort to look into her azure eyes
he theorized why she was alone

He played his waiter's role and talked politely
stealing looks at the stockings that she'd worn
He brought her Beaujolais, upon a silver tray
It was a weekday and the place was empty

He served and he smiled at her laughter
the lapses in formality were more
about to pour a glass of that Burgundy again
she took his hand and spoke very softly

"Dining alone isn't easy
come share a glass of my wine
your willing eyes speak with approval
don't be shy, you're welcome anytime
don't be shy, you're welcome anytime"

So, they talked until the time came for closing
discounting the glasses they had filled
They found they forgot what their places might be
and the keys that she gave to him were sterling

And she said, "Sleeping alone isn't easy
come share a glass of my wine
your willing eyes speak with approval
don't be shy, you're welcome anytime
don't be shy, you're welcome anytime"

The night seemed to slip away quickly
quietly the farewells were past
the parting took place just a year ago it seems
but the waiter still dreams of her saying

"Dining alone isn't easy
come share a glass of my wine
your willing eyes speak with approval
don't be shy, you're welcome anytime
don't be shy, you're welcome anytime"

Tom May copyright 1977 Blue Vignette ASCAP

After the album "Vignette" was finished, I flew to St. Louis to preview it for my benefactor, then back to Boston, where I would wait for another few months until it was released. I figured I might as well work at Able Rug for a few more months and play some more Boston and Cambridge gigs before fame and fortune were sure to come my way!

"I WOULDN'T COUNT ON IT" — CONFESSIONS OF AN UNLIKELY FOLKSINGER

Though I mostly enjoyed working at the rug company, I yearned to devote more time and energy to my music and get back to performing full time. To that end, I made a decision to move back to St. Louis, where the living was cheaper, and it seemed to me there were more performing opportunities at that time than there were in Boston.

I had saved the money for the move out of my meager wages, and I always tried to cut corners where I could.

Oftentimes those corners involved technicalities such as taxes, car licensing, insurance, etc. (I have long since reformed in that area.)

The entire time I lived in Boston I drove around with Nebraska plates. They had finally expired just a couple of months before I had planned on moving, so a buddy of mine gave me his old Massachusetts plates to put on my car for that short period. Unfortunately, I got stopped by an officer for cutting a yellow light a little too close. I handed over my license and registration, which of course did not match my plates, and proceeded to explain to the exasperated officer that I was moving next week.

After telling me how serious my offenses were, and how many fines and penalties would be involved, he said "I don't ever want to see you again: Don't drive this route before you leave, and if you are caught by someone else, don't mention this – and don't run any more yellows!" He let me go, bless his heart. It was a kinder, gentler time than today.

I departed to drive back to St. Louis in mid-December, perhaps not the best time to hit the road in an old Toyota station wagon that was not running particularly well. The road conditions were not ideal, and it was pretty icy as I drove through Pennsylvania. But the real problem was my headlights, which got progressively dimmer as I drove into the frosty evening. A mechanic told me my alternator must be going out and suggested I not turn off the car until I got to where I was going to stay, because it was not going to start again for me until I replaced that part.

I reached Washington, Pennsylvania, where interstates cross and many drivers have had unfortunate breakdowns (or so I have heard since my experience there; it is kind of like the Rock Springs, Wyoming, of Pennsylvania). My lights were almost out, it was 10 degrees, and there were few places to stay. The fellow at the gas station said they could fix the alternator the next morning and suggested either a rooming house up the road, or the Holiday Inn, which he said cost $40 a night.

At that time in my life, $40 was a perilously high amount for one night's lodging. It might as well have been $400, so I went to the rooming house. The proprietor said she was out of regular rooms, but she had one left that had no heat. I gratefully took it and paid her the $10 she asked for it. The temperature dipped to well below zero that evening, and that room was as cold inside as it was outside. I wore as many clothes as I could put on and had a restless, shivering sleep, but at least I wasn't covered in snow when I woke up. I got the alternator fixed the next day and headed for St. Louis.

VIGNETTE: ST. LOUIS

I CERTAINLY COULDN'T HAVE KNOWN IT AS I COVered the last few miles to St. Louis in that Toyota that was running on only half its cylinders, but my luck and life were about to take a dramatic turn.

Moving back to St. Louis with no ties, few possessions, but lofty aspirations, I was about to enter the most settled time in my life. It sure didn't start that way.

I first bunked at Diana's house, the nurse/anesthetist I mentioned earlier. The romantic spark just wasn't there though, and a friend from my earlier sojourn in the area suggested I move out to a spare bedroom of his house in St. Charles, just across the Missouri River.

It was a welcome safe harbor, and seeing as my savings were quickly diminishing while I was waiting for fame and fortune to strike, a necessary one, too. I will always be grateful to Don Fitch for his unflagging belief in me at that wandering time in my life.

As the holidays approached, my parents really desired a visit from me, so my dad flew me back to Omaha for Christmas. I was at an old high school buddy's house there, drinking beer, when he had a call from a mutual friend of ours about a party that he was hosting that night – and we all decided to go. At that gathering, I put on the tape of my album and played a few songs,

Vignette: St. Louis

particularly directing them at a comely, unattended woman who seemed interested.

It was a life-changing evening. Her name was Michaela Reilly, and she would eventually become my second wife and the mother of my son – a 16-year union that I am still so very grateful for. She is one of the sweetest, kindest human beings I have ever known.

After my brief stay in Omaha we did not see each other until she came to St. Louis a month or so later. She was a school teacher, so time off was hard to come by, but she did eventually visit me. We were so in love, as only young people can be.

Michaela came from a large Catholic family in Omaha and had attended University in Ireland. She had experienced a couple of disappointing relationships but was willing to try again, even with a musician with little money and vague prospects. Between my gigs in St. Louis, I would hop on the Greyhound bus and "ride the dog" overnight to Omaha to see her, to steal even just a day or two. It was a whirlwind time of romantic excitement, desire, and anticipation.

Back in St. Louis I was performing frequently, primarily in a newly developed area of warehouses down on the waterfront known as Laclede's Landing. It was located on the Missouri side of the famous Eads bridge, which connected East to West when it became one of the first spans across the Mississippi River in the 1870's. There were many brand-new clubs down there, and a number of them were willing to give me a gig. I remember Kennedy's Pub and Chapin's Restaurant as being fun, regular sources of income.

At my typical engagement during that period I would do a few of my own songs, some songs by Canadians I had met and respected (Valdy, Lightfoot, Cockburn, Peter Mathieson) and a couple of John Hartford songs. I also threw in a smattering of popular songs that I had been able to come up with interesting guitar arrangements for, like "Please Come to Boston" or Joan Baez's "Diamonds and Rust."

There were some songs then that virtually everybody who

"I WOULDN'T COUNT ON IT" — CONFESSIONS OF AN UNLIKELY FOLKSINGER

played guitar in bars were doing, and being kind of stubborn I absolutely refused to learn or do. Among those were "American Pie," (I actually like Don McLean, the writer, but I got so sick of hearing that damn song), "Fire and Rain" (same situation: I like the writer, I like the song, but it has been done!) anything by Cat Stevens, Neil Young or Neil Diamond (I sometimes told folks it was a one hundred percent no Neil show), and I wouldn't be caught dead doing a version of Kenny Rogers' "The Gambler," which was another one I got asked for every night.

I also had begun to hear some of my contemporaries' songs that I thought were memorable (despite the fact they were not on the radio) and I would learn them and incorporate them into my show. I always had just enough popular singer/songwriter material that the audience might hear a song or two per set they were familiar with, The rest of the time, they were just going to have to listen and trust me – or vote with their feet, as happened often enough.

Whether a large or tiny audience, I would practice my spoken introductions and work on them being entertaining, concise and interesting. I was never as glib or effortlessly funny as some of my pals, but I did my best and worked at it. I somehow sensed this would serve me well down the line.

As a young man with no guidance whatsoever, I'm amazed I didn't get into more serious trouble than I did in those years. In the musician circles I had traveled in, everyone drank copious amounts of alcohol before, after and sometimes while they performed. Most places it was considered part of your pay. I had occasionally drunk too much on stage, but I mostly kept that in check.

I do remember a night on the Landing in St. Louis, at Kennedy's, walking in with my guitar after spending all day in a bar in South St. Louis with friends. I was already well lubricated. A writer from the St. Louis Post Dispatch by the name of Jake McCarthy, who had been known to have a few toddies himself, was there to see me and noticed my uncertain gait as I entered. He proceeded to give me the advice to "stay high," and bought me some powerful mixed drinks throughout the evening. I don't know how I even made it through that night: I'm sure it sounded dreadful.

I resolved to never do that again, and pretty much have fulfilled that resolution.

St. Louis was full of excitement about the redevelopment of those historic parts of town and had lots of new venues at which to perform. I wound up being a regular at a place called First St. Alley on Laclede's Landing, and I would play there four to five nights a week. I met and heard some fascinating music and musicians.

One memorable set of performers were the M and M Girls – a quartet of geriatric female traditional Dixieland players, led by an ex-madam of a brothel in East St. Louis. They had some of the filthiest lyrics I have ever heard sung on stage, and they were so much fun, they would pack them in whenever they performed. They used some very interesting word pairings in their version of "Barnacle Bill the Sailor." Visiting with them was a glimpse into another, less ordered, no-holds-barred time.

I didn't travel out of town to perform much during these years, because I had so much work locally. I wasn't doing many concerts, but I was playing plenty of enjoyable gigs where people by and large would actually listen. It was pre-cell phone, pre-internet, and even pre-VCR days, and people were more attentive, less distracted and more social than today.

I did some odd engagements there, too. Three days a week, from 11 AM to 1 PM, I played at a cafeteria in a converted old bank building, named Fourth and Pine. I would have to find a parking spot, feed the meter, haul my PA in there and play a couple of sets – all for the princely sum of $20. What the hell, it was paid rehearsal. An odd little side note is that they would occasionally do large rock n' roll shows there at night, and I wound up opening for Herman's Hermits there – twice! This is not something listed on my professional bio.

On a typical Friday, I would perform at Fourth and Pine from 11 AM to 1 PM. Then, I would play happy hour at First St. Alley

"I WOULDN'T COUNT ON IT" — CONFESSIONS OF AN UNLIKELY FOLKSINGER

from 5 PM to 8 PM. Fortunately, First Alley had its own PA setup. Getting out of there quickly, I would perform at a restaurant-bar in Clayton called The Leather Bottle from 9 PM to 12:30 AM.

This was in about 1981, and altogether on a day like that I would make $135 for my efforts. It doesn't sound like much now, but life was a lot cheaper, and it seemed like a fair sum back in those days. It was a kind of "music by the pound" approach, but I was practicing my craft – and mostly having fun, too.

As I stand on stage, it has always amazed me that folks don't know – or care, I guess – what you can hear and see from your position in front of them. I could pick up conversations all the way from the back of the room, depending on the place. I heard some very interesting arguments, accusations, off-color jokes and stories.

At the aforementioned Leather Bottle, a well-lubricated bunch took the pantyhose and panties off one of their fellow workers, about 10 feet from where I was performing. At that same place, late at night when everyone was gone from the room except for one affectionate couple in the back booth and myself, I watched as they clearly had sex by pulling clothes aside and twisting around in an uncomfortable looking fashion. It made me feel kind of lonesome – and amused – as I sang my tender ballads.

I RECEIVED A call from a production company in St. Louis I had approached about doing some opening acts. One of them was to be an opener for a farewell tour concert by the Midwest favorites Brewer and Shipley, who had hits in the 70's with their songs "Tarkio Road" and "One Toke over the Line." Interestingly enough, I would share a festival stage with them 16 years later. They became notorious for their annual farewell tours.

I also was booked in Southern Illinois to open a show for one of the hot, big hair, power rock bands of that era, a group called

Vignette: St. Louis

Starcastle. The concert was in a big venue with a revolving stage, a layout that was popular back then (and thankfully now has pretty well disappeared). You had to be careful as you walked up the aisle to the stage to meet it exactly at the gap in the railing around it, so you could successfully get to your microphone stand as it kept revolving. Weird.

Now, you wouldn't think that the crowd going to a Starcastle show would appreciate a burly, red-bearded folksinger, but I remember the audience being okay. I almost killed myself exiting that dumb stage, though. I was vindicated in my clumsiness when one of the featured band's members who followed me on during their big entrance fell on his face as the stage revolved, dropped his drumsticks – and yelled a loud obscenity as he tried to crawl onstage. It was the best moment of the show.

I MET ANOTHER one of my lifetime friends in St. Louis during this time, a talented guitarist and singer originally from Minnesota, named Mark Moebeck. Mark was also very busy, performing constantly in St. Louis at that time, and we became close pals. He had a fine voice and was an excellent musician, as well as having a skewed sense of humor, which made him so much fun to be around.

Mark also would do one of the most unusual regular gigs I ever heard of: "Ralph and Charlie's," from midnight on Sunday until 4 AM in the morning on Monday, at a seedy steak house in Granite City, Illinois. I accompanied him there a few times. The place would be empty until about 2 AM, then be packed until 4 AM – bizarre. You took your gigs where you could find them.

In the winter of 1980, First St. Alley talked to me about putting together some Irish music for St. Patrick's Day. Mark knew a couple of Irish songs, I knew one, and we figured how hard could

"I WOULDN'T COUNT ON IT" — CONFESSIONS OF AN UNLIKELY FOLKSINGER

it be to learn more? We lived in the same apartment complex in the central city area, and we decided to practice a whole repertoire for St. Patrick's Day that year.

We learned 30 or 40 songs from Clancy Brothers albums, Chieftain's albums, and other sources, over pots and pots of hot coffee. We had a good time and lots of laughs learning these pieces, and we were loaded for bear when St. Patrick's Day came around. (To amuse ourselves, we made up parodies of those traditional songs – with words like, "The Menstrual Boy to the drugstore has gone, with his beltless shield you will find him.")

I think that first year playing St. Patrick's Day at First St. Alley, we did eight or nine sets. It's hard to imagine that now! The songs were washed down by Guinness, Irish coffees, and later in the evening, chloroseptic mouthwash for our sore throats.

Mark and I would continue to play Irish songs at St. Patrick's celebrations for years to come. I recall one year in St. Louis we began performing at 8 in the morning, at a place called the Blarney Stone on Laclede's Landing. At noon we went over to

TOM, PETER MATHIESON, AND MARK MOEBECK, ST. LOUIS 1980

Vignette: St. Louis

John D. McGurk's (still a legendary Irish pub) to play from noon until 4 PM. Then back to First St. Alley from 5 PM to 9 PM, then off to a place in Lafayette Square called Ronayne's to finish off the night.

We sang, cajoled, croaked, laughed, drank a lot, incited lots of people to have fun and generally deported ourselves in a rowdy fashion. It's a miracle we made it home that night.

One year, Mark and I had a request from the McGurk's management to incorporate an Irish lad who played there occasionally into our St. Patrick's Day sets. His name was Seamus, and I vaguely knew him but was by no means familiar with the songs he played. That was okay – because after he had a few drinks, neither was he. He was embarrassingly drunk the whole day, but we would have him sing a song every once in a while and do our best to accompany him. When Mark and I would do our regular St. Pat's Day tunes and he tried to play along, we just turned his volume down. He didn't even notice.

I had booked an additional private party at a Catholic Church that St. Patrick's Day that we would do after our McGurk's sets. Seamus wanted to come sing with us at the gig, and I didn't have the heart to say no. Besides, he sang songs, although badly, that we didn't want to do. We just plinked along behind him and attempted to appear cool and detached.

Just before we left McGurk's that day in my van to head to the church for the gig, a sold out pre-paid dinner for the parishioners, Seamus picked up this sexy young girl in an extremely short kilt that did nothing to conceal her beguiling attributes, and he invited her to come with us. Now, this pissed me off more than I could say, but she was in my van before I even knew what he had done, So I figured, "what the hell."

The seats were arranged around circular tables, and every chair was spoken for by folks who had reserved for the show/dinner. We got there, and Mark and I set up the PA. Seamus's date was ungallantly reposing in one of those chairs when the audience started coming in. The organizer came to me and said, "one of your 'entourage" is sitting in an assigned seat." I told Seamus to get her the hell out of there and tell her to find somewhere else to light. His reply was "she has to sit down, she can't feckin' walk. But he did get her to move and rearrange her clothes a bit so not quite so much skin was in full view of the old folks.

But it continued to get stranger. As we were packing up to leave after the show, one of the nuns from the connected church school who had been at the concert came up to talk to this cutie. It turns out Seamus's "girlfriend" had actually gone to school there, and this nun had been her teacher. The nun prattled on to the very drunk girl and even more drunk Seamus for awhile, until I hustled them out of there.

The nun's last words to Seamus as we left were, "Take good care of my little girl." I'm sure he did.

AND SPEAKING OF Irish ballads, St. Louis provided an incredibly rich education in that melody-driven form of music. Shortly after Michaela and I moved into our humble apartment on Russell and Grand, the aforementioned Irish pub, John D. McGurk's, had opened at 12th and Russell, a little over a mile down the road from our abode.

I had heard some Irish tunes and ballads in Ireland and some played very badly in the U.S., but the songs, traditional tunes and musicians at McGurk's were a revelation and would become a significant part of my own musical education and identity.

The first group I heard there was The Irish Brigade, featuring Mike Wallace and Gerry Goodwin, both from County Limerick. Their spirited rendition of Irish ballads and their way of getting the crowd to participate was so infectious – I was enthralled by the whole scene. They would spend many of their Sunday nights

Vignette: St. Louis

off drinking and listening to me at First St. Alley, and I would spend many of my off nights at McGurk's.

McGurk's featured music five nights a week, and the bands that played there would lodge in an old row house next door, jokingly referred to as "The Palace" while they were in town. All of them were of Irish descent, and most were from Ireland, many of them on their first trip to the U.S. Most of them were guys, and the whole experience of free alcohol, willing U.S. girls, and a crowd in love with the whole idea of Ireland and Irish music was a life-changing experience for them. Talk about letting the roosters loose in the henhouse!

A veritable Who's Who of traditional Irish music would come through McGurk's, and I made a point to get to know them and listen to them all. It only cost the price of a Guinness and arriving early for a good seat to hear virtuosic, legendary artists in a room that originally was not much bigger than a living room. Later on, McGurk's would expand quite a bit, but in the early days it was just one smallish room and the bar.

Joe Burke, James Kelly, Jackie Daly, Triona Ni Domnhaill and Michael O Domnhaill, Paddy O'Brien and Tony McMahon are just a few of the musicians who would do a month at a time at McGurk's. Often, when the evening's formal music would be done, we would adjourn to the Palace for more drinks and songs until the wee hours of the morning.

I also met another one of my lifetime pals there, the Dublin born and raised Irish singer Peter Yeates, who at that time was performing with the Scot Steve Mulligan. Peter was to figure into my life in many ways over the next 40 years and has always been a good friend.

MICHAELA AND I lived in St. Louis for almost three

"I WOULDN'T COUNT ON IT" — CONFESSIONS OF AN UNLIKELY FOLKSINGER

TOM, PETER YEATES 1982

years. Our time there was spent with her teaching, me playing music constantly and writing songs, and it was by and large a peaceful, happy time. I was performing locally many nights a week, and in the summers, we would go to her parents' summer home between Estes Park and Allenspark, Colorado. I would do a few gigs and concerts while we were out there, as well as a lot of hiking, climbing and generally enjoying the beauty of that region.

In the spring of 1981, through the intercession of Peter Yeates, who hailed from Vancouver, Washington – just across the river from Portland, Oregon, I obtained a three-week gig at a bar in Salem, Oregon. It was a decent listening room, and I had good luck attracting an audience. The daily newspaper there, The Statesman Journal, did an in-depth story on me that graced the cover of its entertainment magazine during that run. It was a big boost to me during that time. I also was reminded again how beautiful Oregon was and resolved to get back there more often.

During that charmed period I also met two more of my dearest friends, Tom Bryson and Claire Levine. Tom was working as a bartender in Salem and Claire was doing freelance journalism. We all became buddies, and though Tom and Claire are no longer together, my relationship with each of them has lasted a lifetime. I would wind up being a welcome visitor at many of the places they would call home in subsequent years, while I worked my way across the Pacific Northwest.

In the autumn of 1981, we found out Michaela was pregnant. The baby was due in May of 1982. We were both happy about the news, though I was concerned about being trapped into a life where I could no longer

have the freedom to travel and perform because of my increased responsibilities. I wasn't willing to give up on the dream of a full time musical career, but it seemed like it was about to get a lot more difficult.

Then, somewhere, somehow, a person emerged to help me get back on the road again. Jerry Rock was a friend of a friend who had ambitions of starting a booking/management agency. He hired a woman, Carol, to do the booking for him and took me on as his first client.

Jerry was a TV producer for the local CBS affiliate, had lots of connections, and had filmed segments on me. He regularly came to hear me perform and committed himself to helping me reach more people with my music.

Carol was very conscientious and hardworking, uncharacteristically so for an agent, and soon I had a tour of the western U.S. scheduled for the spring of 1982. I was thrilled to be going on the road to do concerts again and looked forward to seeing more of the western landscapes – where my heart has always been. If there really is a geography of the soul, then mine has always been the dramatic mountains, deserts, and wide-open spaces of those territories west of the hundredth meridian in North America.

So, in that spring of 1982, I played in St. Louis, then headed for points west after the usual St. Patrick's Day bacchanal, returning home a couple of weeks before the baby was due. Also, since it looked as if I would be traveling more extensively,

Michaela and I made plans to move back to Omaha, where she had family and would have more support while I was touring.

I didn't want to move back to Omaha, but it was the sensible and responsible thing to do, particularly if I was going to be traveling much of the time. So, we made a plan to relocate that summer, after the baby was born.

COMING HOME: NEBRASKA

THE TOUR THAT I DID IN THAT SPRING OF 1982 was an emphatic reminder of the reason I had chosen to play and write music for a living. I left St. Louis that March with a slew of dates from Omaha to Seattle to Portland and Sandpoint, Idaho, and lots of places in between.

After having reverted to primarily being a tavern singer (though there is certainly no shame in that) in those St. Louis years, it was so energizing to be performing my own songs again in front of people who were really there to listen, in a concert situation.

That being said, I do still believe the best experience, for both performer and audience, is an atmosphere where
most everyone is attentive but people still feel relaxed and can have a glass of wine or a beer, or a coffee or tea, in what's often called a "cabaret" setting. Concert halls are beautiful places to play your music but can feel kind of stiff. An intimate cabaret style listening room, with tables instead of rigid rows of seats, remains my favorite kind of venue.

The year 1982 had a typical western U.S. springtime: some occasional beautiful weather, intermittent snow, white-knuckle drives – and a windshield full of what I consider to be the most gorgeous scenery on earth.

In April on that trip I was booked to play at a tavern in Portland, Oregon, a place whose owner Peter Yeates and Steve

Mulligan knew well and where they had performed themselves various times. It was called the Horse Brass Pub.

I used to fancy I could find most places in big cities just by reading road signs and going on instinct. Though that method sometimes got me into trouble, it worked well this particular day. I saw an exit off I-5 that would lead me to Belmont Street, and the address I was looking for was 4534 SE Belmont.

It was an early Saturday afternoon, I had no gig that night, and I was due to perform at the Horse Brass the next evening. I parked right in front of the establishment and walked in. It was a lovely afternoon, and almost no one was inside the pub.

What first struck me as I walked in was the sense I was back in England again, at a cozy getaway in a small village. The place was fairly dark, but had big windows in the front letting in lots of brilliant Oregon sunshine. It was, and is, a totally unprepossessing storefront that one could easily miss, with just a modest sized pub sign – illustrated with a horse with a collar and the name of the pub.

It was woody throughout, with old clear fir flooring and post and beam construction. The tables were Victorian-style cast iron and dark mahogany, many of them true antiques, as were the chairs. The bar itself was long, with an awning over the back bar. It was lit by a few lamps that were covered in the Victorian style by colored fabric.

The scent of cigarettes, beer and good times hung in the room, kind of like an exotic perfume. The walls had started out white textured plaster, but now were a soft muted brown, testimony to the thousands of pipes and cigarettes enjoyed there. Right up until the time smoking became illegal in pubs and restaurants in Oregon in 2006, the Horse Brass was always an incredible smoky place, just like pubs in England and Ireland. Even though I have never smoked, I appreciated the ambience.

Overall, the effect was quite comfortable, rustic, unassuming – and quite unusual for the U.S. of A.

Behind the bar that day was a hale and hearty, red bearded teddy bear of a man by the name of Clay Connolly.

He was expecting me and began by pouring me a glass of Bass Ale while he called the owner, who I would be staying with that weekend and who lived in a house just steps away from the pub.

In a few minutes, a thin, bearded man with short black hair and black horn rim glasses joined us at the bar. Don Younger was his name, and he had owned the Horse Brass since 1976. He and Clay proceeded to give me an international beer tour without us ever leaving our barstools. This was before the days of local microbreweries.

Don later wound up being very instrumental in the regional and national microbrewery explosion, but at the time the Horse Brass had Bass Ale and Guinness on tap. It also offered a large variety of international brands in bottles, including Samuel Smith's, some of the Belgian beers, Anchor Steam and many others.

So, after a number of hours of stimulating conversation, numerous pints, and what can only be called an amazing welcome to Portland, the Horse Brass Pub and the secrets of the nascent real beer revival that was underway, I stumbled over to Don's house and the extra bedroom he had there for me to collapse in. This turned out to be a prelude to decades during which I would stay with Don when I came to the region. Wherever he moved, he made sure he always had a guest bedroom available and invited me to stay for as long as I was in the area.

The next night, when I performed at the Horse Brass, the place was not full but had a respectable crowd gathered. Among the folks there was Terry Prohaska, another fine musician who would become a longtime pal and musical compatriot. This night marked the first of what would be more than 30 years of my appearances at the pub. As to the number of beers consumed during that time, I wouldn't even hazard to make a guess – but I can tell you that the worst I ever tasted there was wonderful!

Don hosted occasional music at the Horse Brass in the years

before I showed up, but as the years went by he pretty much cut back to no music at all, except for the few nights a year I would perform there. Interestingly enough, Don wasn't overly fond of folk music, but he loved my songs and also enjoyed Peter Yeates and Terry Prohaska.

Mostly though, he considered musicians a pain in the ass. In that opinion, he had lots of company in the world of venue operators and promoters.

The rest of that spring tour was also memorable, and I knew I was back on the road where I was meant to be.

A few years later I was in Baltimore, Maryland, performing at a place called Bertha's Mussels. Perhaps you have seen their catchy bumper stickers – "Eat Bertha's Mussels." A couple of traditional folkies, John Roberts and Tony Barrand, had written a song for that establishment, which was one of their favorite pubs. I thought, "If they can do that for their favorite establishment, surely the Horse Brass Pub and Don Younger, two of the treasures of this nation, deserve a song too."

Here is my paean to that unique place. Be sure to stop by if you are anywhere close. There is nothing like singing this at the Horse Brass, with a chorus of happy friends and beer drinkers joining in.

The Ballad of the Horse Brass Pub

If you're ever in Portland with the old hangtown blues
your pockets as low down as a bum's pair of shoes
take the Morrison bridge, head up Belmont way
there's a horse, with a collar, on a sign that will say

Chorus
Have a Grant's beer for me, at least two or three
beneath the soccer flags waving from the ceiling up above
you're a stranger no more, when you walk through that door
you'll find what you're after at last

Coming Home: Nebraska

a drink and a smile at the old Horse Brass

After one beer you'll find that the bartender's kind
but don't play him in cribbage, or darts all the same
for you'll find that if you do, that he's better than you
and you'll have only your bad luck, and the good beer to blame

Repeat chorus

From a ship at the pier, came a sailor for beer
Birmingham seemed such a long ways away
then he walked in the Brass, sat and ordered a Bass
now he's drinking there nightly, 'til this very day

Repeat chorus

Don is at the bar, that Brian is behind
Marge serves the brew with some mischief in mind
Howard moves his pegs, Mike smokes his pipe
here at the Horse Brass, it'll be a good night

Repeat chorus

Now I've traveled this country from pillar to post
there's weak beer and strangers from coast to coast
but there's a bit of old England, kind faces to be found
in the Oregon rain, of old Portland town

Have a Grant's beer for me, at least two or three
beneath the soccer flags waving from the ceiling up above
you're a stranger no more, when you walk through that door
you'll find what you're after at last
a drink and a smile at the old Horse Brass
a smile, and a good friend, at the old Horse Brass
I've gotten in lots of trouble, at the old Horse Brass

copyright Tom May, 1989 Blue Vignette ASCAP

"I WOULDN'T COUNT ON IT" — CONFESSIONS OF AN UNLIKELY FOLKSINGER

The last night of the tour I did a concert in Salem. Time was drawing near to the predicted date for the birth of our child, so I departed immediately after the gig that evening, drove through the night and arrived in Omaha after a 20-hour journey, punctuated only by a short nap at a rest area in western Nebraska. I got some sleep at my parents' house and continued on to St. Louis.

OCEANSIDE OREGON, 1982 "COMING HOME" ALBUM COVER

HAVING OPENED THE door to touring again, my life began to really get hectic. Dylan Reilly May was born May 18, 1982. We had a scare when he was born, and he needed to be hospitalized for a few days before he came home. Thanks to modern medicine, however, he was a healthy, loud voiced, spirited baby boy.

Michaela and I moved back to Omaha that summer, and by autumn she had a job as a teacher. That September I lined up a month-long gig in St. Louis with my old pal Mark Moebeck, to perform a few nights a week at the Blarney Stone on Laclede's Landing. That pub was located in a dank, humid basement. It was hard, sweaty work, but it gave me the funds to record my second album, which I did in early October 1982.

Coming Home: Nebraska

The project was called "Coming Home," and was a mix of my songs and songs by friends that I was performing at that time. It was destined never to find a home with a record company, though I tried hard to accomplish that goal. It was a reminder that rejection is the partner to success in the arts, as well as in other professions and endeavors in life.

The new record was recorded at Technisonic Studios in St. Louis, which was built as a "quadrophonic" recording facility. Quadrophonic sound was a fad of the day that never caught on, but it was a nice facility.

When I have listened to cuts off that album in recent years, it is obvious to me I was still in an early learning phase in my career. Most of it doesn't stand the test of time, at least to my ears. (My son, Dylan, likes it a lot.)

Mark Moebeck sang harmony with me on some of the tracks, and he suggested for the sessions a keyboard player he knew by the name of Avery Grimes. Avery was not primarily a musician. He worked in management for major railroads. He was, however, a fine pianist and added a lot to the songs.

Even more importantly on a personal level, he became a very close friend who would join me on stage frequently through the years. As Avery moved about the country back to Omaha, to the Pacific Northwest and eventually to Denver, he would also offer his home as a refuge to me, and we would indulge in many bottles of good red wine and hours of stories and songs.

I can't recall what enticement exactly coaxed me back out to Oregon after the album was done, but I know I was there because the album cover photo was taken at Oceanside, Oregon, by an old friend from Ontario, Andy Pavuls. I also know that I was still around there in Portland at Thanksgiving, because I attended the very first "Horse Brass Orphans Dinner," a tradition that would carry on until the present day.

Later that autumn I was across the continent back in Vermont, where I pitched Philo records to adopt the new album. It didn't work out, but I made other connections there that would eventually be helpful. So, that autumn I was in St. Louis, the Pacific Northwest, Ontario and New England, traveling by car, making the long drives, singing and performing wherever I could, and trying to make my way in the music business.

Though living back in Omaha was stifling in some ways, it did have the advantage of being right in the middle of the continental U.S. I resolved that I would not only tour extensively in the West, but also in the East, where I still had my connections from the years I lived in Boston and Toronto.

While I was contemplating putting all of that in motion, the rather severe winter of 1982-1983 was coming down around me in Omaha. I was performing at local watering holes pretty regularly and being a full time father and primary caregiver to my infant son while his mom taught school.

Dylan was then, and always has been, one of the lights of my life. However, it was a difficult transition for a guy who had no experience of babies or child raising to come off the freedom of the road and be a house daddy that winter. All the same, I am grateful for the experience and have fond memories of my little guy in his snowsuit that winter, bundled up against the cold as we would do errands together. As I was away from home much of the subsequent years, it was always an ache in my heart to be apart from Dylan and Michaela, despite the refuge and good times of the roads.

One of the aspects of being in Omaha that helped keep me sane was my membership in the downtown YMCA. I had become a Y member in St. Louis and was a devotee of the game of racquetball. That minor obsession continued in Omaha. I even entered some tournaments there and acquitted myself respectably.

I have been fighting a weight problem since I was a young boy. One way to confront this and at least keep it in check was exercise. All throughout my adult life, I would keep that YMCA membership and make good use of it. No matter where I traveled, from

Boston, Massachusetts, to Little Rock, Arkansas, I could go to the local YMCA, work out, and clear out the cobwebs from the road.

The local Y would also reveal some local color about the place you were, and I would strike up interesting conversations with the patrons. Nothing like being naked in a sauna or shower with other men to break down the barriers of geography, race and profession.

Also, the days on the road could be quite long and uneventful. Aside from the town library, the YMCA was the only place I could go where I could not only get my heart pumping, but also sit down afterwards, relax and read the local newspaper in a social environment. It helped fill in the empty hours, and I always felt welcome there. I would belong to the Y for all my extensive traveling years, and it was also an integral part of most every day I spent at home in Omaha.

IN CONCERT 1980'S

IN THE SPRINGTIME of 1983, I would return to New England and do a very important gig through the auspices of my dear friend, Jeff Mclaughlin. Jeff arranged for me to do a weekend at Passim in Harvard Square, which at the time was arguably the most important folk venue in the U.S. The descendant of the famous Club 47, where Joan

"I WOULDN'T COUNT ON IT" — CONFESSIONS OF AN UNLIKELY FOLKSINGER

Baez, Tom Rush and many others started their careers, it was located at 47 Palmer St.

In those days at Passim, there were two shows on Friday and Saturday night, then a Sunday matinee and a Sunday night show. On this, my first appearance there, I would open for Mason Daring and Jeannie Stahl. At the time, they were very popular in the world of acoustic music. Mason would go on to write acclaimed scores for the movies "The Return of the Seacaucus 7," "Lliana," and numerous other documentaries, as well as producing many award-winning albums.

Bob and Rae Ann Donlin ran Passim and were wonderful folks. Bob was the very definition of a quirky curmudgeon, but you just had to love the guy's wry smile and teasing nature. He had been a part of the beat poet movement in the late 50's and counted Ferlinghetti and Allen Ginsberg as pals.

Passim was a gift store during the day, in an alley close to the center of Harvard Square. At night, it became the premier folk club in the nation through the 80's and could seat around 125. There was a tiny, dingy little dressing room in the back of the club. As playful as Bob was, when he put up his finger back at the cash register indicating you were to do one more song, you knew you had better not go over that if you ever hoped to perform there again.

Often on weekends, folks would be lined up to attend the evening shows. It was always exciting, if unnerving, to play for such a knowledgeable audience – more unnerving than even opening for an act like Gordon Lightfoot. After that first weekend I performed there, both Bob and Rae Ann complimented me profusely and expressed a hope that I would come back often.

I took them up on that invitation and would drive or fly back to Boston numerous times during the 80's to play a weekend there, even when I was not specifically on tour in the East. Though I was never a headliner, I opened at Passim for Reilly and Maloney, Jack Hardy, Rod MacDonald and others.

I think Bob and Rae Ann enjoyed my western flavored stories and songs, which were quite a bit different from those of most of the East or West Coast artists who regularly performed there. I was disappointed to never get a weekend headline gig, but I did appreciate all the work and the chance to play at such a legendary venue.

You can't take rejection in the music business to heart. Through my career, I have had some incredible opportunities that few in this alternative music ever were offered, and I took advantage of those. Other times, I was passed over, for whatever the reason.

Somehow, I always wound up making a living at it and meeting people who appreciated the songs I wrote and sang – and really, that is just about all you can ask for. I have come to believe that everything else, including big money, notice in the press, and awards are all relatively unimportant and ephemeral. This lifestyle is a lot more like a vocation than the vacation many imagine it might be.

One truth I was beginning to fully appreciate in the music business was the importance of luck. Luck can take many forms for a traveling folksinger. I suppose the first element of luck is just getting to the gig safely, since almost all travel back then was done via automobile. Bill Staines, the intrepid New England singer/songwriter, used to tape a piece of paper on his dashboard with his name, home phone number and other details in case he was in a bad accident while touring.

Another element of luck would be the weather. Particularly when you are doing an important gig in a prestigious or well-known venue, you had better hope that the weather wasn't too bad – or in some parts of the country, too good. Folks will never remember that a weather event affected your turnout at a venue; only that you didn't draw. You will likely not be asked back to perform there again in a case like that, in addition to having a poor financially rewarding night if your recompense is based on cover charges.

Two situations of that sort come to mind. In the mid 80's,

on my annual East Coast swing, I was booked to play at a very renowned Somerville, Massachusetts, club called Johnny D's. Back then, Johnny D's featured many of the best-known acoustic artists of the day, and I felt honored to get the gig. Unfortunately, the night I was booked to play there, there was an hours-long torrential rainstorm in the Boston area. Walking into the club with my guitar was more like swimming.

The deluge continued all evening, and the audience was tiny. Though I was never asked back there, I had the consolation of meeting the renowned Scottish fiddle player Johnny Cunningham there that night who eventually became a good friend and occasional accompanist.

That illustrates another axiom of the road I found to be true: It is almost always better to be performing, even when the crowd is thin or obnoxious, than to not be working. So many times, as in that situation, something would happen, such as meeting Johnny Cunningham, that would redeem the experience.

Much later in my career, in about 2007, I did a concert in the Rose Garden Amphitheatre in Portland, Oregon, with my band. These concerts were free events sponsored by a trucking company and took place in August in that picturesque outdoor venue.

Huge crowds regularly attended – but not that night, as it was gently and persistently misting, which was extremely unusual for Portland in August. The mist was not quite enough to cancel the concert. They put an awning up over us, but the moisture minimized the audience that came to hear us. When I tried to book us there again, I was told that we simply didn't bring in a large enough crowd. All the rest of those August dates had perfect weather for the performers. Ah well, c'est la vie. Lady luck is either with you, or she ain't.

Coming Home: Nebraska

AUTUMNS WERE RESERVED for my favorite trip of the year, to the intermountain West – Wyoming, Montana, Idaho, Utah, the Pacific Northwest, and later in my career, Alaska.

In that period of time, the early 80's, Michaela, Dylan and I would spend at least part of the summer in Colorado, where her parents had a beautiful old cabin up a rutted mile and half dirt road. It had a fantastic view of the Diamond Face of Longs Peak and was between Estes Park and Allenspark off scenic Colorado Hwy. 7. While we were out there, I would book some gigs at mountain resorts or down in the town of Estes Park. Little did I imagine this would begin a tradition of more than 30 years of performing in Colorado each summer.

In 1980, on one of those trips to Colorado, I climbed the 14,000 ft. Longs Peak. Michaela's brother Don was supposed to join me on the climb, but that morning when I got up at 3 AM to get started he flaked out on me: he had been up late, drinking with pals.

I was determined to go anyway, and I am certainly glad I did. I have not been in shape like that since that golden summer. I hit the trail with a flashlight by 3:30 AM, hiked rapidly above the timberline and summited the peak by late morning – when I felt quite ill from the exertion and depleted oxygen supply.

Thousands of people make that ascent each year, but it was and remains a big deal to me. On that luminous morning I saw no one until after I started back down the mountain, and then there were only a very few folks on the trail.

Even at that age, in the good shape I was in, it took everything I had to climb that mountain. And since I am certain I will never climb another one at this point, I look back very fondly on the experience. My most vivid memory of the trek is the sun coming up over the flatlands of Eastern Colorado and lighting up the peaks all around me, as if a magnificent lamp from within the land had been switched on.

"I WOULDN'T COUNT ON IT" — CONFESSIONS OF AN UNLIKELY FOLKSINGER

♪ ♪ ♪ ♪ ♪

AFTER THAT FIRST appearance at Passim, I fell into a pattern of touring the East Coast every springtime. I would start the trip by traveling to St. Louis to do St. Patrick's Day with Mark Moebeck, then continue from there to whatever concerts and gigs I had lined up on the Eastern Seaboard.

I was doing my own booking. Back in those days, there was no internet and no e-mail. You were pretty well stuck with making long distance phone calls, still pretty expensive back then, and communicating and sending everything (contracts, records, posters, etc.) via regular mail.

I remember months when my phone bill was around $300, a hefty sum in those times. I looked for an agent to take over my booking, but then, as now, it is very difficult to find an agent if you are not generating a really substantial sum of money. Most agents take 10 to 20 percent of your pay, plus their expenses such as phone and postage.

No one likes booking themselves – it is the least fun part of the music business. However, with alternative forms of music, like folk or jazz, you better become good at it or find another line of work. That advice remains just as true now as it was in the 70's and 80's.

Another musician's rule is it is almost always better to book yourself and know what you are getting into than to rely upon someone else's words and initiative. I can't tell you how many times an agent lied about the type of gig it was or exaggerated the financial potential.

Though it is truly time intensive, requires a lot of organization, and really is a pursuit unto itself, it was proven to me many times that it was really the only way to go about actually making a living in music. Other friends, including David Mallett, Steve Gillette, Anne Hills, Greg Brown and others all signed with established booking agencies, only to be severely disillusioned as they waited for gigs – or found the efforts of their emissaries being dedicated to the current "flavor of the month" musician who would bring the greatest revenues into the agent's coffers, rather than themselves. All of those folks again book themselves today.

IN BETWEEN THE regional tours, I would keep busy with gigs in Omaha or a day or so drive from there. Chicago, Kansas City, Denver, St. Louis, and Minneapolis-St. Paul were all close enough you could get there in a day.

The Mill in Iowa City became a regular stop three weekends a year or so. Keith Dempster, owner of the Mill, was cut from the same cloth as Don Younger at the Horse Brass in Portland. Outspoken, opinionated and boisterous, a collector of BMW motorcycles and antiques, he hardly had a good word to say about anyone. But he was generous, helpful, and cared very much about the music. He became a good friend, and I stayed with him many, many times in a farmhouse built by his parents in the 19th century.

Keith had a large book collection in his home (I remember reading the book "American Caesar" there, about General Douglas McArthur) as well as copies of "Broadsides" and "Sing Out" magazines from the early 1960's.

The first weekend I performed at the Mill in the early 80's, I recall Keith wanting me to linger with him at the bar after closing time. We chatted and argued about literature over a rapidly diminishing bottle of whiskey until the sun came up, and then I headed straight for St. Louis with no sleep – taking the picturesque Mississippi River road.

Thanks for the whiskey, the gigs and the memories, Keith.

"I WOULDN'T COUNT ON IT" — CONFESSIONS OF AN UNLIKELY FOLKSINGER

SPEAKING ABOUT BOOKS, they were constant friends and companions to me on those long solo journeys.

There was always a lot of waiting around in this crazy profession – waiting for the venue to open, waiting for the soundman to show up, waiting to make a booking phone call at the proper time – and books helped fill those idle hours. I always made sure to have a few of them stashed in the van.

In 1983, for Father's Day, Michaela gave me the present of a book that Jeff McLaughlin from Boston had told me about: "Blue Highways," written by William Least Heat-Moon. I have re-read it countless times since then, and it really became kind of a bible to me. It is filled with anecdotes of people, places, and legends and customs along the less traveled secondary roads of America.

Decades later, I would write a song called "Blue Roads, Red Wine," inspired at least in part by that book. The cover of the CD by that title features myself sitting at the Horse Brass Pub in Portland, with that book on the table. I sent the author a copy of the album, and he sent me back a very thoughtful and complimentary letter that I treasure.

There are so many authors who have impacted not only my songs but also the way I look at travel and life. A very incomplete list would mention John Steinbeck, Ivan Doig, Jack London, Stephen E. Ambrose, Nathaniel Philbrick, Annie Proulx, Wallace Stegner and so many others. I gravitate toward history, geography and non-fiction, which has been the focus of many of my songs, but I enjoy a well-constructed novel, too.

I don't understand this often-anti-literate, frequently belligerently ignorant world we inhabit today. Aside from music, travel and women, many of the greatest pleasures of my life have come from the hours spent with books.

IN BETWEEN MY touring life, I was always casting about for more local opportunities.

The Nebraska Arts Council was quite active in promoting concerts throughout the state, and I applied for their touring artist program. The application was a maze of paperwork, work samples and other bureaucratic hoops, but I completed it all and was admitted to the program. It was actually quite a good deal. As always, I had to do all the booking myself with the presenters, but as I specified, I was paid a fee of $600 per concert, plus expenses. And album sales were an additional form of income at the concerts, as they were for all the gigs I did.

The Nebraska Arts Council paid 40 percent of that $600 fee, and the presenter paid the rest. I was able to perform in such bucolic Nebraska locales as Loup City, Chadron, Tecumseh, and once I even did a concert in a livestock auction barn for an arts council in Columbus, Nebraska. I generally would score 10 to 15 of these gigs per year, and they really made a difference.

One particular arts council gig experience really stands out, more for the region the shows took place in than the actual concerts. Hyannis, Nebraska, is way out in the Nebraska sandhills, not too far from where my parents grew up and more than 400 miles from Omaha. The concert and high school presentations would both take place in town, but I was to be quartered on a ranch owned by the arts council president, 15 miles north of the town.

Folks think of Nebraska as being very flat, and indeed it is if you follow Interstate 80 along the Platte River, the route of the Oregon Trail across the state. However, much of the interior and west of the state is quite hilly and full of sandstone buttes: Picture yourself in an old John Ford western.

The sandhills are a unique geographical formation, the largest of its type in North America. Charles Kuralt, the renowned travel writer and television personality, rated Nebraska Hwy 2 through the Nebraska sandhills among the top 10 scenic drives in the U.S. There are hardly any trees located within them, and it was

"I WOULDN'T COUNT ON IT" — CONFESSIONS OF AN UNLIKELY FOLKSINGER

so easy to get lost that even the Sioux and Pawnee of bygone eras did not like to venture into that area during overcast times of the year when you could not navigate by the sun.

Turning north from Hyannis up Nebraska Hwy 61, the road rose steeply into the precipitous sandhills of that region. From there my turnoff was a one-lane blacktop road, very hard to spot, that I was to follow four miles to the ranch.

It was February, but I was fortunate that the weather was kind – cold, but not snowy. I remember the sandhills silhouetted against the winter overcast looking ethereal, mysterious and beautiful.

I came over a ridge, and there before me was a scene similar to the set of western television program, The Big Valley, popular back in the 1960's. There was a wide-open plateau with two large homes, stables, various other outbuildings, and horses in the pasture.

I knocked on the door of the larger house: no answer. In a couple of minutes, a fellow emerged from the smaller house next door and introduced himself as the head of the local arts council and the concert promoter.

He explained that he was staying in the smaller house with his mother, who was not well, and that I would have the big house to myself for my three days there.

And what a house it was. It was filled with western antiques, including elaborately crafted hand carved rocking chairs, a pair of crystal boots, handmade spurs and saddles and a wealth of interesting – and I'm sure, very valuable – items. My bedroom was upstairs, and I recall it had a full-size stained-glass window as one of the walls of the shower, which you would see as you climbed the stairs. The house was so big (I think it had six or seven bedrooms on the second floor alone) that it felt a bit spooky staying there by myself. But it sure was a unique accommodation.

As soon as I had dropped my bag and guitars upstairs, I joined the promoter outside. He took me over to the barn and introduced me to the chief wrangler, who asked me if I rode horses. Though I had a bit of experience on horseback, I was by no means a proficient rider. But I sure didn't want to miss out on the chance to survey that wide-open expanse atop a pony. I answered affirmatively, and I may have exaggerated my equestrian prowess just a little.

The wrangler saddled up a chestnut mare for me and gave me a horseback tour of the ranch. I don't think I embarrassed myself too much, though I'm quite sure he caught on that I wasn't quite the Roy Rogers I may have implied I was.

Still, the wrangler gave me the use of that horse and offered to take me riding or allow me to go out solo whenever I liked while I was there. I was sensible enough not to take off by myself, but it was an unforgettable thrill to ride across that still-wild stretch of North America. Cattle were free-grazed there on the rich sandhill grasses, and one day we rode a couple hours each way to a memorable viewpoint over the prairies – the Steppes of the United States. My butt was sore for a week following that expedition, but it was worth it.

The concert and workshops were fine, but that welcome and experience of the hospitality of that fellow who ran the arts council was unforgettable. It turns out he had been an actor in New York, though he had been raised on that ranch. What a dichotomy.

He had returned to help run it when his mother had become ill, and he revitalized the local arts council to provide himself and a few like-minded souls with some cultural stimulation out on the remote high plains of Nebraska. That weekend was one of the unforeseen treasures of a life in the arts, one I could have never anticipated when I started playing and singing for my supper.

IT'S JUST BESSIE AND ME IN BUTTE, MONTANA

IT'S LATE OCTOBER OF 1983, AND I WAS COMING to the end of my fall tour by performing a weekend in Butte, Montana. I had little or no idea about the history and rough charm of the place, but I was about to find out.

I was booked at a place called The Silver Dollar Saloon. It was easy to find – Butte is not that large. The town consists of the older "uptown" historic part of town, with the many mining headframes scattered about, and the "flats" down below, close to I-90, where most of the people live.

BESSIE AND ME IN BUTTE MONTANA-

I walked into the venue and noticed a little glass display case at the end of the bar. Within it was a plaque that said, "Frank Little, murdered by the Copper Kings, 1913. WE NEVER FORGET." It was illustrated by a picture of the unfortunate Frank hanging from a railroad trestle. Also in the display case was a miner's helmet with a lantern and some other artifacts.

That was the introduction to the background of Butte. Once

called "the reddest town in America," it was the site of bitter labor disputes in both the 19th and 20th centuries. Those strikes led to the creation of Miner's Union Local # 1 in the western U.S., as the workers struggled for basic human rights and a living wage on a site that was dubbed "The Richest Hill on Earth" for its deposits of copper, gold, silver and other precious metals.

Frank Little had been an organizer for the I.W.W – the International Workers of the World. He was assassinated in 1913 attempting to organize miners from Butte into that union. That town experienced many cold, hungry seasons as the workers would strike for rights such as a 10-hour day and mining regulations. They also wanted showers available when they emerged from the mine, as too many perished from pneumonia they picked up by walking home in freezing Butte winter temperatures while still soaked in sweat from their work. The Anaconda corporation and its ilk were poster children for the evils of unbridled capitalism.

Butte was so labor conscious that non-union businesses like McDonalds and Wal-Mart were not allowed to operate there until the mid-1980's. No great loss, as far as I'm concerned, and appropriate in a place where men and women sacrificed mightily to achieve things that we take for granted – like the 40-hour work week and workplace safety protections.

Throughout its history, it was known as a place where you could find a job if you could get there, and if you were not too picky about what you were asked to do. This made Butte, Montana, a siren song for generations of immigrants from Ireland, Finland, Wales, China and elsewhere.

Those miners had real guts. Imagine being tightly squeezed into a steel cage with a couple of dozen other men, then dropped free-fall on the cable a half mile to a mile deep in the earth. You would then work eight to 12 hours a day, six days a week, in some of the most dangerous conditions in the U.S.

All of this and more I would learn about over the period of the many years I would perform in Butte. On this first trip, however, the next thing I needed to know is where they were going to send me for accommodations.

(Often, a place to stay was part of the agreement. The lodgings could be anyplace from a plush hotel to a miserable fleabag or someone's couch: what Dave Van Ronk called the "at your mercy circuit.")

Jana Faught, who owned the Silver Dollar at that point, directed me just a couple of blocks over to an old rooming house/hotel run by an elderly, tiny Irish lady by the name of Bessie Mulhearn.

As you walked in the doors of the Towey Hotel, next to an old bookstore, the first thing one would notice was a long, steep set of stairs. I'm not even sure I could make it up those stairs anymore, and even then it wasn't easy to haul two guitars and a bag full of clothes up them.

At the top of the stairs, just to the left, was a wall divider with a glass window and a door. Bessie came out of her little apartment there to say hello and directed me down the hall to a comfortable, old fashioned room. There was no phone, no television, and the facilities were down the hall – all fine as far as I was concerned. I think at that time her room rates were around $10 a night.

I dropped my bags and guitars and availed myself of her invitation to have the first of what would prove to be many cups of tea and interesting, enlightening conversations over the years.

Bessie Mulhearn was born in Ballyhedreen, County Roscommon, in the early part of the 20th century. County Roscommon, the "Gateway to the West" of Ireland, was mostly rural, then and now. Legend has it she had a boyfriend who was killed in the Irish rising of 1916 in Dublin, but she didn't like to talk about it. What is certain is that prospects were bleak in rural Ireland in the 1930's, and she chose to emigrate to America. Her uncle owned a hotel in Butte, where she knew she could work as a maid and make her way in "the land of opportunity."

At that time, Butte, Montana, housed a substantial Irish population. Each nationality had its own enclave there, but the Irish contingent was perhaps the largest. Even Marcus Daly, who discovered the rich vein of copper ore that the town's wealth was based on, was of Irish descent.

So for an Irish immigrant like Bessie, the landscape, customs and occupations were very different from that of Ireland, but you were still among thousands of folks who shared a common tradition with you. Most of the police and firemen were Irish, and the town was run by the Democratic party, again, made up of principally Irish politicians.

After meeting that interesting woman, off to the Friday night gig I went. That first night before I played, I met a rancher who tried to talk me into joining him at his spread on Monday and going to work for him as a ranch hand for a couple of months. He said, "It looks like you are in the kind of shape that you can bale hay."

I declined, as I had the rest of my tour to complete and a wife and son to return to – but I can't say I wasn't tempted. I was 30 years old, and the idea of working on a Montana ranch for a few weeks sounded way more romantic than I'm sure it actually was. And I also knew it was a window of time in my life that would pass quickly, when experiences not taken advantage of would likely not come again.

The gig was a typical, long four-set night. The crowd, however, was colorful, friendly, and enthusiastic. I met folks there who befriended me and, after Bessie's death a few years later, offered to house me when I came through town. These included Lisle Wood, Steve and Kathleen Robinson, and a rough and ready Butte musician by the name of Tom Susanj. They were all engaging folks who made sure I experienced the real Butte, along with its stories and quirks.

Right across the street from the Silver Dollar, the first couple of years I performed in Butte, was the last operating brothel in town, named the Four Queens. Butte used to be full of such places, catering to patrons in all price ranges. The Four Queens even had a little revolving red light on its roof. I was hesitant to enter there and never actually did, though as I look back on it now in my older age, I kind of wish I had availed myself of that quintessential western experience.

The person who had designed and executed the sign that hung on the front of that establishment was not particularly strong in spelling skills. The sign read The "Four Quens." A couple of years later when it closed down, the Silver Dollar saloon salvaged the sign and hung it in the back room of the bar.

The section of Main St. that the Silver Dollar sat on was rich with history. Just up the street a couple of storefronts was The Pekin restaurant, which had been there since the days Chinese workers were considered subhuman and not allowed to vote. Beneath it was a warren of opium dens dating back to the 19th century.

The Pekin had high wooden booths with curtains that the servers would meticulously draw shut after they had taken your order or delivered your food. I'm not sure what had gone on in those booths, but it was an odd custom I have only ever seen at The Pekin.

A couple more blocks up the steep hill was another Butte institution, the M and M Cafe. It was opened during the boom times around World War II, and like many Montana bars, it had "liquor in the front and poker in the back" – not a reference to sexual proclivities. The front part of the M and M had a long piece of tape on the floor, which demarcated the restaurant, where minors were allowed to be, from the bar, about 10 feet away. You could still get alcoholic drinks on the restaurant counter side, of course; but the tape on the floor undoubtedly preserved the morals of the minors on the restaurant side from the focused, heavy drinking at the bar.

I remember that the waitress at the restaurant side's counter was named Elsie. She had been there for decades and remained behind the counter as long as I would visit, perform in Butte and eat there. She wore an enormous amount of makeup and kind of looked like a large Kewpie doll, but she was friendly and efficient. She would call you "dearie" and give back as good as she got to the rough, often inebriated clientele. It was instructional to someone like me to see her work the crowd.

That first year I was in Butte, the economic situation in the town was at a low ebb. The last of the deep shaft mines had closed down a couple of years earlier, and the open Berkley pit had also closed. Montana Power Company was the only substantial employer left in town, and it, too, was threatening to move.

As it turned out, Butte would alternatively flourish and flounder over the next 30 years. I remember so well that first sight I had of it, with the Christmas lights on the old Kelly Mine shining brightly in the bitter cold – and almost no cars or people in sight. In the late 90's, the town would begin to realize some of its significance and establish a historic district, with plaques and interpretive displays throughout uptown.

In the early 80's however, none of that had happened yet, and there were still palpable reminders of Butte's wild, wide-open, quirky past.

It was said when a bar was sold in Butte, Montana, the owner would be given the keys to the joint, then throw them over his shoulder in the gutter. Why? Because the bars in Butte during its early history never closed, so no reason for a key to a door that was never locked. In the halcyon days around and during the World Wars, everything in Butte ran 24 hours a day. Even the prostitutes would have to lodge other than their places of business, as those cribs were in use around the clock.

By time I arrived there, those days were long gone, but there were still plenty of physical reminders of the odd, cantankerous, fascinating place that Butte had been. As you continued up Main or Montana Streets, the hill got increasingly more steep, and all around you were the headframes of the mines where so many men would troop to work each day. Many of these shafts were a mile deep into the ground – as deep below as Butte's elevation was above sea level.

A few houses also remained, many of them at funny angles where their foundations had begun to collapse into the tunneled ground beneath them. As you looked to the south and west, you could see a magnificent snow-capped mountain range. I wondered how that lovely view must have appeared to these hard working, sweaty men, emerging from a 10 or 12 hour shift deep in the earth, out into the 20 degree below zero winter temperatures.

Luigi was a Slavic immigrant who for years operated a bar not far from the Silver Dollar. He was a ventriloquist who had plied his trade across the country during the vaudeville years, eventually settling in Butte. His bar had marionettes that hung from the ceiling all over the establishment. He would amuse his patrons by lowering them to tables where folks were sitting and have them speak to the inebriated customers, throwing his voice across the room and saying something like, "Pay your bill and get out, asshole."

There were tales of violent drunkards so spooked by this experience they would flee the bar in terror and never return. A big picture of Luigi used to be displayed in the back of the Silver Dollar. I hope it is still there.

Up on Broadway was a restaurant called Gamer's, where the cash register was always wide open. You would order and eat there, then be trusted to settle your bill by putting the amount yourself into the register and making change. There were always a waitress and cook there, but the owner was known for leaving for hours at a time, relying on the honesty of his customers to pay for their meals.

Close to the Berkeley Pit mine, the largest open pit in the world at that time, was the venerable Helsinki Bar.

When you went into the Helsinki, there was rarely anyone sitting on the stools drinking. Why? Because they were all downstairs, imbibing in the saunas that you could rent for a few bucks an hour.

An old Butte tradition was to purchase liquor or a 12-pack of

It's Just Bessie and Me in Butte, Montana

beer upstairs at the bar, rent one of the saunas underneath, and consume it all in the 130-degree heat of a Finnish dry sauna. I tried it a couple of times with friends, and as advertised, as you sweated and chatted in the heat it accelerated greatly the effect of the alcohol. It was kind of a "value added" experience. The Helsinki was eventually eaten up by the expansion of the Berkeley Pit, when it got rolling again in the 90's.

A lot of folks were familiar with Butte as the hometown of the maniacal motorcycle daredevil, Evil Kneivel, who was said to have broken every bone in his body at one time or another. He typified the reckless abandon, live-for-the-moment philosophy that was an integral part of the town's identity.

His son, Robbie, also became a worldwide celebrity for his motorcycle jumps over multiple school buses and river canyons in Nevada. One night during a break at the Silver Dollar, a character approached me, obviously in his cups and running on something more than just alcohol. Yes, it was Robbie Kneivel, loud and colorful, profane and jovial.

He asked me if $2000 would be enough to get me to Las Vegas in a couple of weeks and play a couple of parties for him, he loved my music – yada, yada, yada. I replied affirmatively, knowing that he would almost certainly forget about that proposal the next morning. As expected, that was the last I ever heard about it.

He also asked me if I would like to take a ride with him on his fancy motorcycle, which was sitting right outside the Silver Dollar, and have a tour of the precipitous hills of Butte from atop his custom Harley. Valuing my life and extremities, I declined that offer. It might have been interesting though, had I survived.

Altogether, the town was a panoply of intriguing, unique individuals, unlike anyplace I have been before or since.

A couple of years after my first gigs there, I would write a song about Bessie and Butte, Montana, trying to capture some of the history and echoes of the past there. All oddities aside, it had been a place that encapsulated the American dream, a place where an unskilled immigrant could get a job, work hard and provide a life for his family that was impossible to achieve in most parts of old Europe.

The song was recorded on my album, "Open Spaces, Prairie Winds," released in 1987. Numerous public radio programmers picked up on it, and a few musicians added it to their repertoire. The best part of all that airplay was that right up until Bessie passed away, folks would seek out that old hotel, walk up that long flight of stairs and visit her.

Bessie loved to chat with people and was great company. Everyone who took the effort to meet her and have a conversation with her had a unique glimpse into a time and way of life that is long gone.

The year after I wrote the song, the proprietor of the Silver Dollar, Jana Faught, arranged to have Bessie brought to the bar to hear the piece I had written for her. Because of her arthritis and scoliosis, Bessie was unable to negotiate those formidable hotel stairs anymore, so Jana arranged to have her carried down them (Bessie must have weighted all of 80 feisty pounds) and given a ride to the bar, where her table was adorned with a dozen red roses.

Bessie wore a smile as big as Montana when I played the song for her, and the audience gave her a standing ovation after I finished it. I felt so privileged to be a small part of her life and to recognize her indomitable spirit in song.

Bessie passed away in 1996. The folksinger and song collector Mark Ross moved over to Butte from Missoula, and he spent the last couple of years of Bessie's life helping her out, getting groceries for her, and keeping her company. She was a great old gal, and we'll not see her like again. Neither will we see the times that created that bustling, tumultuous American town, the largest city in the western U.S. between Chicago and San Francisco in the year 1900.

Bessie and Me

The middle of Montana, a dirty cold night
I inquired of lodging in a rough looking bar
they told me of Bessie's, they said that she welcomed all
sinner and Saint, from near and from far.

Above an old bookstore, the narrow stairs beckoned
to a tired old traveler, fresh from the road
at the top of that flight stood a weathered old woman
with an accent as thick as a piece of old sod.

Chorus
It's just Bessie and me this evening in Butte, Montana
in her empty hotel, on a cold Friday night
with the ghosts of the miners and the old worn out carpets
40 rooms vacant in the fading twilight
their windows shut tight against the morning

In 1909, these oak doors first opened
to the immigrant dreams, of a thousand strong men
in the thirties young Bessie took the ship here from Ireland
to be a maid for her uncle, and to cook and to mend

she married a man who came from her own country
they carved out a life there beneath the Big Sky
their boarders were hard men who toiled in the darkness
for the copper and the silver they lived and they died

Repeat chorus
Bessie spoke of her youth, and of the Easter rebellion
of a lad that she loved that has never been found
she told tales of the 30's here in western Montana
of the unions who protected the men deep in the ground

"Butte was a good town" I can still hear her say

"I WOULDN'T COUNT ON IT" — CONFESSIONS OF AN UNLIKELY FOLKSINGER

the men were hard working and the churches were strong
but now the churches are abandoned and the buildings are rotting
the Berkeley Pit and the deep shaft mines have been idle too long

Repeat chorus

Tonight I walk down the streets of old Butte, Montana
imagining the Friday nights this town did know
the drinking and the fighting, the spirit of adventure
that summed up this brave land, so long ago

Bessie's rooms now are spotless, the towels are clean
the hallways ring hollow with no one around
like this Friday night Main Street of old Butte Montana
there's the echoes of the past, but there's hardly a sound.

Repeat chorus

Tom May copyright 1986 Blue Vignette ASCAP
from the album "Open Spaces, Prairie Winds"

In 2013 I recorded my favorite version of this song, on an album I did with my pal from Wyoming, Chris Kennedy. Chris's voice and complementary guitar parts give it just the flavor I always imagined for it.

FROM 1982 TO 1984 I drove a Toyota station wagon that Michaela and I had bought new, back in St. Louis. I ran the wheels off that car, crisscrossing the highways repeatedly from coast to coast. My next vehicle was a 1985 Colt Vista wagon, a funny looking, boxy affair with an extra passing gear for down the road journeys.

When I was out the Pacific Northwest in 1984, Don Younger suggested we hop in that then-new car of mine and take a road trip to the first real microbrewery in the Northwest. Bert Grant had started Grant's Brewery and Pub in the original train station of the small town of Yakima, Washington, about three and a half hours from Portland.

Don was already selling Bert's Grant's Scottish Ale at the Horse Brass, and the brew was very popular. Just that year, a bill had passed in Washington State, and would soon pass in Oregon, allowing small brewers to sell their own product on site – the first time since Prohibition it had been legal to do so.

The now-famous McMenamin brothers of Portland, who I had met at the Horse Brass, were at that time in the process of getting their first couple of pubs open. But the first Washington entry into the microbrewery/bar/hospitality sweepstakes was by Bert Grant.

Don and I took off in my new car on a glorious Northwestern autumn day. It was a couple of hours to the Dalles down Interstate 84, then over the Columbia River and up over Satus Pass on Hwy 97, rolling down into Yakima later in the afternoon.

Don had called and told Bert we were coming, and Bert really rolled out the red carpet for us. We sampled his new tasty cask-conditioned ale. At that time, it was only available at the brewery, and it was one of the first cask-conditioned ales in the United States in modern times. Cask-conditioned beers are made without adding CO, typically pulled with an old-fashioned British-style hand pump. We also tried all his other beer varieties and talked until well after closing time, swapping stories, trading lies and trying to solve the world's problems, as drinkers are apt to do.

Don got a motel room for the night. Bert's brew master offered to put me up on the floor of his living room, which was fine for me in those days.

In the morning, we rendezvoused again at the pub, and Bert contributed lots of cask-conditioned ale to take back to the Horse Brass. He put it in milk jugs and whatever else we could scrounge up that would contain beer successfully. Of course, just to make

"I WOULDN'T COUNT ON IT" — CONFESSIONS OF AN UNLIKELY FOLKSINGER

sure it hadn't spoiled, Don and I had to sample some on the drive back home. I recall there being construction over Satus Pass on the return trip and feeling quite uncomfortable as the traffic was stopped – and there were no bathrooms in the area.

We arrived back at the Horse Brass as conquering heroes, transporting all that exotic beer. It wouldn't be too long until cask-conditioned beer could be found everywhere in Portland and also in many other enlightened areas around the U.S. too – but at the time, it was quite a novelty.

By this time, when I came to Portland in the autumn, I would perform three Sunday nights in October at the Horse Brass, between gigs on the Oregon Coast, Washington State and California. Don had moved to a house about a mile from the Horse Brass where he kindly still kept a separate bedroom that he offered for my use.

In that particular abode, my room was up a rickety flight of stairs with a few loose landings you had to watch out for. The room was pretty drafty, and the roof had the tendency to leak a little bit when it rained hard – right onto my foot when I was lying in bed. Still, I was so grateful for the accommodations, and it always felt like home. That little house butted right up against Mt. Tabor Park in Southeast Portland, a lush, extinct volcano.

It also became an autumn tradition in the 80's that I would do a concert with my dear friend, Terry Prohaska, who I had met the first evening I performed at the Horse Brass. Terry is a fine singer and multi-instrumentalist, who at the time I met him was still driving a Tri-Met bus and performing with his folk revival group, the Rite of Spring.

Terry and his lovely wife, Neva, took me in many the night when I was too much into my cups to safely drive back to Don Younger's house. They would also host parties at their house after our annual concert together and make sure I had a good home-cooked meal while I was in Portland. They remain dear friends.

Terry is a master of the autoharp and more than competently

plays at least another dozen types of instruments. In recent years he has had a very full schedule of teaching music, as well as performing the music he loves. He has given tirelessly of himself to all levels of musicians trying to improve their skills.

Terry and I would meet at the Horse Brass or Digger O' Dell's in Portland in those early days and demolish significant amounts of beer, as young men are wont to do. We did our yearly duo concerts at various venues in the area, including the Old Church, The Northwest Service Center and others. Terry was and is fun to work with as well as being a tremendously knowledgeable and talented artist.

One evening, when my yearly sojourn of the Pacific Northwest was finishing up, Terry and Neva had a small gathering for me at their house, which at that time was not far from the Horse Brass Pub. Terry and I were the last ones standing, after having enjoyed a goodly amount of Henry Weinhard's Ale, Scotch whiskey, and probably some other substances too. The sun had already been up for a couple of hours by this point, so I just decided to start the long drive to Omaha – plenty of time to sleep when I was old.

I did okay until I ran into a dense fogbank while I was

TERRY PROHASKA, TOM, DON YOUNGER, PORTLAND OR 1986

climbing into the Blue Mountains in Eastern Oregon, where both the lack of sleep and road visibility demanded I pull over and doze for a few hours. Those were the days.

IF IT'S ALL THE SAME TO YOU: RIVER CITY FOLK

IN THE SPRING OF 1985 I RETURNED FROM MY annual tour of the East Coast, buoyed by good crowds at the concerts and full of ambition. That year I had traveled to my usual Northeastern locations and as far south as Georgia, Alabama, Florida and Mississippi performing my songs.

As I traveled, I listened (as I still do) primarily to public radio. There seemed to be a dramatic increase of programs on that band that were featuring the kind of music that I played and wrote. It was wonderful to hear those broadcasts and listen to the music that I loved in far flung places like Indiana and Maine. I had also been featured on many of those same public radio stations that promoted folk music and musicians during that tour.

It occurred to me that though my hometown of Omaha had two public radio stations, neither of them featured a folk music program. I thought I was the person to remedy that. Who better to put a show together than someone who actively did acoustic music for a living and who got to hear such talented fellow artists as we all traveled around the country?

I had no experience in the medium except as a performer and no idea of how one went about putting a program together

"I WOULDN'T COUNT ON IT" — CONFESSIONS OF AN UNLIKELY FOLKSINGER

technically, but I sure knew the kind of music I wanted to feature. The early 80's were a very active time for my alternative trade, with artists such as Bill Staines, David Mallett, Nancy Griffith, Bryan Bowers and many others putting out an album every year or two on labels such as Philo, Flying Fish or Rounder.

There was also the burgeoning Celtic music renaissance, with virtuosic artists like Touchstone, The Bothy Band, The Battlefield Band and Christy Moore, all producing inspiring music that was bringing a whole new audience to acoustic music. Folks in Omaha deserved to hear this kind of music on the radio!

I asked my wife, Michaela, which station she thought I should approach about doing a radio program. She suggested KVNO Radio at the University of Nebraska at Omaha as her preferred public radio source, which was probably because they programmed a lot of classical music – her favorite. As luck would have it, KVNO had just hired a new general manager, an Englishman by the name of Peter Marsh.

I went to his office to speak with him about my idea for a program, and he was very open to the concept. I met with him in late May, and after a few days of talking to his staff he got back to me and agreed to begin airing a program I would produce and host in early July 1985.

I was astounded I would be on the radio that quickly. I had explained to him that I did a great deal of touring for my music and that almost always the program would have to be taped in advance to accommodate my schedule. He was amenable to that proviso, and I began to figure out how to do this whole venture. The pay scale for the program was sadly familiar to me after being a folksinger for a few years – zip. Still, I considered it a great opportunity.

I came up with the name "River City Folk," combining a popular Omaha nickname with folk music, and also being aware that most towns in the U.S. are situated on riverways, those being the original highways across the continent.

On the show, I played selections from the new wave of recorded folk albums coming out around the country at that time. Occasionally I intended to sneak in a classic, too.

The process of taping a radio program in advance was not easy at that time. Back then, KVNO radio was located on the second floor of an old house adjacent to the campus. I would use turntables for the records, then record those selections and my intros onto a massive old Ampeg machine that used quarter inch tape. Those tape machines were so heavy that the floor in that room had bowed and was disturbingly unstable.

The show was slated to be an hour broadcast, and this technique of recording it was clumsy, very time consuming and archaic. While I was getting familiar with using the equipment, I frequently made mistakes and had to start all over again. Add to that the fact that no matter how at ease you are with talking on microphone in front of an audience, speaking into a microphone for a radio broadcast adds a whole other dimension of anxiety to the equation. Sometimes I wondered if I would ever get beyond that confused, tongue-tied, inarticulate stage.

I PERFORMED AT the Omaha Summer Arts Festival that year, and posters were placed throughout the city to promote the new radio program, which would begin to air just a couple of weeks after the festival.

A wandering soul had just moved to town, after landing a gig teaching at Creighton University. His name was Chris Kennedy, and he had noticed some of the posters with my picture promoting the new radio program around Omaha. Chris was a gifted, original singer-songwriter himself. He had been kicking around the country for years playing his own songs and those of others he admired, in all sorts of situations, including street corners and passenger railroad trains.

In between getting a college degree and doing graduate work, he had hitchhiked from Maine to Alaska, and Florida to Alberta, living out a Woody Guthrie-inspired, Jack Kerouac literary-fueled lifestyle, writing great songs, seeing the country, voraciously reading and living life to the fullest.

One of his recent homes had been Spokane, Washington, which in the end didn't work out so well for him. So, he decided to accept a teaching job in Nebraska. He had seen a poster for me out in Spokane when I was booked to play at a great listening club there called Ahab's Whale – owned by an effusive, friendly Norwegian by the name of Harris Helgeson. Chris wasn't able to attend that night, but he remembered my name. So, when he saw the River City Folk poster in Omaha with the same guy's name and face on it, he decided to look me up in the phone book and give me a call.

CHRIS KENNEDY

We met for a beer at a place called Sullivan's Bar in Omaha, and Chris has been an integral part of my life's script ever since. I have always been grateful to him for taking the initiative to make that call. His friendship is one of the most valued treasures of my life.

We traded songs at his efficiency apartment close to Creighton University. He had just written his fine song about the writer Jack London, and I had recently finished my song "Bessie and Me." We were both young men, just getting underway with our eventual life's journeys, and we would wind up sharing many roads, songs and laughs together.

BACK IN OMAHA between tours, the family bills still needed to be paid, and I needed to contribute. I always had local gigs, but the money for those was minimal. So, in those early years I did temporary jobs painting houses, working for a telemarketing firm, selling watches at a kiosk in a mall during the holidays, all sorts of stuff. I just figured it was paying my dues for getting to do what I wanted with my life most of the time.

Not that being on the road was without its less-than-encouraging stretches. One week in the spring of 1986, when I was performing in North Carolina, I noted in my journal that I played concerts in four towns during the week – to a grand total of 20 people. To reach that impressive number of folks, I had to drive 540 miles and sleep on a few kitchen floors. My take from those shows, including record sales, was $135.00 before expenses.

Who does that? Surprisingly, I don't remember being overly discouraged at the time. It was again just part of paying your dues, and I was playing my music, meeting folks, having fun and seeing the country.

There were also glimmers of hope. The radio show was picking up steam and seemed to be popular, and all that touring had inspired a pretty good crop of new songs. I had met a recording tech, Steve Ozaydin, who was doing a lot of work with American Gramaphone records back in Omaha, and he invited me to come by and check out their studio.

American Gramaphone was founded and run by Chip Davis, who established his touring group Mannheim Steamroller there in the early 1980's. After a couple of audiophile releases, they had a platinum-selling hit record with their first Christmas album. Chip had raised his initial seed money for all of this by working on radio and television commercials and as a co-writer of the #1 hit "Convoy," a ballad about the Citizens Band radio craze sweeping the country at that time. His background was in classical and jazz music, but he was conversant and appreciative of all forms – and was a really nice guy.

The name of the studio Chip had built was Sound Recorders, and it was state of the art at that time, featuring all the latest technology. One of Chip's employees was a fellow by the name of Clete Baker. Clete was primarily a mastering engineer – the person who takes the finished, mixed recording, smoothes off the sonic edges, equalizes the volumes of the tracks, and generally readies it for pressing. This was pre-compact disc, back when vinyl records were still the standard.

Coming from a commercial radio background, Clete also did a little bit of everything else around the studio, including recording and producing commercial jingles and working on various music projects. He was classically trained on the cello and was an outgoing, friendly, positive figure who would soon become one of my closest friends.

With Steve Ozaydin and Clete, I began to plot how I could record my next album at Sound Recorders. Both of them figured there was a chance that Chip Davis might put the American Gramaphone imprint on it if he liked it after we were underway. So, I began to make plans to do the project there, with Clete as producer and Steve as the recording engineer. This was a risk, as the studio time there was quite expensive (as I recall, around $100 per hour, way steep back in the 80's), and I would be liable for the bill if Chip Davis did not spring for it.

We began to work on the album in a piecemeal fashion, recording when it was possible for everyone to work, usually on weekends. Steve recruited a drummer, and Clete rounded up a musical couple who played violin and harmonica, Debbie Greenblatt and David Seay. They would eventually work on a number of productions I was involved in. Other talented studio cats would join in, too, throughout the project.

As it turned out, my type of music just didn't fit Chip Davis's vision for his label, so he never picked up the tab for the recording time. It meant I had to work harder than ever and book myself more aggressively so I could pay the recording bill, as we were far enough along that I wasn't going to give up. I made monthly payments to the studio, just as if I were buying a car. Due to this slow but steady approach, it took more than a year to finish the recording and mixing.

It was worth it. Clete produced the album and wrote a couple of beautiful string arrangements for the songs, and working in that manner gave us a lot of time to consider what instruments and voices fit the melodies. Working with Clete was a delight and would be a prelude to the decades we have spent since collaborating on various projects.

The production was recorded on two-inch wide analog tape, in that capacious studio enclosure, using Neumann microphones. At the end of the process, the album "mother disc" was "cut" on the coolest machine I have ever seen, before or since – a Neumann lathe. This tool alone cost more than $50,000, and the operator (Clete, in this case) viewed the grooves through a scope as they were being cut into the mold, making sure they were the correct depth for maximum fidelity.

Folks are always confused on what the role of a producer is.

"I WOULDN'T COUNT ON IT" — CONFESSIONS OF AN UNLIKELY FOLKSINGER

CLETE BAKER

An album producer works with the artist on the songs, making suggestions on instruments that would be appropriate to color the compositions when they are recorded. He will also suggest musicians to play those instruments. He is in the studio while the recording is going on, trying to ensure the song is sung in tune with the desired dynamics.

The producer will also often write specific parts for the musicians to play on the arrangements and help choose the songs for a popular artist. He will also assist the engineer track the instruments in such a way that it will be easier to mix, when that part of the process comes along. Essentially, the producer is like a field general on a battlefield: coordinating all the various parts of the project and holding everything together. Thus, the artist is left to concentrate on his most important responsibility – giving life and sparkle to the songs by doing the very best performance that he can.

Even though synthesizer technology was available at that time for sounds such as orchestra strings and drums, I made a decision to stick with real instruments always. I have stuck with that determination through all of my album projects. Though it is generally more expensive in both time, personnel costs, and even when you get to the mixing phase, I am happy when I go back and listen now that I went that route. Not only is the real resonance of the instruments more pleasing, but I can remember fondly the fine musicians who put down the tracks with me. If I couldn't afford the real thing, I didn't need it.

"Open Spaces, Prairie Winds" was released in the fall of 1986. I had no label for the release, but I sent out dozens of copies of the record myself to public radio stations, and many of them began to play cuts off it.

There are a number of songs off that album I still perform, notably "The Heart of the Appaloosa," written by Fred Small, and "Bessie and Me,"

When I listen back to the album now, my favorite production is the song "If it's All the Same to You," backed by a gorgeous string quartet part that Clete wrote, directed and performed in. It kind of sums up those years when I was often on the road months at a time.

If it's All the Same to You

If it's all the same to you, I'll leave now when I can
miss most of the traffic, hit Kansas City about 10
I know it's hard to understand, the reasons for goodbye
but what we don't know won't hurt us, so it's better left this way....

Chorus

Now the way I've come to see you, it can't be defined or phrased
or neatly written out in a lover's poem
or packaged up in paperback, or carefully carved in stone
so even though I love you, let's leave well enough alone

If it's all the same to you, I'll write you when I can
let you know the latest news and when I'll be back again
I know it's tough to wait 'til then, but it's the best that I can do

"I WOULDN'T COUNT ON IT" — CONFESSIONS OF AN UNLIKELY FOLKSINGER

and the same sky smiles above us as I write these words for you

Repeat chorus

If it's all the same to you, I've never felt this way
like a tongue tied wanderin' minstrel who's unsure of what to say
so, without another word, I'll leave you as before
wonderin' if all this is worth it as I close another door

Repeat chorus

*Tom May copyright 1986 Blue Vignette, ASCAP
from the album "Open Spaces, Prairie Winds";
re-released on "From the Prairies to the Past"*

THROUGHOUT MY LIFE, I wrote songs I believed in. They were songs that reflected my beliefs, geography I was enthralled by, history, remarkable characters or imagined or memorable romances. Looking back at my lofty ideals now, it might not have been such a bad idea to devote some time to writing a hit single in the 70's or early 80's, when radio was still king.

Today I hear a steady diet of 60's, 70's, and 80's music at the gym, the grocery store, and all kinds of other places – realizing that every one of those spins represents money going to the writer or the writer's estate. Who knew that music from that time period, even the preponderance of bad music, would have a seemingly interminable shelf life? Who knew that 20-somethings today would be just as familiar with such baby boomer tunes as "Sweet Caroline," "Brown Eyed Girl," and "Taking Care of Business" as folks were way back then?

It would be as if we who grew up in the 60's and 70's all embraced and danced to the music of Al Jolson, Rudolf Valentino, Cab Calloway and songs like "Pennies from Heaven" at our high school proms: It just didn't happen, and we thought all music from 20 to 50 years previous was impossibly dull and irrelevant.

So, perhaps some efforts on my part back then to write and market a song that would have become part of the inescapable nostalgic pablum that infiltrates every pore of the contemporary world might have paid off in the long run. I might have had more freedom to do and write what I truly cared about. I prided myself on holding tight to my ideals, but perhaps a little more pragmatism would have served me better.

As a teenager in the 1960's, I was impressed by a recording that rose to number one late in that decade, "Classical Gas" by Mason Williams. Chip Davis signed Mason Williams to his label right around the time I was working on "Open Spaces, Prairie Winds" at Sound Recorders, and Mason came to Omaha to do a remake of his famous song and also to record some newer compositions.

Clete was working on the album with John Boyd, who had engineered the original version of "Classical Gas" in California back in 1967, and Chip Davis had composed a Mannheim Steamroller arrangement for this remake. By that time, everyone at the studio knew me, and I was invited to those recording and mixing sessions. It was a thrill to hear the song I had aspired to play as a 14-year-old kid being played (over and over again) in the studio by the artist/writer.

I had the opportunity to meet Mason during those sessions, and I invited him out for a beer at a local watering hole. He had started his career as a writer on the Smothers Brothers television program and had fascinating tales to tell about those times and his career in music. I'm afraid I was a bad influence on him, as he was a little wobbly when I dropped him off and he walked up the stairs to the Residence Inn where he was staying.

When I talked to him years later (he lives in Oregon, close to Eugene), he remembered the evening – and how he felt the next morning, too. Sorry, Mason. It was a night to remember, as he regaled me with vivid stories of the music and comedy business in Los Angeles in the 60's.

"I WOULDN'T COUNT ON IT" — CONFESSIONS OF AN UNLIKELY FOLKSINGER

CHRIS KENNEDY WAS in Omaha only one year, teaching at Creighton University; but we shared lots of songs and stories during that period and also exchanged gig leads. The Reilly cabin in Colorado was going to be sold, which meant an end to my little family's gratis summer trips to those majestic, cool, beautiful mountains. Chris had mentioned a resort lodge on the other side of the continental divide from Estes Park, close to the bucolic little village of Grand Lake, that he had worked and performed at.

The Grand Lake Lodge was set on a rise overlooking the village, the largest natural lake in Colorado, and magnificent Rocky Mountain National Park. It was owned by the James family, who had been in possession of the property since 1953. The original lodge and cabins were built in the 1930's after the national park was established.

The younger son, Ted, had just taken over as food and beverage manager. Chris knew him well and gave me his contact information. I did my usual dance of calling first, then sending promotional materials and a cassette (of the "Coming Home" album) and following up with phone calls.

Ted James and his brother Reed, who was head of the grounds crew there, were active, exuberant, enthusiastic young men. Ted in particular loved folk music, played guitar and sang himself. He hired me to play at the lodge a couple of weeks that summer. It paid a small stipend, but also came with meals and rustic accommodations for myself, Michaela and Dylan.

This would mark the beginning of more than 20 idyllic summers I would perform at that lovely old edifice. My son Dylan would grow up traveling out there every summer and eventually worked in the dining room of the lodge as a busboy and waiter during his high school and college years.

The Grand Lake Lodge was at an altitude of over 8000 feet, which made carrying the PA system up the stairs quite a heavy-breathing experience. The natural beauty that surrounded the lodge was stupendous, but inside the scene could sometimes be less than concert-like. Each night, partway into your first set, the vacuum cleaner would compete with you to see who was louder. It sometimes seemed the vacuum cleaner got more attention than I did.

You performed on a stage right next to the kitchen grill, and aside from it being really hot when it was busy, there was always a loud sizzle when the steaks hit the fire. I did, however, have some decent audiences there, met a lot of enthusiastic folks, and in later years Chris Kennedy would join me on that small stage, as would my pal Avery Grimes on piano, Cliff Jones on bass, and even my son Dylan on bass, when he was older.

The employee cabins there were rustic, to say the least – but they kept you dry, if not warm. Cabin 42 was my two-week summer abode for all those years, when life was simpler, and it seemed I had all the time in the world. The Grand Lake Lodge has changed owners now, and the employee cabins have been torn down.

It's a shame they could not have recorded all the stories of the young, vital people from around the world who called those rustic shacks a temporary home. Now that would have been a memoir. I know my son, Dylan, only told me a little about the wild and uproarious times those kids had there, but I can certainly imagine.

IN THE MID-80S I attended a kind of songwriters retreat outside of Milwaukee, Wisconsin. It was a chance to share songs, booking information and strategies, and get to know some other folks like myself – all trying to accomplish the difficult task of making a living doing this music. It was a fairly intimate gathering, probably no more than 30 people total. I recall Peter and Lou Berryman, Dan Hart, and Chuck Mitchell (Joni Mitchell's ex-husband) being among the attendees.

It was a friendly and educational weekend. By and large, you do this profession in such a solitary way – from writing the songs, promoting yourself, and finally performing them, you are almost always on your own. It was illuminating to visit with artists who had experienced some of the same struggles and learn how they coped with those obstacles and that solitude.

I also met a woman there from Philadelphia, Charlotte Britton, who booked some dates back east as well as a series of humanities concerts in Kansas. Through her auspices I began to do a bi-yearly series of appearances, in elder care facilities, high schools and the occasional community college in and around Coffeyville, Kansas.

I have lost track how many times I did that circuit, but I must have made between 10 and 15 trips down that way.

Again, it was all part of foraging a living in this up and down business. Playing at a nursing home in Coffeyville, Kansas, might not have been what your dream was when you started all of this, but it was integral to being able to make a go of it. I also believe, particularly for young musicians, it is almost always better to be performing somewhere rather than not performing at all. There are lessons to be learned about your material, relating to audiences, and not least of all, yourself.

That first trip down to southeast and south-central Kansas was actually a two-week series of gigs, the first week being in and around the town of Pratt. I remember those appearances in Pratt being an enjoyable, diverse mix of schools, senior living, and active older folks. Unfortunately, that leg of the humanities tour lost funding after that first year I performed in the area.

Coffeyville, Kansas, on the other hand, could be a very long week. The town itself had been a railway and commercial hub in days gone by, but not much was left of those times. Like so many Midwestern communities, it had a population and activity level far less than had been the case 50 years earlier.

There was a community college, one of those places big NCAA

schools would send athletes to raise their grade point average so they could play big time football or basketball at the University of Nebraska or Oklahoma. A small museum downtown commemorated a bank robbery by the Dalton Brothers (which ended badly for them) that occurred in the 1880's. Aside from the usual fast food joints and one of the first Wal-Marts in the U.S., that was about it for the towns attractions. Oh, and there were lots of senior citizens and living facilities for them (which seems to be the primary employer in many rural communities these days).

One of the great ironies of Coffeyville was that you couldn't get a decent cup of coffee in the entire town.

That in itself added insult to injury.

You were paid a set amount for the week. I remember during one of my last sojourns there that number was $1100. Out of that you had to cover your own lodgings and meals. The motels ran from $30 to $60 a night, and it was up to you how much luxury you wanted (I generally selected the low end). There was also the option of staying in an old, stately, three-story Victorian house, with an elderly woman named Stella. Her extra bedroom was way up on the third floor, in kind of an attic, but I availed myself of that choice on a couple trips too. She was friendly and only charged $15 a night.

The closest thing I ever found to a decent meal in Coffeyville was a joint called The Pig Shack, a barbeque place that, you guessed it, was located in a dilapidated, leaky shack. The culinary choices in town were dreadful, even being used to getting by on a very limited food budget, as I was. I think Coffeyville had the worst Chinese restaurant I ever had the misfortune to patronize.

Your week in Coffeyville would start out with a program at the community college. The students were polite, but you wouldn't call them enthusiastic by any means. The rest of that Monday you would have one more show, at a nursing home, early in the evening.

For all those performances, I would have a repertoire I designed for the listeners. For the senior centers, I would include "Home on the Range" (written in Kansas in the 1890's), a couple railroad songs and other western favorites like "The Red River Valley," and an Irish ballad or two, introduced by a pennywhistle piece.

The pennywhistle had been an important addition to my act. It was a totally different sound from guitar and caught people's attention. It could also be quite lovely when I was playing it well – which by no means was always the case! "Danny Boy" on the whistle would be a tune I would also frequently slip in at the older folks' residences. They all knew it and would even sing the words.

The rest of the days of the week in Coffeyville, I would do four to five shows a day, 45 to 60 minutes each, and each in a different care facility. These shifted through the years, but you would perform at a senior meal site, where folks would be chatting; the Alzheimer's wing of a nursing home, where you would be escorted through locked doors to sing for a mostly mute, unresponsive group; to deluxe assisted care sites, to apartment buildings where seniors would gather in the common room to hear you. (You had better not interrupt The Wheel of Fortune television program by arriving too early or playing too long!)

It was a humbling, sometimes discouraging, but also a gratifying experience. I got so I recognized folks who liked particular songs on my return visits, and there were always those sweet older residents who would ask me to come back soon. It was a reminder of the temporal nature of life and how lucky I was to be young and still able to play, sing and travel. It was also a reminder of the debt we owed to those who came before us and how often human brings are warehoused and forgotten in less than ideal circumstances.

It was consistently a difficult week and not overly profitable, but I felt it was part of my responsibility as an artist to go there and perform – as well as it being another piece of making a living in music.

The worst gigs of that week would be when you drove over to Caney, Kansas, about 20 miles west of Coffeyville. The care facility there seemed particularly bleak. I recall pools of urine on the floor from the residents that had not yet been cleaned up. Nothing wrong with the folks that lived there though. They were kind, friendly and trying to make the best out of a bad situation. I played my best for them and made a point of lingering and visiting at that facility after my show.

The high school in Caney, however, was a different matter. You would do a presentation in their auditorium for 100 to 200 students who would be intent on chatting and making fun of the songs and your introductions to them, despite the best efforts of their teachers to get them to behave. I remember clearly one performance where I was thanking students for listening as they exited the hall. Two of the boys, probably 15 or so, just looked at me and started laughing at me, as if what I was doing was the most ridiculous, mindless thing they had ever seen. Perhaps it was, but their rudeness just floored me.

You would finish the Coffeyville circuit on Friday afternoon, and I was always out of there immediately after the last set of songs – on my way to somewhere, anywhere, that was not Coffeyville, Kansas.

KANSAS IN THE 80's wasn't all bad though, mostly because of a listening room called The Iron Horse in El Dorado, not far from Wichita. The owners/operators were Don and Marianne Koke, sweet folks who had a longtime history with and love of folk music. They had played in St. Louis extensively during the folk revival of the early 60's on the DeBaliviere strip and told captivating stories about folks they had worked with and met.

El Dorado was a lot more lively than Coffeyville. Like Coffeyville, it had a community college, where Don worked, but it also was a larger town with significantly more industry and population. Don promoted a concert each week through the school year at the Iron Horse, and lots of my friends performed there: Dr. John Walker, the fine country bluesman from Lincoln, Nebraska; Chris Kennedy; Bryan Bowers and many others.

Don and Marianne were very hospitable people. Marianne was an excellent cook, and there was never any shortage of alcohol. Beer was served at the concert and in their comfortable home where they would put you up, and there would frequently be a party after the festivities that usually wouldn't conclude until the wee hours of the morning.

When you awoke on that Sunday morning, Don would have been up already so he could catch Charles Kuralt on the CBS Sunday Morning program. Even when I got up to leave for Omaha early, it was impossible to awake before he was already bustling around. He would offer you coffee and a concoction called an Old Fashioned, made with gin, to start your day. I always opted for just the caffeine, as I was generally still feeling the effects of the night before.

Marianne passed away in the early 90's, but as far as I know Don is still running the Iron Horse as a venue in downtown El Dorado. He is one of the unsung heroes in this country who has kept this music alive and vital by presenting it and playing it himself for little or no monetary gain – simply because he believes it makes a difference. His dedication to the music and community has made an impact in El Dorado, Kansas, over the decades and in the lives of the musicians who enjoyed his fine stage, hospitality and friendship there.

IT SEEMED AS if every year I was traveling more and enjoying the shows more, too. When I was away from home, however, I sorely missed my wife and son. It was always worst just before I departed for a long tour. There was that half of you that just didn't want to leave – and your other half that couldn't wait to hit the road again and see what adventures lay ahead. It was a kind of schizophrenic existence for everyone involved.

When I would come back from an extensive journey, Michaela would comment that she had just gotten used to me being gone and was running everything fine. Then I would return, her day-to-day life would change radically again, and we would each have to relearn our roles in the household – and the relationship.

For myself, I had a lot of mixed feeling as I drove back into the city limits of Omaha. Nebraska remained stubbornly conservative and Republican, and I always felt like a fish out of water there.

Of course, you rarely garner the kind of crowds at home you receive at concerts on the road. At home, you suffer from the curse of being just too familiar to folks. This would somewhat change for me a few years later, but in the 80's it was a jolt to revert to playing in scuzzy bars after being feted in concerts around the country. It was good for my humility but tough to see how it was advancing my career.

One time in particular, I remember stopping at Louis' Bar, a few blocks away from our house, after I returned to town from a long tour. I had to have a drink before I faced the reality of being a husband, father, and Nebraskan again, even though I dearly loved Michaela and Dylan and missed them very much. It is hard to explain, but over a shot of schnapps and a beer, I entertained the thought of what it would be like to be ceaselessly on the road doing shows – just keep on going and fantasizing about finding a patron who would finance me to do so. The thought quickly faded, and I went home to my home and loving family, but the transition to a more "normal" life was becoming more difficult for me.

Though I would have chased this elusive musician's existence in any case, I knew I owed much of the comfort and security I had when I was out there to Michaela. I don't think I ever adequately thanked her for that, but I realized it was true and

"I WOULDN'T COUNT ON IT" — CONFESSIONS OF AN UNLIKELY FOLKSINGER

appreciated it always. Looking back, though, my actions didn't always indicate that gratitude.

♪ ♪ ♪ ♪ ♪

AS FOLKS LOOK over their lives, it is said most people regret the things they did not do or dreams they did not pursue rather than what they actually did. I by and large do not experience those sorts of second thoughts, because for the most part I bullheadedly followed the path I was passionate about. There are a few exceptions, however, where I still kick myself for the decisions I made.

One of those was when a place called The Speakeasy opened in New York City. Rod McDonald, who I had met in Boston at Passim was booking the venue. He was a nice guy and liked my music. I called him up and inquired about a booking there. The Speakeasy was staffed by a co-operative of musicians in New York City who were putting out a vinyl record a month profiling the artists that had played there. They were making quite a splash in the Eastern-centric folk music press, such as it was – magazines like "Sing Out" and "Dirty Linen." I thought it would be a good move to take the train down from Boston on one of my tours out that way and perform there, if they would have me.

The Speakeasy featured Friday and Saturday night shows. I inquired with Rod about the pay and possibility of doing both days on a weekend down there. Rod was amenable to me performing there but said he never booked someone for both nights of the weekend. He said he couldn't even book himself for both nights in one weekend. His fellow musicians would string him up if he took two nights in a row, he said – way too many fine pickers and songwriters, way too few venues. As for the pay, it was $50 for a night – extremely low, even in the mid-1980's. It would barely cover the train fare from Boston.

If it's all the same to you: River City Folk

I was in the Northeast on tour at the time and chatting to Elijah Wald about this deal. Elijah was a very interesting, inquisitive young musician who often hung out at Jeff McLaughlin's place in Cambridge. He lived a few blocks away, and his father was a Nobel Laureate in physics. Even though he was only 17 or so, he had already hitchhiked through India and had experienced a lot of wild adventures. Later, he would go on to become an acclaimed author and write biographies of Robert Johnson, the famed blues guitarist, and Dave Van Ronk.

His collaboration with Van Ronk on the book, "The Mayor of McDougal Street" is, in my opinion, the finest musical portrait of Greenwich Village and the folk music scene in the late 50's and early 60's. Elijah assembled it from numerous interviews he would do with Dave about his life and times.

In any case, when I told the young Elijah of the situation in New York, he said, "Well, you should go down there and perform the one night at the Speakeasy anyway. I can call Dave Van Ronk, and you can sleep on his couch for the weekend. I am sure he won't mind."

Though I was familiar with Dave Van Ronk's music, I wasn't overly fond of the idea of spending a whole weekend in Manhattan on someone's couch. I really didn't know much about Van Ronk's history, except that he and Bob Dylan had been pals in the early days. I appreciated Elijah's offer to arrange it for me, but replied "Thanks, but no thanks."

Then, 20 years or so later, after Van Ronk had died, I read the book that Elijah authored with and about him. It is full of humor, history, politics, the music business, personalities, and a unique viewpoint on an interesting and revolutionary time in American life and arts. Looking at it from this end of my life, what an experience it would have been to spend a weekend kibitzing with a guy like Dave Van Ronk and getting to know him. I think we would have gotten along famously, and just because of the lack of what I considered to be adequate bucks and comfort, I missed out on it.

What a dummy I was.

THE YEAR 1988 would be a very busy one for me and really represented progress in my career, though it was all happening so incrementally it didn't really feel like it at the time. It reminds me of what Garrison Keillor, of The Prairie Home Companion used to say: "It wasn't appearing on that radio program, or any one event that would make a career. It was a thousand small positive steps, some of them even disguised as setbacks, that made a career in the arts possible."

Many musicians in my tiny subculture of music would travel with just their guitars, a few clothes and a box of records to sell, but traveling with a PA system gave me the maximum amount of flexibility to fill in between concert dates at clubs. Of course, this wasn't possible when I flew somewhere, such as when I jetted to Boston to do a weekend at Passim, but except for those rare occasions, it was very useful to travel with your own equipment.

This was also extremely handy if you found yourself in a situation, as I did many times, where the venue had a dreadful PA. Though it was a lot more aggravation to set up your own sound in a concert setting – I remember hauling the heavy speakers and PA head up lots of steep stairs or long distances – you knew you would sound good with your own equipment, and folks would remember that.

The Colt Vista wagon I had driven since 1984 was reaching the end of its useful life and was threatening great expense and breakdowns if I held on to it. So, I traded it in and purchased my first real van. It was a truly unique vehicle, a 1986 Ford, short wheelbase (they used to call them "shorties") six-cylinder van, with a four-on-the-floor manual transmission.

Boy, was that vehicle fun to drive! It had a fold-down bed in the back, lots of space, and I really felt like King of the Road shifting through the gears in that box-on-wheels. Because it was a manual transmission, it got pretty good mileage, and it was really adept at going through the snowy, mountainous terrain I often found myself in. Gasoline was under a buck a gallon in those days, which allowed you to just hop in the van and drive to a concert hundreds of miles away, say, in Chicago or Kansas City, and still make it pay.

I was fortunate to be able to drive long distances with very little sleep. Seventeen and 18 hours behind the wheel were no problem for me. When I would feel really tired, I would continue on for five more minutes, then if I still felt as if I was falling asleep, I would pull over and shut my eyes for a bit. I became a master of the power nap: In those situations I would fall asleep immediately, doze for almost exactly 20 minutes and then wake up on cue. After I got out of the van and stretched my legs, I was good for at least a few more hours of white line fever.

The springtime of that year saw my longest tour to date, almost three months, transpire successfully on the East Coast. While there, I met McShane Glover, a very aggressive, efficient agent, who was working with some folks like Alan Damron and a folk revival group, The Hard Travelers. She would later work as an agent for me on the East Coast, as well.

As always, I was able to do such a long tour by being able to bunk at the houses of dear friends between performing dates, particularly at Jeff McLaughlin's in Cambridge, Al Feetham's in Avon, Massachusetts, (Al was an old buddy from Able Rug days, and he and his wife tolerated me in their lovely home many times), and Al and Anita Avery in Virginia Beach, Virginia.

In between the comfortable beds that my friends kindly provided, my old journals show that I also spent a good many nights on floors, in my sleeping bag. I guess it must not have bothered me, as I have few clear recollections of terribly uncomfortable circumstances. Linda Ronstadt once said, "Touring for music is an expensive means of being uncomfortable." At least for me back then, it was an inexpensive way to travel in discomfort.

Occasionally, after I thought I had everything in place for my lodgings along the way, plans would fall through.

In the early days, before I arrived in a town, I would ask the proprietors of venues I was performing at if could stay with them or someone they knew the night I was there. This casual approach to setting up a place to lay my head sometimes resulted in misunderstandings. Before I had my Ford van with the bed in the back, or when the weather was cold, this could be problematic.

One night, in Olympia, Washington, I was performing at a place where the owner/booker had confirmed I could stay with him the night I was in town. He wasn't there when I arrived, and I asked one of the waitresses if she would call him and ask him if he was coming to the show and what I should do about the lodgings that he had promised. Halfway through the first set, I got a note from the waitress that said, "The owner says you need to announce from the stage that you need a place to stay tonight." Say what?!

Needless to say, I was less than thrilled about that, and I'd be damned if I was going to beg for a place to stay from my audience on microphone. I don't actually recall what I wound up doing about a bed that night, but I was more specific in the future about those kind of arrangements.

I would play that spring at Passim in Boston; Old Dominion University in Norfolk, Virginia; a folk club in Morgantown, West Virginia; the Eagle Tavern in Greenwich Village, and many other venues of all sorts. A couple of the gigs particularly stand out – the Iron Horse Concert Hall in Northampton, Massachusetts, and an appearance on the nationally syndicated Mountain Stage radio program in Charleston, West Virginia.

The Iron Horse in Northampton was one of those plum gigs

that everyone was chasing in those days. It still exists today and is thriving. When I contacted them, Jordi Herold at the club told me flatly there was no way I would play there. He worked almost exclusively with agents and "name" artists. Be that as it may, he told me to go ahead and send a record and promo to him. At that time my most recent recording was "Open Spaces, Prairie Winds."

I phoned a couple of weeks later, and he said, "I get dozens of submissions every week, but I heard something different in your songs," and he engaged me as an opening act for Claudia Schmidt, the popular singer from Michigan. It went very well, and I even got an encore, which opening acts rarely get – remember, they are not there to see you – and an invitation to return.

It seemed there was even less chance that I would get on the syndicated show Mountain Stage. Again, the producer, Andy Ridenour, preferred to deal with agents. They paid very well for a short set, $400, as I recall, and included accommodations in a nice hotel. At that time, they were carried by almost 200 stations across the U.S.

Again, somehow, I beat the odds and was contracted to appear on the program. It was to be on Mother's Day, 1988, which was also the date of the Kentucky Derby that year. (I found out that was a very big deal in the South and in border states like West Virginia.) The other guests on the show were Maria Muldaur, who had a big hit in the 70's with the song "Midnight on the Oasis" and had been an esteemed singer since the Greenwich Village days in the early 60's, and The Battlefield Band, a very popular ensemble at that time from Scotland who put on a smoking, raucous show of Celtic music, complete with bagpipes and dance moves.

I had performed a couple of hundred miles north of Charlestown, West Virginia, the night before, and the pre-show production meeting was at 11 AM, so I needed to awaken early and start driving to make it there in time. I didn't sleep at all that night, in anticipation of the next day's festivities.

With my customary anxiety, I left way early and got to

"I WOULDN'T COUNT ON IT" — CONFESSIONS OF AN UNLIKELY FOLKSINGER

Charleston in plenty of time. The pre-production meeting was fun. All the guests on the program that day attended, and Maria Muldaur was there in the tightest jeans I had ever seen on a woman. She had staff with her. (I thought to myself she must have a lackey just to paint those trousers on.)

I also rehearsed with "The Twister Sisters," a couple of singers who were fixtures of the program, who often joined the artists on a song or two. I was the only one on that day's lineup who had consented to that. They and the Mountain Stage band played and sang my song, "Open Spaces, Prairie Winds" on the program with me, and they did a fine job. I recall I also played "Bessie and Me," with a pennywhistle introduction, along with a couple of other songs.

Mountain Stage was taped in front of a big, live audience in a fancy concert hall, and the crowd was particularly receptive to my set that day. I was tired after having no sleep, but I couldn't have been happier when the broadcast concluded. The producer, host and band leader all invited me to return, which was a big lift to me at that time.

A filly won the Kentucky Derby that day, evidently a rare occurrence that was considered good luck for the year ahead. Because it was Mothers Day, almost no restaurants were open in town. The show's staff and the musicians wound up congregating at a sushi bar in Charleston, and I had my first sample of that seafood delight. It was an acquired taste that I had not quite yet acquired.

Later that evening, the guys in the Battlefield Band and I went out to a roadhouse just outside of town that featured a country band, even on Sunday nights. All of us sang and sat in with the ensemble on various old country tunes and had a good, rowdy time. As always, spending time and sharing stories with Scotsmen stimulated the thirst, and we quenched it in a celebratory fashion with lots of Scotch whisky and beer. It was just a memorable day in every sense.

If it's all the same to you: River City Folk

AFTER THE YEARLY summer stint in Colorado, I was off to the western U.S. in early autumn. One of the places I would regularly do a concert was the venerable East Avenue Tavern on Burnside Street in Portland, which featured many of the traveling folk artists of the time, with a particular emphasis on Celtic music.

Mike Beglen had recently bought the place. Mike was a talented button accordion player from Ireland with a wry sense of humor and healthy disdain for the foibles of the musicians that performed for him. He would own the establishment for more than 15 years and came to be a good friend. He even joined me a couple of times at my gigs with his accordion.

While I was preparing to play there that evening in 1988, I got in touch with old friends Tom Bryson and Claire Levine and let them know I was in town. Turns out Tom was leaving that very day to go on a sailboat trip in the San Juan Islands. He said there was room on the boat and encouraged me to pack up after the concert and take off for Anacortes, Washington, where the sailboat was docked. I told him I was too low on funds for such a journey, but he said he would take care of whatever added expense there was.

It was a crazy thing to even contemplate on such short notice, but after giving the proposition a little thought I decided, "why not"? I had a few days off until the next weekend, and I could figure out how to get back to Seattle from the San Juan Islands where my next performance was booked. I had always heard about the beauty of that region of North America and decided I would be a fool to pass up this chance.

After the concert that night, I drove up I-5 through a torrential rainstorm to Anacortes, about 200 miles north of Portland. I located the marina where the vessel was docked and caught a couple of hours sleep in my van.

The next morning, I found the boat and met the captain, a gregarious, outgoing Minnesotan by the name of Chris Courneyer, who Tom Bryson had become good pals with. Chris was

"I WOULDN'T COUNT ON IT" — CONFESSIONS OF AN UNLIKELY FOLKSINGER

IN THE SAN JUAN ISLANDS (TOM BRYSON)

very welcoming, and I was excited to be onboard. Chris said they could drop me in Friday Harbor later that week so I could catch the ferry back to Anacortes, retrieve my van, and get back for the gigs in the Seattle area.

It was late September, which can be a dicey time in the Pacific Northwest weather-wise. The sailing journey started out in the rain, and there was a pretty good chop in the water as we crossed the international boundary into the Canadian Gulf Islands. Small craft advisories had been issued, and at times we couldn't see land because of the rain squalls. On the other hand, there was lots of wind for sailing!

The sailboat was a 39-foot French-built schooner, very seaworthy. After a damp, cold day, the skies cleared and we were graced by one of the most spectacular sunsets I have ever witnessed as we anchored at Annette Cove close to Active Pass, between two of the Canadian Gulf Islands.

I was having the time of my life. Being from Nebraska, I had essentially no experience with sailboats (an honorary organization back in the Cornhusker State called "The Nebraska Navy" doesn't have much to do with water), and I found such joy in being able to help tack (after instruction) and help out with sailing tasks.

Chris was very tolerant of my rank ignorance of boats, knots and procedures. I had brought my guitar so I could play a few songs for ships company at night, and I had also brought a few jugs of wine to contribute to the alcohol stash. Every evening we had a hot, delicious meal that one of the culinary-gifted crew members would prepare, followed by wine and song.

The weather the rest of that week improved and was as superb as it could be in the Pacific Northwest in late September. Warm days and cool nights were the rule, and at every place we stopped for the evening we would grab an anchor buoy, take the dinghy into shore, and hike around the lush, beautiful islands. That late in the season, there was not a lot of competition for the anchor buoys, and we were one of the few ships enjoying the perfect autumn temperatures. (The San Juans and Canadian Gulf Islands get quite crowded during the summer months.)

Getting into the dinghy on that boat was a challenge for me. The sailboat itself had what was called a raked stern, meaning it was angled back toward the boat rather than going straight down or at an angle toward the water. This made mounting the dinghy (the small boat or skiff used to row into the islands) particularly daunting. You kind of had to launch yourself in its general direction from the rear of the boat and then land in the dinghy without falling into the water.

I'm sure I must have looked as ungainly as a moose attempting to climb into a canoe as I made that jump – it truly was a leap of faith. I never actually fell in the water, though I came perilously close many times.

I will never forget the magnificence of the scenery on that journey nor the kindness of those folks who shared their voyage with me. I would wind up going on many other sailing trips with Chris Courneyer as captain, particularly after he bought his own boat, the Jenny Gordon. On one other memorable cruise, Tom

Bryson himself would captain a chartered sailing vessel and my son, Dylan, then in his senior year in high school, would join us.

Without the songs, I never would have met Tom Bryson and Claire Levine, Chris Courneyer or Mike Beglen – and certainly would not have had the experience of this sailing voyage in the luminous, picturesque waters surrounding the San Juan and Canadian Gulf Islands of the Pacific Northwest.

The last day I was on that sailing journey we were surrounded by a pod of Orca whales, so close it seemed like we could almost touch them. They frolicked and played for the better part of a half hour. It was a spectacle my heart will never forget, as was the entire tour that year.

OPEN SPACES, PRAIRIE WINDS: WINTERFOLK

THE YEAR 1988 WOULD ALSO MARK THE BEGINning of one of the most important traditions in my life and part of my musical career where I have been able to make a positive impact beyond just the songs.

Mary Barclay was a fan and friend who had been coming to see me at the Horse Brass in Portland for years.

On my last couple trips, she had been talking about how she would like to fly me out to play at the pub for her 40th birthday. As always in those situations, I said I would love to do it, but took it with a grain of salt. Most proposals like that just never happen. I think folks mean well, but alcohol ramps up their enthusiasm and powers their rhetoric a bit farther than their pocketbooks can follow.

In this case, however, it actually worked out. She paid for my roundtrip airfare from Omaha and a modest honorarium, and I played for her party December 11th, 1988. I invited my pal Terry Prohaska and a couple of other friends to play some songs that night, too.

Toward the end of the gathering, Mary passed through the

"I WOULDN'T COUNT ON IT" — CONFESSIONS OF AN UNLIKELY FOLKSINGER

pub taking a collection up from the listeners and patrons for a cooperative that she was working for that helped the homeless.

This was the unassuming beginning of Winterfolk, a benefit concert now in its 32nd year. It spent its first five years at the Horse Brass Pub as an all-day Sunday festival with many acts. Utah Phillips – the Golden Voice of the Great Southwest, as he used to be called and one of the most original, brilliant humanitarians and performers I have ever known – would first play Winterfolk at one of those Horse Brass events.

In year three, I named the event Winterfolk, and it became a benefit for Sisters of the Road Cafe, an innovative organization that provides low-cost and no-cost meals in the Old Town area of Portland. They also provide information on area resources, job training, and most importantly, they give folks hope. It's all wrapped in the Dorothy Day/Catholic Worker philosophy of non-violence, no proselytizing, and a commitment to addressing basic needs. Sisters of the Road Cafe operates under the credo that without food, clothing, and shelter you simply can't move on to live a productive, happy life – so take care of first things first.

Over the first 30 years, funds raised from Winterfolk fed more than a quarter of a million folks who have had a tough time. I feel so honored to have been allowed to devote my time, energy and talent to making that happen, and I am proud of every performer who has played a song at the annual concert.

Sisters of the Road Cafe was about more than just food. The restaurant is a real gathering place in the community, a refuge of respect and positive connections, and for a buck and a quarter you can get a filling, tasty meal. If you can't afford the price, you can work 15 minutes in the cafe for your lunch. No one is sent away hungry. There is no obligatory sermon to hear, no hoops to jump through save one – no violence of any kind is tolerated there, either in deeds or in words. Everyone is treated with friendliness and dignity.

In my travels, I have witnessed so much basic need in this

country. There are pockets of near-Dickensian poverty in every large city and in many smaller communities across the U.S. It doesn't have to be that way. Compare how many homeless there are and how many appeal signs there are (or aren't) in Europe or Canada, and you will begin feel a bit queasy if you have a conscience. The safety net continues to shrink, and the stories from this segment of society don't make the papers or the evening news unless violence or sex is attached to them.

Attempts to slightly level the playing field via a decent minimum wage or health insurance are met with the same cry of "socialism" or "communism" and "jobs will disappear" as have been used and disproved since the 1930's, when my father was young and Western Union flatly refused to honor new federal wage standards until they were threatened with severe penalties.

I don't know how right-wing, prosperous, pompous Republicans who use these spurious, debunked arguments against basic living standards can look at themselves in the mirror in the morning. Many of the homeless are working poor, slaving away at more than one job, attempting to live on a minimum wage that in real dollars is far less than it was when I was a young man and it was pegged at $1.60 an hour.

There have been many times in my life, as there have been in most people's lives, if they are honest with themselves, when I was only a heartbeat away from homelessness and hunger. I am grateful to have had a chance through Winterfolk to make a real difference in people's daily lives through music. Winterfolk has always been a true benefit – every dollar goes to the beneficiary, and every artist performs gratis, whether they are unknown locals or nationally known folksingers like Utah Phillips, Anne Hills or Tam Paxton.

After five years at the Horse Brass Pub, Winterfolk (always with the foursquare support of Don Younger, who became an enthusiastic partner in Sisters of the Road Cafe's efforts) eventually moved to Portland's lovely Aladdin Theatre, an old Vaudeville hall that until the 80's was principally known for screening the classic "Deep Throat" for more than a decade. When that cinematic milestone ended and the renovation of the lovely old theatre was finished, the Aladdin became the home to all sorts of folk, bluegrass, jazz and alternative performers. Winterfolk was a natural there, and that theatre became an invaluable partner of the event.

But as the years rolled along, the Winterfolk crowds somewhat diminished. The graying of the audiences of this gentle, literate music in this rough age is a real thing. A new, smaller theatre opened in the Alberta St. area of Portland that seemed to be a better match for the event. After dear pal and gifted soundman Rob Folsom passed away in 2016 (he would drive down from the Seattle area every year to help out), Winterfolk moved to the lovely 400-seat Alberta Rose Theatre, where it has been ever since.

In 2019, the beneficiary also changed to a multi-dimensional social service organization, JOIN PDX. Staff and policies at Sisters of the Road had shifted, and it was time to make a move as their priorities changed. Thanks to my dedicated musician friends and volunteers, the event carries on in its work of making this area a bit more equitable for those who are struggling to get by.

AS THE DECADE of the eighties moved into its final year, I was staying quite busy. I would perform that winter in Boston on two different trips, and McShane Glover from Annapolis, Maryland, would take over my bookings on the East Coast for a couple of years. Despite my rants about agents, she actually was quite responsible and effective. I still handled the majority of my business myself, though, as she was quite occupied with better-heeled clients that could pay her more than I could.

I would stop in Ithaca, New York, and perform on the long

running radio program, Bound for Glory, run by Phil Shapiro. Lance Heidig, a close friend of Chris Kennedy's and another veteran of the Grand Lake Lodge, would provide me a place to stay there and a tour of the campus, town and lovely waterfalls. Then, on to Beverly, Massachusetts; Rehoboth Beach, Delaware; Baltimore, Maryland; Norfolk, Virginia; Philadelphia and other crowded locales.

Two highlights were performing at the beautiful Birchmere in Alexandria, Virginia, and at The King of France Tavern in Annapolis Maryland, a historic and acclaimed music venue which had been on that site since the Revolutionary War. It is now a Starbucks – not surprising, given the importance most Americans accord history.

Ever since I was a young boy I have been interested in history. One of the unforeseen benefits of this trade was finding myself in places where great events had occurred and having the time to visit them or the museums that commemorated them.

In the East, there are so many Civil War and Revolutionary sites, and I tried to explore as many as I could. As I look back now, I wish I had taken more advantage of my proximity to those sites than I did. The most evocative of those sites for me was the massive battlefield at Gettysburg, where the largest engagement ever fought in the Americas raged from July 1 to July 3, 1863.

When I first visited Gettysburg at the close of the 1980's, a motel was located just outside of town, directly in the path of the famous Pickett's charge – the decisive afternoon in the Confederacy's loss of that battle. It was called the Home Sweet Home motel.

The price was right in a folksinger's range, 30 bucks or so, and the location was amazing. Gettysburg National Park is spread out over a huge area, but from that motel you could just take off walking across the fields and get anywhere on the battlefield, from the Little Round Top to the cemetery and central interpretive buildings.

The motel was sited next to the Emmitsburg Pike road, which

"I WOULDN'T COUNT ON IT" — CONFESSIONS OF AN UNLIKELY FOLKSINGER

would have been directly in the path of Pickett's men as they marched that mile and a half to the Union breastworks and attempted to break through. In the motel parking lot, there was even a stone memorial to one of the Confederate regiments that had suffered grievous casualties.

Imagining that such pain and death had occurred not so very long ago on the very spot I was sleeping made for a restless night. Still, it was an ideal place to venture out from and see some of the hundreds of monuments and names that are etched forever in American history.

I visited the battlefield two different years on April weekdays. Both times I stayed at the Home Sweet Home motel. When I visited again a few years later, the motel was gone. Gettysburg National Park had done a land swap with the owners and demolished it, so there would be no commercial establishments on the park grounds. I was fortunate I had gotten to experience that emotional site from that convenient – and inexpensive – lodging while it was still there.

It was just another instance where you were reminded that money was not your only recompense for doing this vocation. In all my travels, it was rare to see a museum packed or a national or state memorial site teaming with people. Generally, if you just got out and walked a couple of hundred yards you had the place all to yourself.

THE RADIO PROGRAM was ticking along, and I think by this time I was even being paid $10 a show – $40 a month. That was okay, I certainly wasn't in it for the money.

In the summer, in addition to Grand Lake, I had some festivals and county fairs booked. One of them reminded me why I carried a PA in my van at all times when I headed out.

The Dodge County Fair took place north of Omaha, just outside of the whimsically named town of Wahoo, Nebraska. I was assured by the organizer they had a PA that was more than adequate for my needs and that I didn't need to bring a thing except my guitar and myself.

When I got there and was pointed towards the area where I was to perform, it turned out the PA was a lectern with a cheap microphone attached (not the first time I had encountered this). There was no provision for a guitar mic, and the speakers were the cheesy ones located in the podium itself. Fortunately, I had my PA system in the van and was able to set it up, despite her protestations that I didn't need it. In a noisy fair setting in an outdoor venue, where the sound travels out and bounces off no walls, ceilings or glass, it is impossible to be heard without a PA.

I guess the fair organizer liked me well enough, because the next year she again booked me and my trio to play the fair. By that time, Cliff Jones on acoustic bass and Avery Grimes on keyboards were performing with me when the money, geography or degree of fun they would have doing it made sense. The organizer assured me that they had a "brand new PA" which would be splendid for the whole band to use.

This time the PA turned out to be a Fender guitar amplifier with a 12-inch speaker. It did look new, I will give her that. A guitar amplifier might be adequate for a public speaker, and you could conceivably hook up a microphone to sing, though the quality would not be very good, as well as play an electric guitar through it. But it was wholly inadequate for an acoustic guitar player with a band. Thank goodness, again, I had my equipment with me in the Ford van.

We set the PA up in front of some bleachers, right next to an antique fire engine display. Throughout the set, kids would come along and ring that damn fire engine bell, which was extremely irritating. But it's kind of funny too now that I look back on it, thinking

"I WOULDN'T COUNT ON IT" — CONFESSIONS OF AN UNLIKELY FOLKSINGER

about some of the more serious songs I was doing at that time being punctuated by a loud bell at the most inopportune times.

Also, at one point during the performance, a determined fellow grabbed hold of Cliff while he was playing his big upright bass and shouted in his ear "Too loud!" I purposefully had the PA level at a low volume. That stupid fire bell was way louder than we were. But this character decided he needed to put in his two cents worth. I thought he was going to knock poor Cliff down.

I ignored the farmer's demand, and we stumbled through the rest of the set. The paycheck certainly was not as large as the amount of aggravation we encountered that day.

It was during occasions like this however, that you were particularly glad to have other musicians with you. Misery loves company, and we laughed about it all the way back home after we picked up some liquid refreshment to lubricate the return journey.

I think that was the same summer I was engaged to do a community celebration day at one of the ethnically settled towns north of Omaha.

In the 19th century, the railroads competed for immigrants to buy and settle the lands the government had given to them after they laid the tracks. This was a major source of profits for the railroads, both in the selling of the lands and the eventual shipping of the crops that were produced from them. Hence many towns along that old right of way were still primarily Czechoslovakian, German, Polish, etc. The town I was to perform at that day was on the old Chicago-Northwestern Railroad line and was primarily of Czechoslovakian heritage.

It was a hot summer day, and Michaela and Dylan drove with me to the gig. When I got there, a large ensemble was on stage. I got out my guitar and waited by the side of the stage to go on next. After the group finished its set, I counted 31 button accordion players trooping one by one off the stage. Their costumes were beautiful, hand made from multi-colored fabric. The accordions themselves were works of art, all constructed of brightly colored,

Open Spaces, Prairie Winds: Winterfolk

cheerful combinations of flashy greens and reds – and they had dancers who waltzed and twirled to their upbeat folk melodies.

Follow that with one cowboy-booted, vested folksinger toting an acoustic guitar and a bagful of songs about history and romance. They were a tough act to follow. My reception from the older, ethnic audience was just as you might imagine it was.

The life of a freewheeling singer/songwriter might look like a glamorous one, but the majority of the time it was challenging, difficult and sometimes downright discouraging. No matter the situation, though, you had to focus on doing your very best, singing the songs and telling the stories with sincerity and passion. You never knew who was going to be listening and how your performance might change their life – or yours.

♪ ♪ ♪ ♪ ♪ ♪

AS I MENTIONED earlier, there have been numerous times in my career that I have been double-booked, when two artists are booked for the same night. It is always an uncomfortable situation, but usually after some confusion it is sorted out equitably. So, I don't ever recall ever being as outright agitated by something like that as I was in Langley, Whidbey Island, Washington, that year.

I found out a couple of days before my concert at a place aptly named The Doghouse that I was double booked with Country Joe McDonald. He is the singer/guitarist mostly known for his appearance on the Woodstock movie and album (Give me an F, give me a U, blah, blah, blah). The proprietor said we could split the night and I would still get half of the door. Country Joe would go on first, I would go on for the second set.

Country Joe was not friendly to me in the least: He was actually kind of surly. He did his set, just he and his guitar, which consisted mostly of stories of how he had written such and such

"I WOULDN'T COUNT ON IT" — CONFESSIONS OF AN UNLIKELY FOLKSINGER

while he was shacked up with Janis Joplin, what he had written when he was living with Jefferson Airplane, yada, yada, yada. I found the music to be simplistic, corny and amateurishly performed, heavily reliant on dropping names, unimaginative, and sounding only marginally coherent.

But a funny thing happened. The audience (the place was full) made up almost entirely of aging 60's hippies thought his songs and renditions of songs by others were fabulous. They couldn't get enough of him. The applause was thunderous, and they whooped and hollered through the cigarette/marijuana smoke haze.

It was the first – but not the last – time I saw the phenomenon up close of a crowd responding in that way to an artist for who he had been or how famous he was in their eyes, rather than the actual performance or music.

It seemed to me the reaction of the audience was antithetical and just the opposite to what was actually, physically occurring in the room. And it was not that he was funny or looked sexy or some of those other factors that will often affect a listener's judgment.

He was none of those. He was just a once-famous, arrogant old hippie who couldn't really play guitar and who could barely sing. He wasn't particularly warm toward his listeners, either, refusing to sign albums or chat with them before or after the show.

I found all of this very disturbing, as did my bass player, Cliff Jones, who was touring with me that autumn. We adjourned to the front bar for refreshment, to try to take the edge off before our set – which we succeeded in doing.

Country Joe McDonald wound up playing almost twice as long as his allotted time. To add insult to injury, when he finally finished and left immediately, almost the entire audience departed, too. Cliff and I were left with a crowd of fewer than 10 to play for. It was a dismal night. But after the concert a couple of friends I had met there on a previous trip took pity on us and took us back to their place, and we salvaged the evening while making acerbic comments about what had happened to us at The (aptly named) Doghouse. It was an interesting case study on perception, reality and fame. At least I got half of the door.

After a busy time the remainder of that autumn in the Pacific Northwest, Avery, Cliff and I finished out that decade performing at a First Night Celebration in Lincoln, Nebraska. It was 20 degrees below zero that evening, as I recall, but we were fortified with plenty of antifreeze and the enthusiasm of young men. After we froze getting our equipment inside the venue, we finished the year with a well played, well-received performance.

BLUE NORTHERN

THE 90'S WERE UNDERWAY, AND I HOPE I enjoyed them, as they sure went by like a flash. I kept busy playing locally and working on the radio broadcast. I would typically record programs months in advance, knowing I would be gone from Omaha for long periods of time. By this time the station at the University of Nebraska at Omaha had moved to roomier, more appropriate digs in the engineering building. No more sagging floors.

In March of that year I did a concert at Midland College in Fremont, Nebraska. An Associated Press writer by the name of Joe Ruff attended the show and wrote and published a syndicated, in-depth article about me, my travels, and folk music that was printed in many newspapers around the country. Back in those pre-internet times, stories like that were really a boost – and this one did indeed make a difference.

I became aware early on in my music life of the power of the press. I had always been diligent about sending out publicity releases and photos to newspapers and periodicals and following up with phone calls when practical. As I result, I received lots of attention – dozens of stories and photos of me were published in newspapers from Boston to Juneau. I never relied on someone else to send out that publicity for me, I did it myself.

Once in a while a fortuitous connection would be made by

chance, and a writer would serendipitously do a story, but by and large you really needed to court those kind of articles through your own efforts. Since this all played a vital role in getting folks out to the gigs, which many times determined your pay and whether you would be asked to return again, you had better become adept at it.

I understand it was different back in the days of the folk revival in the 60's, when there was lots of money floating around. But in the era I was working in, you really had to learn to take control of your career and do the detail work to make it happen. This included booking yourself, sending out publicity, making cold calls to new venues, sending out contracts and negotiating fees, and constantly following up on all of this. Though I would periodically avail myself of the efforts of agents like McShane Glover, it would quickly become apparent that "no one had more of an interest in me making a living than I did myself." That's a direct quote from folksinger Tom Rush, spoken on a long night the two of us spent investigating various taverns and pubs in Harvard Square in the early 1980's. I have always remembered his words.

Back in these pre-cell phone days, I memorized the locations of many car-payphones around the country. These were coin pay phones mounted in a parking lot or lay-by on steel poles, with a small cover over the apparatus that you could use while sitting in your vehicle. They were just the right height. I would have my long distance phone card handy, with a prepaid code you would dial to access the minutes you had bought, my calendar, a list of numbers I needed to call about gigs, and notes about all of them.

I could pull up to one of these conveniently mounted phones and have the privacy of my car and a little shelter from the weather as I haggled about money, dates, and all sorts of other details, as well as checking in with home every other day or so. It was quite a contrast to the smart phones of today, which puts the advantages of a complete office in everyone's back pocket.

I had no patience – and still don't – for the constant bitch I heard from those musicians who carped, "I could be so successful if I had an exclusive agent or manager to book me." No one likes to do that part of the job, but working in an alternative form of music like folk or jazz or functioning in any kind of music at a level below say, $50,000 a year, there is just no way that paying an agent or manager makes any sense. And nobody I knew in this segment of music was making that kind of dough.

Plus, what kind of an agent can make a living on 15 percent of that, and what kind of a job do you think they will do for you? With the exception of a very few talented, lucky, inordinately prosperous individuals in this subculture, everyone who has ever had an agent has eventually gone back to booking themselves and taking care of their own affairs. It's either that, marry a rich spouse, or figure out some other way to make a living. Seeing the latter two options as unappealing, I worked at being a good steward of my own business.

I HAD READ an article in the daily newspaper about Nebraska establishing its own regional public radio network, similar to the sort that existed in Minnesota, Montana and other states. I made an appointment to meet with the newly minted director of that network, which was to be headquartered at the main campus of the University of Nebraska in Lincoln. His name was Steve Robinson, and he would become an extremely important catalyst to the growth of River City Folk.

As well as being very knowledgeable about classical music, Steve was a folk and jazz fan. He was from the East Coast and was a good choice for network general manager – aggressive, bright and full of ideas. He agreed this new state organization might have a place for something a little more roots-oriented than the typical NPR mix of classical music and news.

The new network was entirely separate from KVNO, where I was producing the show, but I figured it couldn't hurt to try and push things along and see what happened. After many discussions with Steve Robinson, he invited me to the sign-on celebration of the Norfolk, Nebraska, transmitter in May of 1990. When I attended that event, he informed me they had decided to carry River City Folk, but he wanted it to be a weekly two-hour broadcast rather than the current one-hour format.

I immediately said I would do it, without being too concerned about the details. I talked to the KVNO general manager, Howard Lowe, about the offer I had received. He did not want to see River City Folk leave KVNO, and he made a counter offer. The show would stay there but also be carried by the Nebraska Public Radio Network. I would continue to produce it in Omaha, and KVNO would pay me the fee that I had negotiated with Steve Robinson for the expanded broadcast.

Mind you, it wasn't a fortune – I think it was $150 a program – but it was a hell of a lot more than I had been making on that venture, and it was going to reach a lot of listeners throughout the state. Steve Robinson agreed to this arrangement, and River City Folk began as a two-hour show across the state of Nebraska in the summer of 1990.

The first time I had the opportunity to read the names of all the translators across the state on the air – Ogallala, Alliance, Norfolk, Grand Island, and a couple more I can't recall – I was quite pleased with the results of my politicking to take River City Folk to a wider audience.

Every little bit of progress feeds another in the music business. My Nebraska Arts Council bookings picked up immediately as I was heard weekly throughout the state, and the radio show was gaining more attention from folk record labels across the country, which would also wind up giving my own career a boost.

"I WOULDN'T COUNT ON IT" — CONFESSIONS OF AN UNLIKELY FOLKSINGER

THOUGH I LOOKED forward to the extensive fall and spring tours, in between I tried to stay within striking distance of Omaha as much as possible. Between Omaha and Chicago lay the great state of Iowa, and I found myself performing there frequently.

I recall being struck by a concert I did in Mt. Pleasant, Iowa, in a weathered, red brick hotel that once had been owned by Robert Todd Lincoln, Abraham Lincoln's eldest son. The building looked very similar to the way it must have appeared during Robert Todd Lincoln's day – very Victorian, with old musty smelling wallpaper and lots of small rooms. I swear I could feel the resonance from those times when the small Mississippi river towns like this one were vital and lively crossroads of commerce and culture.

I have no recollection how many people were at the show that night, but the aura of antiquity clung to the walls like old cigar smoke. More so than in any museum, I could sense both the common and famous people that had trod those floors before me.

Another performing highlight in Iowa was The General Store in Stone City. Stone City was where Grant Wood had created many of his famous paintings and founded the new American painting school of Regionalism. The General Store was a quaint little place that put on concerts seating maybe 50 folks, and I played there numerous times. They would also put you up a short distance away at a luxurious bed and breakfast as part of the deal.

I had some friends in the area who were farming land their family had grazed and cultivated for generations.

Like me, they loved good wine and good food. I have a very fond memory of going to their home, fueling up on young lamb expertly prepared, exquisite French red wine, and some very potent marijuana, and heading to the General Store in Stone City to see Leon Redbone perform.

It was kind of a foggy night, both inside and outside, as I sat in a rickety lawn chair in the back of their cargo van. Leon sounded fine as I recall, and looked dazzling in his white suit, but I think I was in a particularly non-judgmental mood that evening.

That summer Michaela, Dylan and I would return to Ireland on a trip that was partly vacation but also consisted of quite a few performing dates. It wasn't the best year to perform in Ireland in June - their national soccer team got to the semi-finals in the World Cup for the first time in history, and soccer mania swept the country, effectively reducing listeners at my concerts to very small numbers. It always seemed as if my shows were on a date when Ireland had an important match.

Ireland, however, never disappoints. Despite the national hysteria about their team, we had a wonderful trip, and Michaela's father, the well-respected teacher and author, Bob Reilly, who had written books and articles about Ireland for decades, and many of her siblings met us there that summer.

In Dublin, I performed at the renowned club called An Beal Bocht (The Poor Mouth). Though the crowd was sparse, the owner was enthusiastic and shared some wicked small batch "poteen" (Irish moonshine, made from potatoes) from County Clare with me. The stuff tasted like the fires of hell, but it sure relieved any anxieties you might have been experiencing. I wouldn't recommend adding it on top of six or seven pints of Guinness, though. The later results were projectile and technicolor in nature.

Ireland always offered glimpses into a simpler time, particularly in the west of that country – especially back in those days before the "Celtic Tiger" economy kicked in. After visiting with my dear friend and fine songwriter Martin Sneyd in Dublin and doing a couple of dates there, we pointed our borrowed car towards County Kerry.

We spent the night in charming Dingle town, with its old pubs and traditional music. The next day, before heading to another concert I had scheduled, we decided to drive out to Slea Head on the Dingle Peninsula – the furthest western sliver of land in Europe.

"I WOULDN'T COUNT ON IT" — CONFESSIONS OF AN UNLIKELY FOLKSINGER

After we passed the picturesque little village of Dunquin and arrived at what we perceived as the end of the road, we saw a farmhouse and acreage to the west, on a high cliff overlooking the ocean. We parked at the thatched stone cottage, and an old farmer came out to say hello.

We asked him if he would mind if we walked to the edge of the cliff where Slea Head ended – and there was nothing between Europe and the New World except the broad North Atlantic. He was very friendly and said, "Walking out there would be fine. Just please don't chase any of the sheep, as they sometimes get spooked, go over the cliff and fall into the ocean."

So, we strolled out to the edge of Europe, staying well clear of any sheep we encountered. Surrounded by incomparable scenery on all sides – mountains behind us, the majestic Atlantic and cliffs in all other directions – our little family enjoyed a lovely vista and memorable ramble.

When we returned to our car, the farmer asked if we would like a cup of tea. I replied that I really needed to get to Killarney that evening to do a show at the Glen Eagle Hotel, and so regretfully we had to keep moving.

Killarney is about 60 miles or so from where we were. His response was, "A pity you have to rush off and we cannot have more of a visit. Killarney, eh? What's that town like?"

Like many farmers at that time in the west of Ireland, he had no automobile. He had a bike that he would ride the 10 miles or so into Dingle to get supplies, or I suppose a neighbor would give him a ride and help him out.

You cannot really get anywhere in that part of Ireland without being forced to negotiate the tourist bus-snarled, kitschy, cart-jammed streets of Killarney. He had never been there, though it was only 60 miles or so from his home. He, his father and his grandfather had lived their whole lives in the beautiful but secluded countryside where they were born, and he had never married. He had never been as far as those 60 miles distant from that property.

I wish we could have stayed all day and drank tea with that kind, soft spoken Irishman. I would have enjoyed hearing more about him and his life there, his joys and disappointments. When I returned years later, his place was torn down and there was no sign of the fieldstone and thatched roof house that his family had occupied for generations.

Like his cottage, there are few traces left of that part of Ireland today. Much of the lovely farmland and coastal acreages have been bought by well-heeled folks from mainland Europe and America. The Emerald Isle of the small subsistence farmer with a cow, chickens and donkey, who rides his bike to the village for a pint, has mostly vanished. Throughout the west of Ireland, people used to like nothing more than to while away the day by telling stories and singing a song in a country pub, with a Guinness next to them to quench their thirst. Now it seems everyone is in a hurry, and the songs and stories have been largely replaced by multiple televisions in every pub, which all have numerous Budweiser advertising displays.

Some may call it progress, and of course I never actually lived there or experienced the hard times they confronted, so this may be presumptuous for me to say. But as an outsider who has been there often, I still can't help thinking something rare and important has been lost with all the modernization and corporatization of that lovely island. I am glad I got to see Ireland, to spend a good deal of time there, and to get to know its people and rural landscapes before the radical changes of the late twentieth century really kicked in – when they turned places like Killarney and other parts of the country into nostalgic theme parks.

"I WOULDN'T COUNT ON IT" — CONFESSIONS OF AN UNLIKELY FOLKSINGER

IN JULY, THE folks at KVNO threw a five-year celebration party for River City Folk at Trovato's Restaurant in Omaha, a place where I regularly performed. It became kind of a mini-folk festival, with acts I had invited from the area doing a set to celebrate with me. An administrator from a downtown museum attended, and it gave her an idea about hosting a similar, but larger, event. Her thoughts would blossom into a full-fledged folk festival in a couple of years, which I was asked to direct and coordinate.

During the Pacific Northwest tour that autumn I would begin performing at a venue in Portland, where I would play frequently for more than 20 years: Kells Irish Pub, close to the old town area that Sisters of the Road serves. Kells had been open in the Pike St. Market in Seattle since 1982, operated by the McAleese family from Belfast, Northern Ireland. It was decided that the oldest son, Gerard, and his wife would open another Kells Pub in Portland.

Peter Yeates, my Irish pal from the McGurk's days in St. Louis, told me about the new pub and suggested I give the owner a call. I did so, and despite the fact that the cassette I sent him had no Irish music on it, he took my word that I knew some Irish ballads and hired me to play a few dates that September.

Who could have guessed that Kells would become such a significant part of my life and income over the next decades? I would eventually spend hundreds of nights on that stage – about 80 nights a year. Gerard McAleese always paid well and was more than fair to me.

Originally, I would just play some dates in the autumn when I was out there on tour. When his St. Patrick's Irish Festival started – which later became the largest Celtic festival on the West Coast of the U.S. – he would pay my airfare to Portland, whatever fee I requested, and provide generous accommodations for me.

In 1992, he honored my request to have Mark Moebeck, my old St. Patrick's Day partner from St. Louis, join me in Portland, and he paid his airfare, hotel and honorarium, too. We were put up at the Benson Hotel, the grande dame of Portland hotels, with fancy doormen, turn-down service, and room service we couldn't afford. Life was good.

Kells was not an easy place to play, however. The pub was cavernous, and the large, built-in PA system was difficult to work with. Over the years, however, I learned so much there about how to get an audience fired up and participating – even young people in their 20's whose priority certainly wasn't listening to Irish ballads.

Many nights, particularly on the weekends, Kells' patrons were the furthest thing from a listening, concert crowd that you can imagine. The clientele was mostly very young, affluent white college suburbanites or 20 somethings, drinking to excess and attempting to get laid. Be that as it may, particularly in later years, my band would have them boogying on the dance floor.

Mostly I performed there solo. In the early years, Cliff and Avery joined me for a couple of weekends there, and once Terry Prohaska and Rich Gillette kept me musical company for a Friday and Saturday night. I think Terry and Rich were shell-shocked by the noise in the place. It was tough to get used to.

And yes, Kells could be noisy. When I would wake up on the morning following a particularly raucous night there, my ears would be ringing.

Mark Moebeck would join me there at the early St. Patrick's Day festivals: two guys, two guitars, two voices. At that event, they mounted a couple auxiliary stages. The largest was just behind the pub, in a massive tent that covered the entire back parking lot with a capacity of over 1000 people. Mark and I never fared well on that stage. The audience was detached from you, and there were no chairs, so people had to stand and hold their drinks, which makes it difficult to applaud or clap along. We preferred the more "intimate" (only 350 or so screaming people) atmosphere of the pub.

When my son, Dylan, turned 18, he would join me and Mark on bass at the St. Patrick's week gigs. Having that bottom reinforcement to our sound made a big difference, and Dylan got a kick out of the scene. Years later, he would join me frequently on stage there and also thumped his bass with another group that performed there regularly.

CHRIS KENNEDY HAD taken a job as associate professor of communications at Western Wyoming College in Rock Springs, Wyoming. It seemed natural that I would begin to play in that community, at the college and elsewhere. Chris and his lovely wife, Sue, were always tolerant of my presence and invited me to stay for as long as I liked.

Chris and I began doing some songs together when I was there. We enjoyed each other's company immensely and seemed to know all the same artists and songs, as well as enjoying the same literature and authors. I even remember once for fun doing a little gig with him at the local Daylight Donuts in Rock Springs. I wouldn't have done it by myself or with anyone else – but Chris and I had such a good time picking and singing together.

I also began to incorporate his talents and companionship, when I could afford to do it, into some of my concerts in that area and beyond. For years I had been doing an October show in Logan, Utah. I lined that up with the intercession of a woman I had met at the Horse Brass, a gardener for Utah State University nicknamed Swede. I had an engagement at Eccles Hall at the Utah State University in Logan that year and asked Chris to open the show for me.

Chris and I headed for Logan together in my Ford van. I think the crowd was pretty good, but I really don't remember much about it – except that Chris and I were invited to the library before the show by the fellow who was promoting the concert. He was the university archivist, Brad Cole. Brad had mentioned they had a large collection of first edition, signed Jack London books, and even an original copy of Jack London's tramp diary, written in pencil.

Chris had written his fine song, "Jack London," and we were both fans of London's books and short stories,

though Chris had read many more of them than I had. Brad left us alone in the climate-controlled room with the priceless first edition London books, signed to the author's darling wife, Charmian. What a thrill it was to thumb through the original tramp diary of London's days before he achieved success as a writer, as he traveled in the roughest fashion imaginable through late 19th century America.

Jack London died at age 40 after writing more than fifty books and dozens of articles and reports. He was the most famous author of his day and was at one time a millionaire from his writings, while also being a renowned socialist. His was a life of contradictions, action, risk, hard work and daring. Holding that diary, reading his words and feeling his spirit was one of the best perks I ever got from this crazy business, and I know Chris was deeply touched by the experience, too.

LIQUOR LAWS IN Utah were, and are, odd. I used to go into a beer bar in Logan, where until recently they were only allowed to serve weak, 3.2 beer, that had a memorable sign Chris and I got a kick out of: "No women served. You have to bring your own." We could find humor in the most unlikely places. For years we would laugh about an adult magazine cover headline we saw at a convenience store on that trip: "Best Bendover Action in Print," featuring the posterior of a comely young woman. We were easily amused.

The weather as Chris and I left the Cache Valley and headed back to Rock Springs was idyllic. The day was sunny, warm and golden, and the evening was well below freezing, but clear. I had just the one day to relax with Chris and Sue at their comfortable home before I headed north to do a concert at Central Wyoming Community College in Riverton, Wyoming, close to the majestic Wind River Mountains.

That concert was scheduled for November 1. The weather was still pleasant that day, but the forecast for the upcoming miles back east didn't look promising. I needed to be back in Nebraska for one of those well-paying Nebraska Arts Council concerts by the 3rd, specifically at the high school in Ogallala on I-80, where the Platte River divides, about 330 miles west of Omaha.

I woke up early in Riverton after the concert, and it was apparent that the weather had radically changed. The wind was coming from the Northwest, and the sky was the color of Pittsburgh steel and getting darker all the time.

From Riverton, Wyoming, there are very few reasonable routes if you are trying to drive east. The only sensible option is US Highway 20/26, which cuts across the Great Basin of Wyoming through towns like Powder River – population 6. The sleet began falling hard, icing as it hit the pavement. Hwy 20/26 in this stretch is a two-lane road, and as it is the only route east-west in this part of the country, when you don't see another vehicle going the opposite direction for a long while, you realize you might be in trouble.

It seemed as if my tires were going flat. I tried to pull off the road to check, but the sleet had accumulated in the wheel wells and frozen, preventing me from turning the steering wheel without great effort and a terrible sound, as I coaxed my van to the shoulder of the road.

I could sure see why my tires felt like they were going flat. The heavy sleet was freezing all along the walls of the van, adding god knows how much weight to the vehicle. The ice all over the vehicle was an inch thick and quickly freezing thicker and more solid. The road was becoming a skating rink. It was time to take a deep breath and some emergency measures. I had chains, but chains are almost no help on ice.

I got out the big tire iron and carefully began knocking huge chunks of ice off the side of the van, the wheel wells, the roof and the engine compartment. I tried not to inflict any large dents on my vehicle while I smashed away at it. I was worried. There were no towns of any size I could stop at, and in any case, I really needed to get to Ogallala.

I drove those hundred or so miles to Casper at about 15-20 MPH, stopping frequently to do more surgery on that ever-accumulating ice. I managed not to slide off the side of the road, though there were some close calls. At Casper, Wyoming, you pick up Interstate 25 and head south to Cheyenne, where you hook up again with Interstate 80 into Nebraska.

I-25 south of Casper was treacherous, but at least the precipitation turned more to snow instead of that damn sleet and ice. The wind out of the west blew me right across the Wyoming border into Western Nebraska when I got to I-80, and I pulled into the Pump n' Pantry (I got the last of their six rooms – whew) just outside of Ogallala as nighttime closed in. It continued to snow inches per hour with a vengeance.

There had been times that day where I seriously wondered if I was going to make it, and I worried about running off the road and flipping over. I had encountered fierce snowstorms before on my drives across the country and had occasionally even been delayed by a day or more when the roads had gotten too bad, but never before had I faced the conditions I found myself driving into that day or felt so helpless and alone out on the highway.

It was senseless to turn around, so you just kept going and hoped St. Christopher was riding shotgun with you.

When I returned to Omaha after a few more shows, I wrote a song about that experience that would become an album title and a remembrance of that white-knuckle day. It is possible I romanticized the experience beyond my real feelings at the time!

Blue Northern

I woke up this morning, there was snow upon the ground
it's cold here in Wyoming when November comes around
I packed up my goods and gear, climbed into my van
now I'm out on Hwy 20 on the way to old Cheyenne

Chorus

Like a Blue Northern from the Wind River Mountains
I sweep across the prairies, and the miles I'm a countin'
past the highway signs and railroad lines and towns I have been
I'm a Blue Northern til' I'm in your arms again

there's snow upon the roadway, snow upon the hills
there's a hawk that flies in circles lookin' for its winter kill
now some folks don't like winter, but they're not here with me
as the big sky decorates the plains with white embroidery

Repeat chorus

There's beauty in the white Cascades and a fall New Hampshire day
but there's nothing quite as pretty as the antelope at play
beneath these granite hills and grasslands, covered from the cold
by a great white frozen blanket gleaming white as miner's gold

Repeat chorus

Listen to the sound, of the quiet on the plains
as night falls hear the old coyote sing his sad refrain
there's no one out upon this lonely highway now but me
and though this journeys almost ended, I know I'll always be

Repeat chorus

Tom May copyright 1990 Blue Vignette Music ASCAP
from the album "Blue Northern"

Blue Northern

BACK IN OMAHA, KVNO radio had used a grant to purchase a multi-channel mixing board and a two-inch, 16-track tape recording machine, and had built a studio in what had been a kitchen to house it all. They also had obtained two recording-quality microphones, AKG 414's. I didn't know it at the time, but this all was a prelude to big changes that were about to take place in my life.

I had that new song "Blue Northern" in my song bag, a bunch of others I was anxious to record, and the core of a recording band with Cliff Jones on bass and Avery Grimes on piano. Now I had access to a brand-new studio that I could use for a fraction of the money I had spent on "Open Spaces, Prairie Winds." Just three weeks after that hair-raising journey from Riverton, Wyoming, I recorded the album "Blue Northern" at the new KVNO studios.

Dave Cwirko was the engineer of the project. Dave would go on to be the primary sound and lights guy for Chip Davis at American Gramaphone. My friend Clete worked as a consultant on the album, but I pretty much produced this one myself. Other musicians would join us on the arrangements, including Debbie Greenblatt, David Seay and Michael Fitzsimmons on percussion.

The new song, "Blue Northern," was the title track, of course. It seemed appropriate with all the traveling I was doing at that time. I also recorded the song I had written for the Horse Brass Pub and some other newer tunes.

Chris Kennedy consented to let me record his "Jack London" song, and I sang Rob Quist's "In Without Knocking" – an exuberant tribute to cowboys in Montana hitting the bar after the long dusty trail.

We finished the recording in less than a week of evenings, plus a full weekend. The era of compact discs was upon us, and I was excited when I placed the order for the first 1000 copies. I had decided I would not even try to peddle this album to a label as I was doing well with selling product at my concerts.

Essentially, the way a standard record contract works, you receive a recording budget from the label. It is only an advance, however, and has to be paid back out of sales. Whatever promotional costs are incurred to promote your product also must be paid back, before you receive any royalties. Royalties are negotiated when you sign the contract, but most times in the folk music world they were a buck or so a unit after all costs had been recovered.

The principal advantage to being with a record label was they would send your album out to hundreds of radio stations throughout the U.S. If it was on a respected folk imprint like Philo or Rounder Records, its chance of actually being listened to and played were much better than if you did the legwork yourself. Also, when you booked concerts and festivals, being on a established record label gave you a certain folkie seal of approval.

The big disadvantage was you had to buy back your own records from the label to resell at your shows. At a usual cost of $6 to $8 a copy, lots of musicians, including myself, got into deep debt to their record companies. You were doing all the work – writing the songs, booking the gigs, driving all the miles – yet you still didn't really own the fruits of your labor. It was a deal with the devil you had to weigh carefully.

So, even though at that point I felt I could get a record deal, I decided I would release "Blue Northern" on my own imprint, Blue Vignette. It wound up to be was a good decision, as I would eventually sell a few thousand of the CDs. The profits from the first tour alone, after the album was released, provided me with the funds to buy what is still my most cherished guitar – a 1990 Martin D-41. She still looks and sounds fantastic more than 25 years later.

The photography for the CD "Blue Northern" was done by a high school friend, Tom Gehringer. I was a lonely, isolated kid in high school, and given my family background I really appreciated the kindness of guys like Tom and Dave Laferla, who both had remained staunch friends and allies – despite the fact Dave was a rock-ribbed Republican. When I got together with my school friends, I was always the oddest, most liberal among them, back in deep red state Nebraska.

Tom Gehringer had taken my earliest promotional photos when I was just a kid in a gray suit, longish hair, improbable ambitions, with a big twelve string guitar. He also took many later photographs that I used on "Vignette," "Open Spaces, Prairie Winds," and "River and the Road." He only ever let me pay for his materials, declining money for his time and skills, knowing that I was financially operating close to the bone. He was talented, kind, and most of all, valued as a dear friend. He died way too young in 1999. Thanks for your work and companionship, Tom.

TOM MAY PROMO, 1980'S (TOM GEHRINGER)

IT'S ALL FOR THE BEST: RIVER CITY FOLK ON NPR

NOT LONG AFTER 1991 GOT UNDERWAY, I WAS summoned to Howard Lowe's office. Howard was general manager of KVNO Radio and University Television. The board had decided that they were not going to continue carrying National Public Radio news and entertainment programs. Instead, they would produce more of their own broadcasts.

Most public radio stations in the country receive funding from the Corporation for Public Broadcasting, depending on the size of their listening audience and population area. Some of this

RIVER CITY FOLK LOGO (SCOTT DOCHERTY)

money comes in the form of what was called then a National Program Production and Acquisition Grant (NPPAG). Typically, this money would wind up going directly to NPR or other syndication services to pay for such programs as All Things Considered or The Prairie Home Companion.

Howard had been impressed with my initiative in getting River City Folk on the new Nebraska Public Radio Network and had a proposal for me. How would I like to produce a program that would be offered to stations nationally, using some of that NPPAG money?

I was stunned, and it must have taken me all of 10 seconds to accept his offer. Jim Payne, who I had been working with at KVNO since I had started River City Folk five years earlier, had an idea for the format. Why not record a different folk musician performing live every week, then have him or her choose recordings that have influenced them? I would conduct an interview with the artist to stitch those parts of the broadcast together. I also suggested that I could play a song with the featured artist toward the end of the program, and Jim and Howard agreed that was a worthy idea and could be a viable format.

Thus was developed the basic structure of the national version of River City Folk, a framework that has remained unchanged now for almost 30 years. This was going to present new challenges to me, as I still needed to get done all my work while I was in Omaha between performing tours.

Parking at the university was always a royal pain. Many of the days I was working there I would get to the Engineering Building before 6 AM and work through the afternoon so I could get a decent parking spot. I always had to haul in a large box of record albums from my collection for the statewide show, and all that damn vinyl was heavy, as I usually recorded three or four shows at a sitting. (I must have been already getting older to remember this so clearly. My pal, Professor Dan Murphy, used to say, "students obsess about sex, faculty worries about parking.")

"I WOULDN'T COUNT ON IT" — CONFESSIONS OF AN UNLIKELY FOLKSINGER

Each week I had to complete two programs – the all-recoding version for the local and statewide audiences plus the nationally syndicated broadcast. These needed to be "in the can," whether I was going to be in town or going to be gone on tour for a month or longer.

Initially, we began the national show by recording programs with folksingers who lived in the area, people like Dr. John Walker from Lincoln and Curly Ennis from Omaha. Through connections I had made on the road, we soon were doing broadcasts that featured New Hampshire's Bill Staines, Colorado songsmith and fine picker Chuck Pyle, and American Gramaphone wunderkind guitarist Doug Smith. Each guest on our program received a small honorarium and a motel room, all of which came out of the NPPAG money.

We also were the very first to feature Iris Dement from Arkansas on the airwaves. She had just signed a contract with Rounder Records and would go on to become very successful. She was one of David Letterman's favorites on his popular television show.

The first time she came into the studio, Iris was so shy and unsure of herself I'm sure she would have burst out crying if I had been the least bit brusque or unsupportive. She was a sweetheart, though, and had that unique hill country twang in her voice – and the ring of truth in her songs. For a time, she lived in Kansas City and would always come out to hear me play when I performed in that area, which I greatly appreciated. When Iris appeared the first time on The Prairie Home Companion, Garrison Keillor said they were absolutely swamped with mail inquiring about her and her songs.

We also were fortunate to have as a guest, in her very last radio performance, the country music legend Patsy Montana. Patsy had a hit in the 50's with her song, " I Want to be a Cowboy's Sweetheart." When she did River City Folk, she was not in good health and had pretty much lost her voice. But it was still fascinating to hear stories of those days when she, Gene Autrey and The Sons of the Pioneers had ruled the airways.

The recording and assembling of the program in those days was quite a laborious process. We would put down the performances and interview direct to quarter-inch tape. Then we would record the album cuts the artists had selected as influences, again to quarter-inch tape. Each influence then was razor-bladed into a shorter piece of tape, spliced into the program next to the interview segment that referred to it, then bookended by one of the artist's live performances. The show's intro and close were also spliced into the production.

At that stage, we knew what we were dealing with as far as total time. The finished length of the syndicated version of River City Folk needed to be between 57 and 59 minutes. We went back in and edited the dialogue to get to those specifications. With a razor blade to tape, we would edit out language stumbles by the guest and myself, as well as long-winded or irrelevant segments to get to that goal. We kept little pieces of tape with breaths on them to be able to splice in and make some of the cuts sound more natural.

The whole process was incredibly time intensive, as you might imagine. Recording one radio program and the influences took between 90 minutes and two hours. Editing the program and getting it ready for final broadcast took between three and six hours.

Thinking back on that past production technique, this is one time I am not nostalgic for analogue days gone by. Digital recording and editing has been an unmitigated blessing in this instance.

I wrote and performed an instrumental to be used as the show's open and close. I titled it "Cliff's Whiskers," as it was composed during a week my erstwhile bass player, Cliff Jones, had cut off his trademark beard (he was soon to grow it back). It was a sprightly little tune that has been used ever since – on radio first and eventually on television. It was difficult to play on the guitar (I don't know why I wrote tunes that were so damn hard to play), but I managed to get through the recording of it. Avery Grimes and Cliff joined me on the effort.

"I WOULDN'T COUNT ON IT" — CONFESSIONS OF AN UNLIKELY FOLKSINGER

We worked diligently to stockpile programs before we went up on the NPR satellite on April 5, 1991. Jim Payne worked with me as program co-producer and as its primary engineer and editor. It would have been impossible to get the show off the ground without his help and dedication.

In addition to paying me more for my work on the broadcast, the NPPAG funds were also used to hire a radio publicist who contacted stations throughout the country and made them aware of this new public radio offering.

Within a couple of months, more than 100 stations across the U.S. were carrying River City Folk. Some of the earliest affiliates were WDCB in the Chicago suburbs; KEMC and its network, headquartered in Billings, Montana; and WSKG and its network of stations in Northern New York state. They still carry the program, all these years later. The Nebraska Public Radio Network would continue to carry both hours of the production – the one-hour show playing recorded music produced for local outlets, and the second hour, nationally syndicated version.

The first national broadcast of River City Folk beamed to affiliate stations from the NPR satellite featured the country blues singer, Dr. John Walker. Within the first two months, we had also profiled Jack Gladstone, a Blackfoot tribe Native American singer/songwriter; Rosalie Sorrels, the legendary "traveling lady" from Idaho; and the fabulous guitarist Doug Smith from Portland, still a dear friend and musical accomplice, who had just released an album on American Gramaphone records.

Word was getting out, and we had interest from folk artists throughout the U.S. and beyond, both famous and infamous.

It took me time to settle into this new role of being an interviewer as well as a folksinger. I read a few books by people who I considered to be masters of their craft in that area, folks like Charles Kuralt and Dan Rather, and those sources gave me some insight into communication techniques.

It was sometimes difficult to keep your guest focused,

particularly in the interview segments, which we tried to keep in the two to three-minute range. Some artists you had to draw out, and they had very little to say outside of their music. It was hard to get others to stay on a topic, such as talking about the recording influential to them that they had chosen to play. Still others were almost impossible to shut up and to convince we had a finite amount of time. The latter were nightmares when we got to the editing process, as we would wind up having so much cutting and tape splicing to do.

After a while I began to be more comfortable, but it remained – and remains – a challenge. Conducting a good on-air interview is just like performing a concert: To be entertaining, it should be paced well with some humor and spontaneity. Initially I would write out the questions I would ask after reading the guest's biography and promotional materials. I later found that after the opening question it was more effective to focus on the direction the conversation was going, adding in details to provide background as we went along. Having those recorded influences in the program also gave me kind of a roadmap to work from.

The guest would generally perform five to six songs live, and in addition the radio listeners would hear the four "influence" songs that week's artist had chosen. Sometimes we would feature a cut from the guest's latest album too, especially if it was quite different from their live studio sound.

On the second to last piece on the program I would join my guest on a song. I encouraged them to choose a commonly known folk or folk-pop song, and I would invite the radio listening audience around the country to pick and sing along. I would name the key we were doing the song in, invite everyone to pick up their guitars, banjos, or autoharps, etc. and help us out. I regularly got mail from people around the country saying how much they enjoyed that segment and that they did indeed join us.

Singing harmony has never come naturally to me, but I always tried to add a contrasting vocal and guitar line to the song my guest chose. Listening back to some of those old duo recordings from the broadcast, I was really surprised at how good many of them were. In 2014, I released an album called "River City Folk Duets with Tom May" on my own label, featuring duo performances almost completely from the early days of the national broadcast in the 1990's.

It has always been odd, then and now, producing and hosting a program like River City Folk. I have recorded the show in Omaha, Portland, and at remote locations like Kerrville, Texas or Haines, Alaska. At one time in the 90's an Arbitron survey showed the actual listeners to the broadcast each week to be well over a million people – but I had no real sense of that.

The show was taped weeks, often months in advance, and then the process would begin to get it on the satellite. I rarely got to hear the program unless I was home or by chance picked it up on a radio affiliate when I was touring. Every station that carries a syndicated show like River City Folk chooses its own time slot to air the show, so the time and day of the week that the broadcast would air greatly varied. Because of that, you really didn't get a sense that anyone was listening. Even when I responded to all the mail we would get, I felt very detached from actually having people tune in. It was a weird sensation.

Having the program reach a wider national audience did make me more saleable to venues around the country, and I slowly began to perform in many towns and cities I had not been to before and draw larger crowds at places where I had performed many times.

I was by no means a "star" however, nor would I ever become one. It was just a little easier to make ends meet. It was also gratifying to play my songs for more folks and have a chance to go to regions and towns I hadn't visited before.

The greatest benefit to me of River City Folk was that it was a splendid learning experience. I had the opportunity to meet and hear songs by the most committed and talented people in my genre of music. Talking to them about their work and the recordings they selected, I was further educated in the tradition and lore of this grassroots form of expression. No amount of reading or books could have passed along the knowledge and stories those folks imparted to me. I am certain it kicked my own songwriting up a notch, as I listened live to the best of the best from just a few feet away, in that little studio.

In addition to this rich trove of advantages, many of the artists became good friends. We would network about gigs, travel routes, decent restaurants on the road and promoters to avoid. When I began to produce festivals, I would use the artists I knew well and respected from the radio program.

I have been congratulated often for keeping River City Folk going all these years. But whatever I gave of myself to the broadcast, it has returned to me many times over – and I could have never kept it going all this time without the dedicated, talented support of so many others.

SHORTLY AFTER THE national debut edition of River City Folk kicked off I would have a chance to spend yet another week in the new KVNO studio, recording music. Chris Kennedy had been contemplating making an album of his own for years. I convinced him that our new studio just the spot to do it – and that I would be glad to help by producing his songs.

Within the first month that the KVNO studio was completed, I had produced an album for Chicago singer/guitarist Marty Pfeiffer. I found I really enjoyed coming up with arrangements for the songs and ideas for the musical lines that the accompanying instruments would play. It was then an interesting challenge to mix the tracks together to create the finished sound. I had also been the primary producer on my own recent CD, "Blue Northern," with help from Clete Baker.

So, I was happy to facilitate Chris's project and attempt to put the very best light on his excellent compositions. Avery and Cliff agreed to help out, too. Chris's old friend from the Chicago Old Town School of Folk Music, Mike Miles, added his expressive clawhammer-style banjo parts to the mix. I played some lead guitar, and a few other musicians chipped in. Dave Cwirko again engineered the undertaking.

The album was titled after a song Chris had written for friends of his who were living outside the small town of Farson, Wyoming, 40 miles north of Rock Springs. It was also a song for all the folks who reside in the small communities of the West, living life as people hurry by them.

Chris and I have worked on three more albums together since that first effort and played many songs together on stage, but the title song of his first recording remains one of my favorites.

Away from it All

It's a town to pass through, a blinking light
a windy place slowly dying
quiet like a memory, even on a Saturday night
mostly old folks who stopped trying

Chorus:
That's what the strangers see as they pass on by
at 55 miles per hour, in the dusty blink of an eye
but what they don't see, as they head for the interstate
is you and me falling in love away from it all

No fancy boutiques, no celebrities
just a general store with plenty of time for bidin'
and a few old shacks from the turn of the century
an old motel out where the two lanes widen

> Repeat Chorus
>
> staring into my coffee at the Oregon Trail Cafe
> plotting routes to Denver on the way to Santa Fe
> You stumbled upon me, and said "feel free to stay"
> and I fell free into a world I thought had slipped away
>
> Now we made ends meet, for just about a year
> making time for silence and some thinkin'
> unsure of the road, but you know we gotta hear, the sound of each
>   other smiling as the sun goes sinking
>
> Repeat Chorus

> *copyright 1991 Chris Kennedy-used by permission
> from the album "Away from it All"
> re-recorded on "Before the Time Slips Away"/Chris
> Kennedy-Tom May*

"Away from it all" contained more songs Chris had written about spacious, windy Wyoming. After the album was released, the Wyoming Arts Council honored him with a monetary award for his work chronicling people's lives and the geography of that wide-open, windy, beautiful state – still the least populated of the United States.

The sum of money was enough for him to purchase a gorgeous new Gibson J-200 guitar made in Bozeman, Montana. I was proud to have been a small part of that accomplishment and had thoroughly enjoyed working with him through the production process.

YOU HAVE READ me talking about Avery Grimes and Cliff Jones who were playing with me more frequently and becoming integral to the sound I would create on stage in larger venues.

They also added color and depth to many of the music projects and performances I would do in the nineties.

Cliff Jones was originally from Huron, South Dakota, and had a music degree from Augustana College. He played upright bass with the Omaha Symphony Orchestra and also worked as a cameraman at the NBC affiliate in Omaha. He had a cynical sense of humor and was always generous with his time and talent, even when I wasn't able to pay him much – or anything! Cliff loved to "play his fiddle," and he would do it whenever he could, in whatever kind of situation, classical music or otherwise.

I mentioned I met Avery through my pal Mark Moebeck when we recorded "Coming Home" in St. Louis. Avery worked in the railroad business as an executive with Union Pacific Railroad and would move from there to Portland, Oregon; Kansas City, Missouri; and eventually back to Omaha, headquarters of Union Pacific. (My dad caustically used to call it "Union Pathetic.") Like Cliff, Avery loved to play music, and he dragged his keyboard to dozens of concerts and gig, or he would rent one when we were far away from home. He and I would become close friends, and we shared a lot of laughs and heartaches through our respective misadventures through the years.

We all liked to partake of beer and wine and enjoyed playing the songs. They would travel with me to some early Winterfolk concerts in Oregon and performed with me at a variety of clubs and other shows when they were able. Having folks join me on my tunes was a new experience for me, and I enjoyed not only the musical embellishment, but also the camaraderie. It's hard to overstate how solitary much of my life was. I traveled alone, except when Michaela and Dylan would join me in the summertime, I worked alone on stage, composed the music alone, etc. I never much minded any of that, but found I did enjoy the company of Avery and Cliff immensely.

It's All for the Best: River City Folk on NPR

IN JULY THAT summertime I landed two days of concerts down on the Kansas-Nebraska border, in the town of Brownsville. That's where the abolitionist John Brown had lived before his depredations in "bleeding" Kansas, before the Civil War.

The financier of the series was a very wealthy Coloradan who had an abiding interest in the arts. He had built a church-like structure for the shows in that historic community and had been bringing in nationally known classical, jazz and folk acts. I felt honored to be included in the lineup that year.

Michaela traveled down there with me, and I was pleased she had a rare chance to feel special and valued at one of my gigs, as they furnished us with accommodations at a very elegant Victorian Bed and Breakfast. With her teaching schedule and motherly responsibilities, she most often was not able to come to the very best engagements such as this one. They were all far from Omaha and mostly took place during the school year. I did two shows each of the weekend days in Brownsville, and the presentations were sold out.

Those concerts were unusually lucrative, and on the Saturday night the organizer/sponsor of the show hosted a gourmet catered dinner for us served in the cupola of the arts building. It was a thoughtful, lovely touch and one of those memorable weekends that I hope Michaela recalls fondly, too.

Cliff Jones would join my little family on our Grand Lake, Colorado, sojourn that year, and he fell in love with the lodge and the folks who worked there. For him, it was an ideal, all expenses paid vacation. I couldn't pay him for the gigs, as my amount of recompense there just wouldn't allow it. However, they gave him his own little cabin and all of his meals free in the employee dining room for playing bass with me during the evenings. It was a chance to get out of stifling, hot, humid Omaha during the depths of summer to a cool mountain retreat with some of the best views in the Rocky Mountains. The lodge also had a heated pool, which he availed himself of often.

Reed James, who now managed the lodge, was very generous in allowing anyone who worked with me to have an employee cabin and meals. Avery Grimes would also take advantage of the offer many times in the summers to come. Cliff just adored the Grand Lake Lodge, and I was happy that he made getting there each year such a priority. It was one of the highlights of his calendar. Since he did so much for me for little or no pay, I was especially delighted to be able to offer him this perk, and he wholeheartedly took advantage of it.

WHEN I LEFT home for my tour that autumn, my first stop was at a festival in Gordon, Nebraska, way up in the northwest corner of the state. My parents had lived in Gordon for a short time when they were a young couple, and I had always appreciated the topography of that part of Nebraska. which consisted of mostly sandstone buttes and wide open spaces.

Gordon was also the epicenter of a lot of tension between the white ranching community and the original Native American inhabitants of that country. Just a few miles to the north was the South Dakota border, and beyond that was the Pine Ridge Sioux Indian reservation, often cited as one of the poorest and most forgotten areas in the United States.

There is a memorial on the reservation to the Wounded Knee massacre which took place in 1890, an event that marked the end of the Indian wars of the 19th century. The massacre was a horrible milestone. Mostly old folks and women and children were shot down in the snow in an unprovoked attack by the 7th U.S. Calvary, some say in retaliation for the headstrong, arrogant George S. Custer's calamitous defeat at the Little Bighorn in 1876. Those vengeful troops rode the train from my hometown of

Omaha and marched north through Gordon before perpetrating the slaughter.

The festival was well attended, but there was still palpable tension between the Anglo residents and their Native American brethren. I could feel it. Twenty years earlier there had been a confrontation between the FBI and Sioux activists, and two agents were killed, as well as many Native American residents of the reservation. There had been an occupation of some buildings in Gordon, and a few folks were willing to talk to me about those days. Wounds in that town were ancient, yet they were still so raw.

An excellent book about the atmosphere in that community and area is "The Death of Raymond Yellow Thunder," by Stew Magnuson. Through interviews and newspaper accounts, he gives a fair-minded picture of the complicated web of racism and injustice that has infected those lands for generations. My own parents, when I was growing up, would make disparaging remarks about "drunken and shiftless Indians." They unfortunately reflected the majority view of whites in that region.

Between my shows at the festival, I drove up to the Pine Ridge reservation and had a look around. The soul-killing poverty that began when the people here were stripped of their traditional living and language was only too evident. I saw a weathered memorial at the Wounded Knee site, but it was obvious visitors weren't courted, or even particularly welcome.

Looking as Anglo as I do, I was not able to strike up any conversations on my journey that day, but I was able to see a lot. Anyone who says they have answers to such desperation on our poorest Indian reservations is deceiving themselves, but I was greatly saddened to witness such ongoing, terrible conditions in our nation.

Back in Gordon, the ranchers were more communicative in their complaints. I wrote a song inspired by a story one of them told me, called "Silence in the Wind." It is a tale of a fellow who loses the water on his home place, where his family has lived for decades.

"I WOULDN'T COUNT ON IT" — CONFESSIONS OF AN UNLIKELY FOLKSINGER

As surface water dries up and the Ogallala aquifer is consumed, the high plains are once again becoming a very lonely location.

Oil exploration and drilling may keep some areas going for awhile, but without water, the "Great American Desert," as early 19 century cartographers called it, could in the not-so-distant future revert to the empty region it was before railroads and white settlement. But missing from that time would be the millions of bison and the magnificent horse culture of the Sioux, Crow, Peigan, Blackfoot and other plains Native American tribes that we managed to rub out so effectively and unconscionably in less than a hundred years.

That festival was another occasion where I was fortunate to deeply experience a place, its people and history. Traveling for this profession was very different than the business travel most executives refer to, where they only see the inside of airports, conference rooms, and the familiar floor plan of a cookie-cutter hotel.

After heading northwest from the Willow Tree Festival, I would share a concert with Native American songwriter Jack Gladstone in Kalispell, Montana, at a show the United Way organization there presented. I had originally heard Jack's music when my friend, Jana Fought, owner of the Silver Dollar Saloon in Butte, had played for me the first cassette he recorded. I loved his songs about wolves, history and his Blackfoot heritage. Our paths eventually crossed, and we became friends, and I featured him on the national radio broadcast and on later productions I was in charge of as well.

Jack Gladstone was one of the tallest Native Americans I have ever met. He was muscular and an imposing presence at about 6 feet 6 inches tall. He is also the only folksinger I have ever known who played on a major college football team. He was a linebacker on the National Championship University of Washington football squad in 1988. Not many folksingers were football players – or even like football! (I am in the distinct tiny minority of singer/songwriters who have that particular character flaw.)

Jack still performs, and you can find him these days at presentations in Yellowstone Park and other venues in his beloved state of Montana. His father, Wally, traveled with him as his road manager for years and was one of the nicest, most interesting guys I have ever run across. Wally was full-blooded Blackfoot and had distinct memories and riveting tales of life on the reservation from when he was a young boy.

The Kalispell concert was a success, and it led to a prosperous run of gigs that autumn, including the first radio station-sponsored concert that was promoted and paid for by an affiliate carrying River City Folk. KEMC in Billings, Montana, had numerous translators throughout the state, and agreed to have me do a live show that would be broadcast across their network.

It took place in Cecil Hall at Eastern Montana University, and I had the opportunity to meet folks who were now listening to the program each week. Marv Granger was the general manager at KEMC in those days. He was a larger-than-life character who had given Garrison Keillor (of the enormously popular Prairie Home Companion radio broadcast) his first job in radio. Marv had a wife 30 years younger than himself and an infectious joie de vivre. We got along famously, and I would return to Billings to perform for him many times.

Just before I returned to Omaha and a lot of work recording the next batch of radio broadcasts, I did a Nebraska Arts Council-sponsored concert in the town my where my parents had met and grown up – Scottsbluff, Nebraska. Scottsbluff is way out west close to the Wyoming border and is a commercial hub of the region.

Unfortunately, the concert was scheduled at the Western Nebraska Arts Center, located in the old Carnegie library there, on a Saturday, at exactly the same time as the University of Nebraska's biggest football game of the season that year against arch-rival Colorado.

College football in Nebraska is the state religion. Almost nothing moves throughout that area when a game is taking place, and to be scheduled for a gig at the same time as the most important contest of the year is the kiss of death for getting folks out for the engagement. However, it was a Nebraska Arts Council-sponsored show, so I would be paid the same no matter how many folks attended.

I have seldom been mistaken when I have anticipated the worst for a particular gig or concert, but I sure was wrong that day. The hall was absolutely full, and people stayed all the way through the performance. I don't know if it was from the effect of the radio program throughout the state or if all the folks in town that disliked the over-emphasis on football came to my show (I wouldn't have thought there were that many). But I was pleasantly shocked and surprised at my reception on that beautiful, Indian summer afternoon. It was a memorable way to end the autumn tour, still in the springtime of my life.

I would finish out 1991 with concerts at Peru State College, Kansas City, Missouri, and in Red Cloud, Nebraska, hometown of the author Willa Cather, in between gigs at local Omaha watering holes. It had been the most promising year of my musical career thus far.

♪ ♪ ♪ ♪ ♪

EARLY IN THE new year I received a call from The Western Heritage Museum in Omaha, asking me to help put a folk festival together for later that summer. This was another venture I knew little about, but I figured, how hard can it be? We came up with the name, Trackside Folk Festival, since it was to be located at that museum that had been the old Burlington Northern passenger terminal.

The dates were set for early August 1992. I booked the well-known singer/songwriter Tom Paxton as the headliner, and myself and a number of other local and regional acts would fill out the rest of the bill.

So, I was cranking out radio shows for local and national broadcasting, producing my own and others' albums, writing and performing songs, booking gigs and tours, and now directing a new folk festival. I wasn't getting rich, but life certainly wasn't dull.

In Omaha, aside from Cliff, Avery and Clete, probably my closest friend was a university professor by the name of Dan Murphy. Dan taught psychology and statistics at Creighton University and was notorious for a course he taught on human sexuality at that Jesuit institution. Over the years, the powers that be had tried to get him to tone it down, but he had tenure, and there wasn't much they could do.

He was introduced to me at a concert by a mutual friend, Ruth Beyerhelm, a student of his – and who he eventually would go on to marry. Dan had an irrepressible smile and laugh, an irreverent nature, and an ever-present twinkle in his eye. I think he was drawn to me as I was so different from other folks in his social circle. I was 30 years his junior, but sometimes I felt that he was younger than me!

He loved a drink, Nebraska football, and poetry and music. Dan was thoughtful, witty and always willing to question the standard mores of polite society. Michaela, Dylan and everyone else I was close to grew to know and love him. He made a point of attending as many of my shows as he could and coming to the house concerts that we presented. One of the pleasures of returning to Omaha was to again share a glass of red wine with him. He passed away far too young in 1999 from a brain tumor. My life was richer by his presence in it. I think of him often, and just recalling his laugh and gentle teasing makes me smile.

"I WOULDN'T COUNT ON IT" — CONFESSIONS OF AN UNLIKELY FOLKSINGER

WHEN I RETURNED to the Pacific Northwest for Winterfolk in 1992, I would do a full week at Kells in Portland. Cliff and Avery would join me for those gigs, and we rented a piano and upright bass for them to use while they were in the area. After playing the Friday night at Kell's, where we performed until 1:30 AM, we got up at 6 AM on the Saturday, and a friend drove us to Seattle to appear on the Sandy Bradley Potluck show. It was also syndicated on NPR, live across the U.S. from Seattle's Museum of Science and Industry.

It was a fun experience, but as soon as we finished our set we were back in the car, driving back to Portland for the Saturday night gig at Kells. Winterfolk started at the Horse Brass Pub the next day at 1 PM, and as director I needed to be there way earlier than that. No sleep for the wicked, but back in those days I prided myself on not needing much rest. However, after the party that night when Winterfolk wrapped up at 10 PM, even I felt a little weary. Happy, but weary – and also probably a little tipsy.

March was also full of dates and travel. Gerard McAleese at Kells again paid my roundtrip airfare and my fee to perform at his Irish St. Patrick's Day festival, and he also agreed to bring Mark Moebeck out from St. Louis to join me again for the actual dates of the festival. I did a marathon stint, performing 10 nights – and many days – in a row. Mark joined me during the actual festival days and evenings, but the subsequent nights I was solo.

It was a good chunk of change for me, and I used some of the money I made during that time to purchase a vintage 1965 Gibson B-45 12-string guitar at a Portland shop. It was similar to the guitar pictured on Gordon Lightfoot's "Sundown" album. I always had thought that guitar of his was a handsome instrument. Like his, the one I purchased had an attractive sunburst finish on the top. Unlike his, mine had a trapeze tailpiece to provide the guitar with more stability. Many of the pin-bridge models, such as the one he had, encountered the grievous problem of having the tops peel off from the high-tension of the 12-string design. I still have that Gibson guitar and play it frequently.

When I returned to Omaha from that demanding schedule, I was back in the van a week later, heading to both North and South Dakota, where I would play a concert for each of the public radio networks in those states.

The fine North Dakota songwriter, Chuck Suchy, a working farmer from just outside Bismarck, North Dakota, would open the show for me there. In South Dakota I had guests join me for my concert, which was broadcast across the state from Sioux Falls College. Other public radio-sponsored concerts I would do that springtime included shows for WDCB in Glen Ellyn, Illinois, just outside of Chicago, and WXPR in Rhinelander, Wisconsin. I still remember the superb raspberry muffins at the B and B in Rhinelander.

WHEN HIS LESSON'S LEARNED

AFTER I RETURNED FROM AN EAST COAST SWING of dates in 1992, KVNO asked me to attend the Public Radio Convention in Seattle. I was joined by my co-producer, Jim Payne, and general manager Howard Lowe.

We had a booth there to promote River City Folk, and it was fascinating to meet and chat with people I had listened to for years, such as the Car Talk brothers. We also had a lot of interest in our broadcast and signed up a number of new affiliates that wanted to carry it.

It was an appreciated perk to get flown out the Northwest and learn more about the way Public Radio actually works. Right about that time the current format of 90 percent news and information and 5 to 10 percent everything else was being developed by consultant Peter Dombrowski as the most efficient way of extracting pledges from members. Music was being discouraged as a format choice.

Finding this out made me somewhat cynical about the purity of public broadcasting being an entity whose primary goal is to reach underserved populations and give alternative arts a voice. KVNO was fortunately a college licensee, however, which gave them much more freedom and latitude in programming decisions.

When His Lesson's Learned

THAT SUMMER CLICKED along with the by now usual parade of gigs: The Summer Arts Festival in Omaha; a couple of weeks in Grand Lake Colorado; a weekend in Iowa City at the Mill, etc. I also made a trip to a festival in Rapid City, South Dakota, way out west, close to the Black Hills, and performed a delightful arts council concert in the park in Kearny, Nebraska.

For the River City Folk national broadcast that summer I recorded Ian Tyson from Canada; Cozy Sheridan and Bill Staines, both from New Hampshire; and Jim Salestrom from Breckenridge, Colorado. Jim was a nice guy, another kid from Nebraska who did good – going on to play with both John Denver and Dolly Parton along with many other artists. I really had to keep pushing when I was home to be ahead on the broadcast before I went out of town for work, now that I had the obligations of both the national and statewide hours.

All of which reminds me that almost all of this work was self directed and organized. As the old saying goes, you had freedom and just enough rope to hang yourself. It was so important to look ahead and always figure out well in advance what needed to be done, and by when.

No one was going to scold you or dock your pay if you blew a deadline, soundcheck, gig, or the countless paperwork details for all the different ventures that needed to be finished and sent – all via U.S. Mail, back then. You would simply lose what you had worked so hard to build.

At the bottom of it all, it was a one-man operation as far as responsibility goes, though I was certainly blessed with lots of indispensable help through the years. That's particularly true with River City Folk. Whenever I got to the point that I just didn't see how it could go on, someone would emerge from the wings with the solution, resolve, or necessary resources to help keep it going.

WITH TOM PAXTON TRACKSIDE FOLK FESTIVAL, OMAHA, NE 1992

"I WOULDN'T COUNT ON IT" — CONFESSIONS OF AN UNLIKELY FOLKSINGER

THE FIRST WEEKEND in August were the dates that had been selected for the Trackside Folk Festival. The festival "grounds" was a parking lot in front of the museum, and on a typically hot summer Nebraska afternoon, you wouldn't call the setting ideal. The folks at the museum footed the bill for the event and also kindly hosted a welcome reception the night before for Tom Paxton, the other musicians and me, guests and sponsors.

Though the ticket price was nominal and the Omaha World Herald newspaper gave it good coverage, attendance was what you might call light. Short of being a complete bust, neither was the first Omaha Folk Festival a resounding success. I figured after it was concluded it would be the end of that particular event.

Heading for the west in mid-September, my first stop would be the Deadwood Jam, in Deadwood, South Dakota. This was the third year of the festival located in the historic "den of sin," where Wild Bill Hickok was shot down, holding a full house of aces and eights, in a poker game in 1876.

The town became famous during those times as gold miners, gamblers and prostitutes flocked there, all in their own way after the large mineral deposits in the region first discovered by the aforementioned George Armstrong Custer, during his agreement-breaking trek through that beautiful country in 1874. The treaty of 1868 had given that land to the Sioux in perpetuity, in exchange for a promise they would not harass or raid the track-builders and immigrants on the Platte River route.

Regardless, the Black Hills were eventually outright stolen by the white man, and the lawsuit regarding that thievery is still working its way through the courts almost 150 years later. The Sioux have declined any monetary settlement, insisting instead on the rightful return of their sacred lands. In the meantime, we have defiled their holy mountains with giant carved graven images of elderly white men, some of whom were at least partially responsible for this egregious theft.

I refuse to visit those damn faces at Mt. Rushmore, and I can't even imagine what it would be like to be a Sioux tribe member and be mocked by their existence. If over the last century the Sioux tribes had only been reimbursed for a fraction of the value of the gold extracted from the Homestake Mine in Lead, South Dakota, in their beloved Black Hills, poverty would not exist on their reservations. The Homestake Mine has recovered more than two billion dollars' worth of gold.

Pardon me, I digress. I am passionate about the gross injustices done to our Native American brothers and appalled at the indifference and ignorance of most U.S. citizens about this shameful heritage of ours. There is a bit of ironic payback at the Indian casinos that relieve mostly older white folks of their money – but nowhere near enough for past and present insults or for each of the 480-some treaties that have been broken by our government.

Okay, back to the subject at hand. The Deadwood Jam was begun by Nitty Gritty Dirt band member John McCuen, who had found his own form of gold in them-thar-hills. He became the very visible voice, visage and song of the recently legalized gambling in Deadwood, South Dakota.

The previously mentioned Jim Salestrom helped me get into this musical gathering, though I was pretty well known in South Dakota at that time on account of the radio program. That year, the musical artists included The Ozark Mountain Daredevils, Dan Hicks, Jim Salestrom, Michael Johnson, myself, and a new ensemble just beginning to gain national attention, Alison Krauss and Union Station.

This was heady company, and I felt lucky to be included. The stage was in the middle of the main street, which was closed off. Orange crowd-control fences came to the edge of the sidewalks, which allowed the merchants to still serve those who had not bought festival tickets.

"I WOULDN'T COUNT ON IT" — CONFESSIONS OF AN UNLIKELY FOLKSINGER

I was on the Saturday bill. When Jim Salestrom and I did our respective sets, the weather was cool, but it was a glorious sunny day, and a nice crowd had gathered in the bleachers in front of the main stage.

After I did my set, I was looking forward to hearing Alison Krauss, who I had been reading a lot about. She and her virtuosic band Union Station, including dobro wizard, Jerry Douglas, labored through a tortuous sound check. When they actually started their set, things still weren't right.

When I had played earlier, the sound guy had been an acoustic specialist who did a terrific job. Since the Ozark Mountain Daredevils were following Allison's performance, she was saddled with that band's PA technician, and it was obvious that guy didn't know anything about doing sound for an acoustic-bluegrass based ensemble.

When they began their show, the sound was terribly muffled, and you couldn't even hear Alison's bell-like, unforgettable voice. Those incredible soloists/sidemen in her band were lost in the mix, and the balance was miserable to begin with. I felt so badly for her. We commiserated together about atrocious sound men later in the evening over some whisky, back at the festival hotel.

She also had a very small crowd to hear her, much smaller than the audience I had earlier in the afternoon, when the weather was sunny. There did turn out to be some poetic justice though. When the Ozark Mountain Daredevils came onstage after her – with their sound volume cranked up to 11 and no way to tell if it was good or not – the grey clouds turned black, the temperature dropped 30 degrees, and it began to snow. The large audience dispersed or pulled their stocking caps over their ears – or perhaps they were just trying to spare their hearing.

Earlier in the day, Dan Hicks and his trio – not really the original Hot Licks, but close enough – performed. Luckily for them, they had the same sound man I drew. When it started sleeting, I retreated to one of the numerous taverns on the street, on the other side of that orange crowd control fence. By coincidence, Dan Hicks and his son, who had traveled with him, walked into the same bar. We had a few sociable drinks and a really interesting chat, while the Ozark Mountain Daredevils rattled the windows and the wet snow fell.

The accommodations the festival provided were really nice, and that evening they put me up at the Bullock Hotel. The Bullock is right in the middle of town, is named after a famous gunfighter-sheriff, and dates back to the glory days of the 1870's. It was one of those places where you could just feel the antiquity and stories seep out of the cracks, and you wondered how many gamblers and gunfighters had slept in the same room you were now resting in.

OTHER UNUSUAL STOPS that beautiful autumn would include concerts at Idaho State University in Pocatello and the Spokane, Washington Art Museum, a show sponsored by the River City Folk affiliate KPBX. There were shows in Omak and Eatonville, Washington; Astoria, Oregon; Bozeman, Butte, and Billings, Montana; and Provo and Salt Lake City, Utah, as well as other stops along the way. Chris Kennedy would join me for the Utah dates, and we had a good time, as we always did. Chris also helped arrange shows for me in both Green River and Rock Springs, Wyoming.

There were some lucrative dates in this bunch, but lest you think I was getting "too big for my britches," as my dad used to say, I will recount the story of a less-than-idyllic night in Seattle.

I had the usual dates at the Horse Brass Pub and Kells in Portland. Avery and Cliff decided they would both fly out to the Northwest, play some songs with me, drink some microbrew beer and have some fun. They were both single guys with disposable income, so why not? They both loved the Horse Brass, too. On the Tuesday of that week I was scheduled to do a show at an up and coming listening joint in Seattle, the Emerald City, called the New Melody Tavern.

We drove up to Seattle together in my van and picked out a cheap motel on Highway 99 for the night. We had good luck at a Seattle concert the year before, doing a decently attended show at the prestigious Backstage club in Ballard, which had since closed, so we were optimistic.

We arrived at the New Melody, but none of my posters were displayed, and the door was locked. The owner turned up a little later and remarked he had almost forgotten we were performing that night. It seems he remembered at the last minute. (Lucky me! I had called him repeatedly the week before and left messages. I suspect this guy was imbibing on a little too much of the white powder.) Good news though! When he finally remembered we were booked, he had called another musician that he knew, who he said had a good local following, to open for us.

A few minutes later this outrageously dressed, flamboyant, drunk, blousy-looking girl comes in with her guitar and proceeds to take over the stage like she built it and owns it. She ignores me except for a couple of snide remarks about folk music, fat guys (hey, I wasn't even fat back then, and Avery and Cliff were downright svelte! Look at that picture on "Blue Northern!") and acoustic guitars.

She has a couple of more drinks, and I suspect a little tete-a-tete with the owner in the back that consisted of communing with the aforementioned white powder. (I have nothing personally against cocaine, but getting high and drunk like that before you play or before you manage your business doesn't bode well for your continued success.)

She gets her electric guitar ready to go and renders a few tuneless songs helpless with her punk-rock attitude and a voice that would effectively strip wallpaper. The audience at that juncture of the evening consisted of myself, Cliff, Avery, one of her friends and the owner. By the time her hour-long set was over and we performed, that audience was reduced by two when both she and her friend took off immediately after she was finished. I can't say I was sorry to see them go.

This was one of those gigs we were doing on spec, meaning you got a percentage of the door. So, we weren't too eager to perform for long, when it became apparent no other audience was likely to troop in. The owner looked like he was about ready to pass out, anyway. We packed up, took our non-existent paychecks, and beat a swift retreat back to Motel "0", after making a stop at the liquor store, purely for analgesic purposes.

The last week of this increasingly winter-like journey would consist of concerts sponsored by public radio stations in Kearny and North Platte Nebraska, then Dodge City and Garden City, Kansas. Michaela, bless her heart, drove out to Kearny on Tuesday, November 3, so we could be together to watch Bill Clinton defeat George Bush in the '92 presidential election – despite the fact she hated driving in bad weather and it was icy that day.

Finally, there was a concert on that Sunday for the Nebraska Arts Council in the town of Imperial, Nebraska, at the restored art-deco Imperial Theatre. It had all been interesting and fun, but I was tired and ready to head for home.

When I was back in Omaha, I had taken to patronizing a new business called La Buvette in the Old Market section of town. It had a very novel approach for conservative, beer swilling Nebraska, especially for that time. Opened by the original developers of the Old Market, Omaha's most interesting and progressive section of town since the late 1960's, La Buvette was located in a characteristic brick-and-mortar storefront in this old warehouse district. Bottles of wine were stacked up against all available walls.

They were primarily French wines – the owners were both originally from France – but there were selections from all over

Europe as well as some esteemed California varietals. The idea was you either purchased wine to go or you could select a bottle, pay a small corkage fee, and drink it right there in that charming, bohemian atmosphere. There was a jumble of mismatched old tables and chairs, and a deli counter with a small kitchen attached where they would prepare bread and cheese plates, soups and other light fare. It was, and remains to this day, my favorite place in Omaha.

Back in the early 90's it was a particularly notable setup, and the good wines and unique atmosphere drew a lot of artistic types. I remember I had arranged to meet Clete Baker and perhaps someone else from the recording studio there, and we wound up being joined by a German by the name of Frankie Boucher. Frankie was the liaison and person in charge of the international dates that Chip Davis and Mannheim Steamroller did when they performed in Europe.

The wine flowed, and Frankie mentioned that Clete had played some of my music for him at the studio and that he had enjoyed it. Later in the conversation, as the company became more lubricated on the good red juice,

I must have mentioned that I would be turning 40 in a few months – in January of 1993. The subject came around to international touring, and I asked Frankie some questions about it. I had only played overseas in Ireland and Scotland to that point.

Frankie agreed I should come to the continent and perform and said, "Let me give you a present of touring dates in Germany for your birthday." He said he would arrange dates with the promoters and make a good little trip out of it for me. As always after such conversations, I took his reassurance of those plans with lots of grains of salt. In this case, however, it actually happened. Frankie kept in close touch after his return to Germany, and I made plans to travel there in the New Year.

THE RIVER AND THE ROAD: GERMANY AND RCF TV

THE HOLIDAYS CAME AND WENT, AND MICHAELA and I made plans for a birthday party on my 40th. It was probably too big of a fuss to make over a relatively unimportant event, but it seemed a good excuse for a celebration.

Michaela and Dylan did everything in their power to make it a memorable date for me. Jeff McLaughlin flew in from Boston to spend a few days, and Mark and Judy Moebeck from St. Louis drove up to be part of the festivities. By this time, we were living in a nice older home on Omaha's north side, with a big finished basement and plenty of room for guests. We hosted lots of house concerts in that basement, which we could turn into a listening hall that could seat about 50.

At parties like the birthday gathering, the basement would become a venue for all the musicians attending to share songs. I would put up a small PA system so everyone could hear the music. There was a snowstorm that weekend, but it didn't keep anyone away. It was an unforgettable bash and a memorable confluence of friends and family.

A few days later after everyone had departed, I had a meeting with Richard Gilliland, president of Metropolitan Community

College. He had attended the Trackside Folk Festival the year before and had enjoyed himself, but he felt it was underappreciated and under attended. He wondered if I might be interested in moving it to the grounds of the school he headed up.

Metropolitan Community College was located in North Omaha, just blocks from where I grew up (I used to pick up the newspapers I delivered as a boy just down the street from there). It was on the grounds of Fort Omaha, an expansive plot of lush green fields and 19 century brick Victorian homes now interspersed with classroom and administrative buildings. The site was rich in historic significance. It still had General George Crook's home/headquarters, which had been turned into a museum. Crook had been head of the Army of the Platte, in charge of basic U.S. policy during the Indian Wars. He captured Geronimo and had led the Calvary in many conflicts with the Native Americans, though he had prided himself on being "humane" toward them.

Immediately next to the Crook House was the field where Buffalo Bill Cody rehearsed and eventually performed for the first time, his Wild West Show in 1883. The show would go on to be the most famous attraction in the world in the late 19th and early 20th century.

Talk about an ideal setting for a folk music festival! I couldn't believe the luck. We agreed in principal after he checked with the folks at the Western Heritage Museum and made sure they didn't feel he was stealing it from them. (No worries there! They had lost a good deal of money on the event and would not have been hosting it again in any case.) We would meet again after I returned from Germany and would thrash out the details at that time.

AFTER I KNEW I was going to be traveling to Germany, I had ordered a German language cassette course, despite all the people who told me, "You don't need it, everyone in Germany speaks English." I wound up being glad I hadn't paid attention to them.

The River and The Road: Germany and RCF TV

I flew out on January 18, 1993, traveling on Northwest Airlines to Frankfurt. I had arranged for a rental car, but Frankie Boucher had taken care of everything else – or so I thought. I would unexpectedly wind up being responsible for a good deal of my own expenses while I was there.

I landed in the rain and cold of a harsh German winter. The round-trip international air ticket was incredibly cheap – I think it was around $250 – and after spending two weeks there I figured out why there was so little U.S. traffic to Germany at that time of year. Typically, the sun would rise and the sky would get gray about 9 in the morning, then begin to darken and turn to night beginning at 3 PM or so. I rarely saw the sun on that journey. It made the Pacific Northwest in winter look like Tahiti. The climate was extremely damp and cold, only a little warmer than it had been back home in Nebraska.

My first concert was in Kassel, followed by gigs in Lohmar, Cologne, Essen, Munster and Aachen in Germany, as well as in Bruge and Leige, Belgium. I was traveling on my own, and I found the speeds on the Autobahn terrifying and difficult to get used to.

Thank god I had gone through that German language course. I really don't know how I would have survived on that trip without it. Yes, many folks did speak English, particularly younger people, but at least half or the country did not. I would not have been able to even follow the road sign directions without some rudimentary knowledge of German.

Most people were helpful but very reserved. The audiences were of a respectable size, but I never felt a surge of warmth or great enthusiasm from them. I played primarily in small halls of 100 to 200 seats, as well as a couple of pubs. The pubs were more fun – at least I could have a drink and meet some folks. The promoters were very businesslike, and I always got paid, but there was not much hospitality outreach from them. I did have one deliciously decadent night with a good audience in Lohmar,

"I WOULDN'T COUNT ON IT" — CONFESSIONS OF AN UNLIKELY FOLKSINGER

where Frankie was personally in charge of the gig and did all he could to make the night one to remember.

Accommodations were provided in the towns I performed in, but I had quite a few nights off where I was on my own. I quickly found that hotels in Germany are by and large expensive and usually lock their doors at 9 PM or so. At least they all seemed to include an extensive buffet at breakfast including meat, cheese, bread, eggs, pastry, etc. You could easily live the rest of the day on what you had at breakfast and just add on a couple pints of lager in the evening and call them dinner.

I spent the days finding museums to explore and took an entertaining drive following historic invasion routes and battlegrounds through the densely forested Ardennes. The towns of Spa and Bastogne were strikingly beautiful and had good museums dedicated to their communities' struggles during the World Wars.

I adopted the compact town of Aachen as my "day off" headquarters. It had been the seat of the Holy Roman Empire under King Charlemagne, and the ancient cathedral where he was crowned still stood. It also had a reasonably priced, modest hotel called the Louisburg, and I spent a number of my free nights there.

The final Sunday I was overseas I went to a mass at the cathedral in Aachen. Though I was still woefully inept at speaking the language with any fluency, after having been there for two weeks and being immersed in the culture, I had the odd sensation of understanding virtually everything the priest said during his sermon.

Aachen was right at the edge of one of the more diverse areas of Europe, where the countries of Germany, Belgium and the Netherlands all intersect. In Aachen, few would speak in anything but German or English. In Leige, Belgium, just a few miles away, the people still had an intense dislike of Germany after having been invaded by them twice in the 20th century. So, they would not speak German, but rather French and their own dialect.

Another few miles (kilometers, sorry) up the road lay Maastricht, Netherlands. The Dutch had the tradition of being the merchants of Europe, and hence historically had become fluent in all those languages, and more. I never met a person from the Netherlands who spoke fewer than three languages. All three towns lay in a triangle, none more than 15 miles away from one another. This was pretty exotic stuff for a kid from Nebraska.

I wished I would have had a guide to answer more questions for me as I toured the area, but I did the best I could on my own. I sampled local bars and restaurants while attempting to be sociable in my halting German and Midwestern US English. I drank good Belgium ale, ate German sausages (it seemed every block had a sausage shop) and even smoked a powerful joint of legal marijuana in one of Maastricht's coffeehouses – all for the sake of sociological research, of course.

One evening, after doing a concert in Essen, I was stopped by the police while following the promoter back to his house where I was to lodge for the night. The officer said he had stopped me because I had been driving with my fog lights on, which apparently was illegal. I did not even know they were on, and I'm sure I had been driving with them on for the entire time I had been in Germany. They let me go with just a warning, but I had lost the fellow I was following. I went to the pay phone (it was the pre-cell phone days) and dialed the number I had for him, but no answer.

It was after 10 PM, and I knew most all the hotels were closed for the night. I didn't want to pay for one so late in the evening in any case. My options were limited. I wound up sleeping in my car at a rest area on the side of the autobahn, covered by just my thin wool overcoat on what turned out to be the coldest night of the year in Germany: It was well below freezing.

So much for the romance of being a internationally touring, famous folk artist, as Frankie Boucher's posters for my appearances there billed me.

Still, it had been a fascinating trip, and I knew I was fortunate to have experienced it. There were no further mishaps during the tour, and I flew out of Frankfort headed for home on February

4. (That year I pushed back the Winterfolk date in Portland to March.) The very early morning return flight to the U.S. was on a Northwest Airlines 747 that only had 52 passengers aboard. With the permission of the stewardesses, I stretched out horizontally on the middle seats, seat-belted myself in, and was asleep before the plane took off.

I TIED IN the fifth annual Winterfolk benefit to my trip to Portland to play for the St. Patrick's Day Festival at Kells. Chris Kennedy took the train out from Rock Springs, Wyoming, to join me at this Winterfolk, and Avery Grimes flew out from Omaha to join us with his keyboard skills. This would be the final year the benefit would take place at the Horse Brass Pub, and the renowned singer/songwriter, social activist, and humorist Bruce "Utah" Phillips added his singular voice to the event.

After those guys went back to their respective homes, Mark Moebeck flew from St. Louis to help me out with his voice and guitar at the St. Patrick's festivities. I was so blessed throughout my career by good friends and fine musicians who were willing to share a stage with me. In between the shows, we also had some raucous times at the Horse Brass and elsewhere.

For the national broadcast of River City Folk that spring of 1993, I would have a stellar group of acoustic artists join me at the studio in Omaha to tape the program. Among them would be: Steve Gillette and Cindy Mangsen from Vermont (Steve co-wrote the widely known and played song "Darcy Farrow"); Beppe Gambetta, (an incredibly gifted flatpicker from Italy); and Alan Damron (a real American character from Texas, co-founder of the famous Kerrville, Texas Folk Festival.)

I was recording two or three of the national and statewide programs each week, trying to get far ahead in the ever-upcoming schedule. I always felt like a kid whose homework was due tomorrow, it was midnight, and I had hardly started on it.

Steve Gillette has always been a favorite of mine, and it was such a pleasure to hear him sing and play.

Since the 1960's he had been touring the country with his eloquent cross picking style and well-crafted songs. For the last 30 years or so he has been joined by his wife, Cindy Mangsen, a fine singer songwriter in her own right. The two of them have a honey-like smoothness in the presentation of their original and traditional material that is just a joy to listen to.

Steve is also a real gentleman and gladly spends time with his audience members and admirers discussing songwriting and guitar techniques. He is so gracious and friendly that Cindy often has to give him a nudge so that they can get some rest at the end of the show! I would employ them at festivals or other events I was in charge of, whenever I had the opportunity to do so.

Steve has a wonderfully informative book on the music business out, and also conducts songwriting workshops across the country, from Oregon to Connecticut.

IN EARLY MAY I was again asked by KVNO radio to attend the Public Radio Conference, which was to take place in 1993 in Washington, D. C. For years, Republicans had threatened to "behead Big Bird" – to defund the Corporation for Public Broadcasting, the funding arm of Sesame Street, All Things Considered and programs like mine. (Each American pays less than the price of a McDonald's hamburger yearly for these programs.) But in 1993, things seemed less dire, as the new administration began its work.

Newly elected president of the United States Bill Clinton wound up attending and addressing the attendees. I had the opportunity to shake his hand after his address, as did dozens of others, and it was a great thrill.

But the most important event at the convention for me came at a private meeting I had with KVNO general manager Howard Lowe. He had been hinting for some time about another development he was interested in pursuing for River City Folk, but he had been very coy about what it was. When we met, he told me he had a tentative agreement with a new television cable network out of Branson, Missouri, to carry River City Folk as a half hour, televised broadcast – if I was interested in hosting it.

Though I sometimes wondered how I would get all these projects done and keep touring, I of course said yes.

I figured I could worry about the details later, after I found out all the particulars.

Another of the highlights of that "PRC," as they called them, was a five-year celebration for the syndicated program Thistle and Shamrock, produced in Scotland and the U.S. by Fiona Ritchie. For her anniversary party, which I'm sure was calculated to boost carriage of her fine program, she had somehow convinced the globe-trotting Irish traditional music legends The Chieftains to perform a set in a large meeting room at the convention hotel that was set up as a pub. There would be free Guinness and fish and chips for everyone who attended, as well as music from Ireland's most famous ensemble.

I had met a couple of the Chieftains on my travels – at McGurk's in St. Louis, where they had a few pints after a SRO concert, and in Portland, where they popped into the Horse Brass for some good beer on a rare day off. I was looking forward to seeing them again, as I was a devotee of their intelligently arranged, spirited tunes.

I wound up being very embarrassed during the set for them. The movers and shakers at the convention talked loudly and by and large ignored The Chieftains, as if the musicians were some kind of second-rate amateurs in a tavern in Toledo. By this time in their career, The Chieftains had played most major stages in the world, from the Sydney Opera House in Australia to Carnegie

The River and The Road: Germany and RCF TV

Hall in New York, as well as sharing bills with The Rolling Stones and other pop legends.

It just goes to show you that rudeness and self-absorption cut across all income and education lines. The public broadcasting employees and executives there that afternoon were probably some of the most literate and well-informed people in the U.S, But after they grabbed their free beers and fish and chips, they gave the music roughly the same attention as the young folks at Kells back in Portland generally gave mine.

After the show, I chatted with my friends in the band, Matt Malloy and Kevin Coneff, and apologized for the insensitivity and boorishness of my colleagues. They were pretty philosophical about it, and there was lots of Guinness left – so the three of us passed the rest of the evening happily recounting stories of bad audiences, good music and pleasant libations.

The following night The Chieftains were booked for a SRO concert at New York's Lincoln Center, so I suppose they could afford to laugh about the afternoon's gig. Those boys were happy just to have a night off where they could enjoy their Guinness in peace.

The other act that I saw at that PRC who I was very taken by was an independent artist who played the harp by the name of Loreena McKinnit. Artists and record companies would book rooms and do presentations, hoping the NPR types would program more of their music, and Loreena was one of these performers. Her compositions and demeanor were ethereal and approachable, and we kept in touch for a number of years.

She would go on to become a popular cult figure in Celtic/alternative music, and rightly so. She is a very gifted and unusually expressive artist.

BACK IN OMAHA, I received a phone call from a fellow in

"I WOULDN'T COUNT ON IT" — CONFESSIONS OF AN UNLIKELY FOLKSINGER

Haines, Alaska, who had a local radio program that preceded River City Folk in KHNS's broadcast schedule. He was an enthusiastic, colorful guy by the name of Mick McCarter. He believed he could set up a concert tour for me in Southeast Alaska, sponsored by stations that carried my show. We conspired to work toward that goal for the upcoming autumn.

I had done one dismal weeklong stint at a rough bar in Juneau in the mid-eighties, at a now long-gone establishment called The Crystal, where the library and cruise ship docks are now. I had not seen the sun or even the mountains the entire time I was there, it had rained so hard. Mick assured me the autumn was different up in those parts, and I was very open and excited about seeing more of the Alaska I had read about, rather than the northland I had experienced that one winter week. (It had reminded me of Northern Ontario, in both the kind of clientele at the venue and the climate outdoors.)

However, before any of that was to transpire I would go to a new event for me, heading toward an entirely different compass setting.

THE KERRVILLE TEXAS Folk Festival by this time was already an annual established happening in the acoustic music world. It was the largest gathering of singer/songwriters in North America.

Spread over 18 days and three weekends, it had started or established the career of artists like Nanci Griffith, Tish Hinojosa, Ray Wylie Hubbard and dozens of others. Peter Yarrow, of Peter, Paul, and Mary and the writer of the classic "Puff the Magic Dragon," had established a song competition there for writers.

Alan Damron, who had recently been my featured guest on the national broadcast of River City Folk and who was a co-founder of the Kerrville festival, had been pestering me to attend for quite some time. I explained to him with all my other obligations – not the least of which was making a living – I could hardly just run away to Texas for a couple of weeks with no recompense or even a guarantee of being able to get on stage to play some of my songs.

I didn't really "get" the Kerrville Folk Festival at that point. Like a normal festival, there were headline performers who were compensated, and an enthusiastic audience from Austin, San Antonio and beyond would attend and pay a daily or weekend admission.

Unlike a normal festival, hundreds of folks came to the festival for the entire 18 days and would never even attend a stage show. They would set up a campsite – the site of the festival is known as The Happy Valley Ranch – and in the evenings the song circles would begin. Some would be very exclusive, consisting of Nashville or established songwriters who were well known. But most campfire circles were more relaxed, welcoming affairs where anyone with a guitar and a desire to share was invited in to play a song when your turn comes around.

Whatever the kind of gathering, listeners could pause and take in the songs at a campfire, then stay put or move on. It was a tremendous community building, unique atmosphere that even spawned its own slang – like "Kerrvert," a Kerrville devotee, and "Kerrvirgin," a first-time attendee. Folks of all abilities and persuasions were encouraged to share their creativity in a nurturing, non-threatening situation at those campfires.

Alan Damron really believed I needed to go there. So, he called up the director at that time, his pal Rod Kennedy, and got me a formal invitation. I would produce two River City Folk broadcasts live on the Threadgill stage there and also perform myself.

Each program would consist of three performers and me in front of an enthusiastic live audience. I chose Chuck Pyle from Colorado, Lucy Blue Trembley from Canada, and David Maloney from California for the first broadcast. Anne Hills from Pennsylvania, David Seskin from Nashville and Alan Damron were on the second show. Jim Payne flew down from Omaha to record

"I WOULDN'T COUNT ON IT" — CONFESSIONS OF AN UNLIKELY FOLKSINGER

AT KERRVILLE FOLK FESTIVAL,

the programs, and everyone, including myself, wound up being paid, thanks to Kerrville and River City Folk monies.

It was all a novel adventure. I drove down there in my van and camped with one of the groups that had staked their claim to a bit of shade days before the festival officially began. (Camp Calm, they called themselves – lovely folks, generous and great cooks.)

Kerrville was hot and humid that year, usually over 100 degrees during the daytime. Nothing much moved or happened from sunup to early evening, just lots of napping and slow movements, as the sweat poured out of you. At night I would sleep in the back of the van on the fold-out bed and throw the rear doors open wide. By time I would crawl into the bunk, it was generally 3 or 4 in the morning, when the heat had diminished to an almost tolerable sleeping temperature.

What made it all bearable and memorable was the absolute love almost everyone showed toward the music and each other. There was a devotion to the song and the principals behind it that I have never witnessed elsewhere. I suppose those were the only reasons a person would spend up to three weeks of their vacation in the tropical heat and torrential thunderstorms of south Texas, camping with legions of fire ants and retro-hippies. It was inspiring, if a little bit nuts.

Somewhere in my conversations with Alan Damron, I had mentioned I had never fired a gun. This was probably when he was talking about his boyhood down by the Mexican border and how important guns were there.

He took this to be a personal challenge to remedy the lack of that particular experience in my life, despite my protestations. At one time he had owned the ranch adjacent to the festival property, and he still had permission to use it. So, he dragged me over there with a couple of revolvers and rifles and good-naturedly browbeat me into firing at a couple of targets.

I was underwhelmed by the afternoon of shooting and have successfully avoided all contact with firearms since. I was, however, touched by his resolve to fill in that hole in my education.

The River City Folk tapings at Kerrville were a big success, and Alan had volunteered to book me a gig in Austin on my way back home, where I could stay with him the evening after the show. The concert was at Saxon's Pub in Austin and was well attended, thanks to Alan.

After the performance we adjourned to his abode, where he told me I could sleep in the room of his housemate, who was gone for a couple of weeks. The bed had a loaded pistol in a holster hanging from the bedpost, which Alan warned me not to move or touch. I asked him if he couldn't put it somewhere else, but I guess nothing irritated his housemate more than when someone moved his gun.

Yes, I really was in Texas. After a restless night's sleep, as far away from that loaded gun as I could get, I pointed the Ford van back towards Nebraska.

THROUGHOUT THAT SUMMER I would toil away' keeping (barely) ahead of the radio show schedule, performing many local shows and making the annual trek to Grand Lake, Colorado, with Michaela and Dylan. In early August I hit the road again to do a few concerts in Sioux Falls, South Dakota; Minneapolis, Minnesota; and Des Moines, Iowa.

"I WOULDN'T COUNT ON IT" — CONFESSIONS OF AN UNLIKELY FOLKSINGER

In August I would do a festival in southwest Kansas, the second time I had performed at that particular event. When I departed the festival on the Sunday morning, I stopped to fill my thermos with rough Midwestern coffee. I noticed that just above the fold of the Sunday Manhattan, Kansas, newspaper, home of Kansas State University, was a picture of a cowboy hat that looked very much like mine. I opened the paper, and there was a large, front page color photograph of me performing at that festival the previous day, playing my pennywhistle as an introduction to one of my songs – probably the song "Bessie and Me."

It was a really dynamic photo, and I was surprised and pleased to see it. You just never knew what was going to happen in this odd business. The festival had been lightly attended that year, and I am sure the fee for my concert set wasn't much. But I had again been paid richly in a totally unforeseen fashion.

The following weekend our first Festival at the Fort would take place in back in Omaha. I had help from Jim and Kathy Wood from the Omaha Folk Song Society putting the program together, and we scheduled the concerts, along with workshops and activities for kids.

Metropolitan Community College not only paid the entire tab for the performances, but their work crews erected tents over the two stages and sun shades for the audience. They also set up and took down all the chairs and did all the other necessary site maintenance, before and after the festival. The stages were set up on a beautiful open lawn, which in days gone by had been the parade ground. The lawn was bordered by stately old cottonwood and maple trees.

I can't for the life of me recall who I engaged as headliner that first year, but in years to come we would host Odetta, David Mallett, Joanne Shenandoah – a well-known Native American singer – Bill Staines, John McCutcheon and many other luminaries from the folk music world. Paid attendance for that inaugural event was more than 500, which was very respectable and more than we had hoped for, so everyone was pleased. Even the governor of Nebraska joined me on air to record some radio spots and television promotion for the festival. All parties involved were excited to make plans for the following year and to it becoming an annual event.

THE NEXT MONTH, Howard Lowe from KVNO would meet with me again about the nascent plans for the national television broadcast of River City Folk. It was all very exciting, if daunting. But right then I was more preoccupied with the final shape of my very first Alaska concert tour that Mick McCarter had put together for me, which was coming up in just a couple of weeks.

Besides producing his own record show at KHNS radio in Haines, Mick was an outgoing character who also worked on the Alaskan Marine Highway System, the state of Alaska ferries. One of those men who never knew a stranger, he had made connections and pals all throughout the southeast part of the state. He took it upon himself to contact people he knew and to cold-call folks he did not know, cobbling together a tour for a guy he had never met.

I will be forever grateful to him for that, and for those unforgettable early concerts of mine in Southeast Alaska. I would wind up going back there many times, but it was all because of Mick's work on that initial journey.

I would play in Evanston, Wyoming, and Sandpoint, Idaho, on my way out West that September, then board the plane for Alaska in Portland. Mick had booked concerts for me in Skagway, Haines, Juneau, Sitka, Petersburg, and Ketchikan – pretty much every town of any significant size in the southeast part of the state. After I flew into Juneau on the Alaska Airlines flight, I would travel on small, single-engine planes from there.

From the first gig in Skagway, it was pretty much a charmed

journey. I felt like Alice in Wonderland much of the time, gazing through the looking glass, or in this case, the windshield of a Cessna, at the stupendously magnificent glaciers, mountains, and the crystal-clear fiords of that largely unspoiled landscape. I remember thinking that in some cases I was seeing ancient lands that human feet had never touched.

It was a humbling, emphatic reminder of our fragile mortality, and I would never fail to be moved by Alaska's wilderness and majesty. The weather on the entire trip was mostly temperate, with many sunny days, and just a touch of southeast Alaska's famous fog and precipitation.

Landing in Skagway in a small airplane is not for the faint of heart. Coming in from Juneau, you follow the Lynn Canal north, unless you are turned away by fog in the Baranoff Straits, then gain altitude to rise close to the tops of the spruce-tree covered mountains that guard the steep, V-shaped valley where Skagway is sited.

At that point you are flying northeast.

The pilot then turns sharply perpendicular on his wing and dives southwest into the always stiff wind, toward the runway. The mountains create an effective wind tunnel for the ever-gusting westerlies, and since the pilot must land into the wind (or, as one of them told me, the plane wouldn't stop until it hit the Lynn Canal) he crabs down using full flaps, losing altitude at an incredible rate.

Landing in Skagway is better than any roller coaster ride, but I wouldn't recommend it for anyone who has trouble with airsickness. The wind regularly blows 30 to 40 MPH as the pilot makes his approach, and even Mick McCarter, who lived in Skagway and has made that landing dozens of times, hangs on for dear life and says a few prayers before the wheels touch down.

By the time I got there, the cruise ship season – in which 2,000 to 5,000 passengers descend upon the small community each day – had ended. So, Skagway had reverted to being a quaint little town of 700 year-round residents. Mick's friends

Don and Sue Plummer had volunteered to put me up at the historic Skagway Bed and Breakfast, a building that had been a brothel during the gold rush days of 1897-1898.

That gold rush is what made Skagway a prosperous village, then and now. In 1897-1898 it had vied with Dyea, now a ghost town a few miles away, to be the primary entry point for the argonauts from the south who were intent upon harvesting life-changing riches. After the steamship "Portland" arrived in San Francisco with a ton of gold from the Yukon, the rush was on – the last great adventure on the American frontier.

The miners would either choose the Chilkoot Pass trail (very steep, but shorter) from Dyea or the White Pass Trail (longer, but not so brutally high) from Skagway.

The Mounties at the U.S. border required miners to have 2,000 pounds of supplies before they entered Canada, so that Canadian officials wouldn't be responsible for them starving to death on their pilgrimage. To get that amount up to and over the border usually required 15-20 trips over the trail. They would cache their supplies at the border until they were all in place to move on.

From there they would get to Lake Lindeman or Lake Bennett after the ice had broken, build a boat, then float down almost 500 miles of the treacherous Yukon River. Even if they made it that far, very few of them ever found gold.

Back in Skagway, however, lots of merchants found their own treasure by equipping the miners and providing them with alcohol and other pleasures to take their minds off the brutal task they were undertaking or returning from. A narrow gauge railroad, The White Pass and Yukon line, eventually was built to Whitehorse, Yukon, and enough people settled permanently at the Skagway terminus to establish one of the first permanent Anglo settlements in the then-territory of Alaska.

The White Pass and Yukon line still exists as a tourist train that goes as far as Frasier, at the border. Chris Kennedy wrote an evocative song about it after riding it all the way to Whitehorse in 1982, called "The Whitehorse Train."

Into the 20th century, the population would wax and wane through economic downturns and the World Wars. A road was built to Whitehorse and on into further north Alaska for defense purposes during World War II, which gave a boost to the local economy. The road connects with the famed Alaska Highway and is still one of the only two roads which actually goes somewhere in Southeast Alaska.

Then, in the 1980's, the Alaska cruise ship phenomenon began. Well-heeled folks from the lower 48 and all over the world would sail from Seattle and other destinations up the inland passage to see the glaciers, mountains and other wonders of the 49th state. Juneau and Skagway were regular stops from the beginning. Both capitalized on their rough gold-mining history to appeal to the tourists, as the merchants there sold them souvenirs, jewelry and legends.

The 1898 gold rush began in those towns, and the most recent one is still happening every summertime as cruise ships unload their thousands of passengers to day-trip in Juneau and Skagway. Today, the cruise ship lines own the majority of the commercial shops in both towns.

But during the season when the big ships aren't arriving, from late September through late April, you can still get a sense of what life was like for those men and women of 1897-1898 as you stroll on the boardwalk of Skagway. Don and Sioux Plummer would become good friends who would promote concerts for me on future trips. Their bed and breakfast was a warm, hospitable refuge that was open to me whenever I was able to travel there.

The concert in Skagway that first tour was promoted by Barbra Kallan, a daughter of gold rush pioneers who still operated the photo shop on Broadway that her parents had established. She was also a folk music aficionado, and said she "never missed my radio program, and taped them all." (Bless her. I think she was the first person to ever say that to me.) An ardent supporter of the arts, she single-handedly produced numerous musical presentations at a gold rush-era Presbyterian Church that she attended.

I would perform through her efforts in Skagway many times and would play concerts in later years at other venues there too. But that first trip made such an indelible impression on me. The icy autumn winds and the high, craggy snow-capped peaks framing the little village gave me a sense of what it must have been like for those headstrong, adventurous souls who took loans from their family or friends and laid it all on the line – and who, in many cases, sacrificed their lives for that improbable dream.

A month or so later as I was returning to Nebraska, I would stop to do a concert in picturesque Livingston, Montana, just a few miles north of Yellowstone. As I lingered at a local cafe, pondering what I had seen and experienced that fall, I wrote "The Boardwalk at Skagway." It was a tribute to the resoluteness, and foolishness, too, of those intrepid souls who were trying to escape from the economic desperation of the Panic of 1893, which would not subside until the turn of the 20th century.

> **The Boardwalk at Skagway**
>
> In the town of old Skagway, the summer ends soon
> colored leaves light the ancient stone ridge
> as we turn on a wing, to land into a gale,
> Alaska seems dreamlike and dim
> I have read all the tales of the men who came here
> on steamers, life's savings in hand
> on the last great adventure, as the frontier was closed
> seeking gold in this beautiful land
>
> Chorus
> But the Boardwalk at Skagway is quiet and cold
> as I walk in this raw autumn wind
> the wood is scarred by the boots of the men who passed through
> never to walk here again, never to walk here again

"I WOULDN'T COUNT ON IT" — CONFESSIONS OF AN UNLIKELY FOLKSINGER

Take a pick and a shovel, a mule and an axe
enough food to last for a year
pack it up to the border, on many long hikes
build a lean-to, to shelter the gear
Then wait 'til the thaw cracks the Lake Bennett ice
and the Yukon winter tales have been told
Time to put in the boat, that you built in the snow,
to float down to Dawson and gold

Repeat Chorus

Now it seems times have changed and most people prefer
To watch their adventures at home
for the descendants of Robert Service, and Jack London
comfort is all that we've known
But I can't help but wonder as I look up that trail
where so many men and horses did die
in the frost and the cold of the harsh northern winter
would I have dared to take the trail that they tried

Repeat chorus

So tonight as I drift off in Skagway Alaska
I dream of the Klondiker's gold
I think I know why they left home and family behind
and bartered what could not be sold
they traveled to see the peaks of the Yukon
to grab that gold handful of dust
for me, like the miners of old 98
this adventure is treasure enough

Repeat chorus

Tom May copyright 1994 Blue Vignette, ASCAP
From the album "River and the Road"

"The Boardwalk at Skagway" was the first

historical-retrospective piece I would ever write. That style eventually becoming my favorite sort of theme to explore in song. From the first time I heard Lightfoot's "Canadian Railroad Trilogy" and later Stan Roger's marvelous musical storytelling of northern sailors, fishermen and ne'er do wells, I saw a songwriting path I could take. That was portraying history and geography (both subjects most Americans are woefully ignorant of) in ballad form, contrasting those men and times to our own.

I would continue to write personal songs too, of course, but doing my bit to remind audiences of great deeds, colorful characters and eras, and the incredible physical features of North America somehow seems more worthy and important. Not many folksingers have followed that path, one notable exception being Bruce Coughlin, the prolific composer from Vancouver, British Columbia. I wish more of that kind of songwriting was being done.

A long time ago, a wise man told me to occasionally "write outside of yourself" – meaning to focus on something other than your own life – and I have taken that advice to heart.

It's hard to pick out some of the other specific highlights of that first Alaskan tour, because the entire journey was one of the best times of my life. I do remember the compact Chilkat Center hall in Haines and the folks who wined and dined me in that charming place. They lodged me at the historic Halsingland Hotel, where I shared some stories and drink with the owner, Arnie Olafsen, an exuberant soul if ever there was one. He came from a Norwegian fishing family that had harvested those incredibly rich Alaskan waters for decades.

The Halsingland is a rambling old clapboard structure that had been the administration building for Fort Seward, the original military post in Alaska. It sits next to a large parade ground, similar to the one at Fort Omaha, surrounded by 19th and 20th century houses that had been officers' barracks.

Arnie hosted a salmon bake and Chilkat Native American

dancing each week. He became a good friend and ally in that neck of the woods.

The concert at the Sons of Norway Hall, which jutted out onto the fishing pier at Petersburg, is another of my favorite memories of that journey. Likewise was a show at a high school gymnasium in remote Sitka.

Sitka sits off by itself on the very edge of the islands and peninsulas that make up most of Southeast Alaska.

This old Russian capitol of that territory is right on the Pacific Ocean, not on inland waterways and fiords where most of the other towns in SE Alaska are sited. When you land on the small island where the airstrip is situated, you see nothing but water until your plane touches the runway.

The public broadcasting station in Sitka is known as Raven Radio, and the staff gave me quite a heartfelt welcome. The concert was well attended, and I had a chance to walk the streets of that old town, which consisted of about half Anglos and half Tlingit, Alaska's largest Native American tribe.

A gentleman by the name of Frank Howes attended the concert in Sitka and joined me and a group of folks from the radio station for a beer after the show. He asked me how much I would charge per concert to do an even more extensive concert tour, including not only Southeast Alaska but also northern British Columbia, the Yukon and the Northwest Territories. I gave him a price that seemed to pique his interest and got his contact information for future reference. As always, I didn't set my heart on bar talk like that, but it sure sounded interesting.

When I returned to Omaha, I followed up with a letter to Frank's Las Vegas mailing address and made several phone calls to the number he had given me. I never received a response, so I figured it was the usual case of dreaming and talking big over drinks.

Before I got back home, however, there was a tour to complete, including the regular shows in Portland, Seattle, Butte and Ronan, Montana, and Green River and Rock Springs, Wyoming. There were also new stops for me in Moose, Wyoming (just north of Jackson), and a show in Bismarck, North Dakota, at the university.

After the Alaska experience, I was on cloud nine all the rest of the trip. Touring in the "last frontier" had given me a buzz like no other, and I resolved to return as soon as possible.

♪ ♪ ♪ ♪ ♪ ♪

WHEN I RETURNED to Omaha, I had an immediate flurry of meetings about the upcoming River City Folk television series, and, of course, lots of radio work to catch up on.

I also had been asked by the Nebraska Arts Council to be the performing representative for them at the National Arts Council Conference in Charleston, South Carolina. Though I was crazy busy after just getting back from the tour, I looked forward very much to heading to such a historic city, one I had never been to before.

The Nebraska Arts Council and Omaha were to host the following year's conference, so their reasoning was that having me play a few songs and be sociable in South Carolina would help raise anticipation and attendance when Nebraska was the conference producer in 1994.

The Nebraska Arts Council was very generous in providing my airfare and an elegant room close to the heart of historic Charleston, as well as my fee. My performance at the conference was well received, and I met lots of interesting folks working hard to keep the arts vital in their communities and regions. I explored the antebellum lanes and houses of Old Charleston and visited museums and Fort Sumter, in between my responsibilities at the convention.

The highlight of that weekend came for me, however, when my Michaela called me at the hotel with stunning news. The conductor and musical director of the Omaha Symphony Orchestra had phoned my house and spoken to her about a proposal for me

"I WOULDN'T COUNT ON IT" — CONFESSIONS OF AN UNLIKELY FOLKSINGER

to appear with the Omaha Symphony at the inaugural concert of its 1994 season. He wanted to speak to me about the details.

Bruce Hangen was the director of the symphony at that time, and he had raised its profile such that it was considered one of the top regional orchestras in the U.S. He had seen me perform many times at Trovato's in Omaha, where he would often have a meal after a rehearsal or concert, living very close to there.

I had also met the development director for the symphony who was a regular attendee at my shows. Her name was Rhoda McIntire, and she encouraged me to drop off a promotional package and CD of "Blue Northern" after it had been released. I had done that, never imagining it would actually amount to anything. Wrong again.

With great excitement I called Bruce Hangen back, and we agreed to the basic framework of the show. Four local artists would be featured with the symphony, and I would be the headliner and closing act. Cliff and Avery would join me for the songs, but all of my pieces would have full orchestral arrangements, written and paid for by the symphony.

Having a talented, experienced arranger compose and write the separate, original musical scores for my songs, for all of the instruments of the orchestra (first violins, send violins, the various horns, flute, bassoon, percussion, harp, etc.) was an incredible gift in itself.

The Omaha Symphony performed its concerts in the ornate Orpheum Theatre, a 2,800-seat renovated vaudeville palace built in the 1920's. It was among the most beautiful theatres I had ever been in, even including the ones I had seen with Gordon Lightfoot.

I was aware of how few artists in any kind of music, but particularly in my little sub-culture as a folk singer and songwriter, have ever been invited to perform their songs with a full orchestra. I felt honored, grateful and thrilled about the symphony dates. There would be three shows in late September 1994, which would coincide with Omaha's annual River City Roundup festivities. They would also be broadcast live throughout the state on Nebraska Public Radio.

So, I flew home to Omaha from South Carolina like a kid who had just opened a package on Christmas morning with his heart's desire inside. Alaska, the national radio program, the Omaha Folk Festival, the new national television program, the symphony performances – all happening at once.

I can't say I had a great sense of accomplishment about any of it. So much of it seemed due to good luck. I was just happy for the work and the chance to do what I had always worked methodically towards doing – making a living in music while seeing the country surrounded by good friends, family and the voices of my steel-string acoustic guitars.

THE BOARDWALK AT SKAGWAY: THE OMAHA SYMPHONY, HAINES AND NAPA VALLEY

AFTER MANY TEDIOUS MEETINGS CONCERNING the television program – a preview of production days to come – a format had taken shape. Like the national radio broadcast, the show would feature a different guest or group each week. Unlike the radio show, there would be no recorded influences and it would be a half-hour broadcast.

I also insisted that I play a song with the guest, and on many episodes, I would perform one of my own songs, as well.

It was being produced as a joint venture between the University of Nebraska at Omaha's television station, KYNE, and a new national cable network in Branson, Missouri, founded by a wealthy entrepreneur by the name of Stan Hitchcock. They contracted with KYNE to produce 16 programs for that first season. Everyone was paid fairly for their work and talent, and knowing that Howard and KYNE-TV must have gotten the lion's share of the dough, it must have been quite a decent sized contract.

The Americana Network was carried on dozens of cable television systems throughout the U.S. It featured programs centered on country music, fishing and other down-home subjects. Branson, then and now, is one of the most bizarre towns in the U.S., featuring older country and religious singers in halls that cater to a senior citizen, ultra-patriotic clientele. It's the only place I know where "breakfast shows" – concerts that take place early in the morning – sell out. Not the kind of audience you think would go for folk music? I didn't think so either, but I was willing to give it a try.

We recorded on video tape the same theme song used for radio show, my composition "Cliff's Whiskers," with Cliff, Avery and Debbie Greenblatt on fiddle helping me out. It was many takes before the producer was satisfied with his footage, another peek into the lengthy process of doing television.

The powers that be consented to fly David Mallett, my old friend who wrote the folk standard "The Garden Song," from Nashville to record the very first River City Folk television program. A set had been built for the show, though it would evolve to become more colorful and interesting as additional programs were produced. It had kind of a front porch theme, with a cracker barrel, rocking chair, butter churn, etc. All it needed was an old guy in overalls spitting tobacco on the floor.

The broadcast was shot with three cameras, and the sound was recorded with microphones attached to our shirts and a big boom microphone that someone had to hold out of sight of the cameras.

The producer of River City Folk for television was quite meticulous, though he had little or no experience doing this kind of program. This meant multiple takes of almost every song and interview segment, plus a full rehearsal for each show for the benefit of the camera people, who were students. It was just about as far away from spontaneous music and chat as you can get.

Lest you think I am complaining too much, consider that each finished program was about 25 minutes, plus the beginning and ending theme. It took roughly four to five hours to tape each program, plus god knows how long to edit it. Thank goodness I wasn't involved with that part of the process.

I used to joke – in all seriousness – that my favorite part of recording the TV show was when the bosomy, very friendly makeup artist, Annie, would fuss and lean over me and try and make me look as pretty as possible for the cameras. Talk about a futile endeavor.

After that, most of the time was spent sitting and waiting on the set, drinking gallons of black coffee, punctuated by occasional periods of cameras actually rolling. It was maddening work. I would try to get the process accelerated a little, only to be met by stubborn resistance.

During that first television taping session with David Mallett, a guest was in the studio representing Wal-Mart, which I guess the Americana Network was courting as a sponsor. David sang a song he has written called, "I Miss Main Street," and the Wal-Mart shill was shocked – and uttered a few profanities. David's song was about small-town local businesses being shuttered by the encroachment of the big box stores like you know who. It had

WITH OMAHA SYMPHONY 1994

the memorable line, "and nobody knows where the money all goes, but none of it stays around here."

To Howard Lowe's credit, he stood up to the guy and said we wouldn't censor our guest's songs for subject matter. The Wal-Mart guy turned on his heel and stormed out, and the Americana representative was quite perturbed. It all could have ended right there, and it would have been fine with me. But somehow it all turned out alright, and we had one show in the can. The premiere broadcast would air in Nebraska and nationally in September 1994, right around the time of my scheduled Omaha Symphony dates.

THIS HECTIC YEAR would finish with a mini-tour to St. Paul, Minnesota; Fort Atkinson, Wisconsin; and Macomb, Illinois; followed by Chris Kennedy's return to Omaha to record his second album, which I would help produce in the KVNO studios.

Chris had an impressive new crop of songs, and we would again recruit Avery, Cliff and a few others to contribute to the effort. The new album was called "Rhythm of the Rails," and it consisted of all original pieces, save the evocative Eric Michaels' Alaska prospector song, "Gold Creek".

I like both of those albums we produced at KVNO, but I think "Rhythm of the Rails" had arrangements that were more complimentary to the music. That's probably because I had more experience composing instrumental parts by that time. "Gold Creek" was so lovely as the arrangement built through the song, with Chris's masterful second guitar part, Debbie Greenblatt's fiddle, and eventually my "D" pennywhistle echoing in the background.

AVERY GRIMES, TOM, CHRIS KENNEDY- GRAND LAKE COLORADO 1996

"I WOULDN'T COUNT ON IT" — CONFESSIONS OF AN UNLIKELY FOLKSINGER

We would use the pennywhistle again, this time a B-flat model, for Chris's song "Abraham Lincoln." It is an emotional look back at folks watching the Great Emancipator's funeral train roll by after his assassination in April 1865 – still one of the pivotal events in our country's history. Chris captures the pathos of those times and the sadness of the moment, mixed with the news of the end of the Civil War, in his well-crafted composition. His recording of that song would wind up being used for various historical programs.

After we finished the project, Chris was riding the Dog – the Greyhound Bus – back to Wyoming on Christmas Eve, nursing a wicked cold. It wasn't a particularly pleasant journey home, as he tells it, but at least we got some fine music put down while he had been in Nebraska. Chris Kennedy's "Rhythm of the Rails" would be released in the New Year.

In the meantime, I had my own folder of new songs I was anticipating recording on a fresh album. Flush (relatively) with profits from all the touring and sales of my earlier titles, I made plans to begin work on a new CD in early January at a studio called Digisound in Omaha. Tom Ware had bought and renovated the old Sound Recorders Studio A, where I had done "Open Spaces, Prairie Winds," when Chip Davis of American Gramophone had moved to a new location in the suburbs. The renovated studio felt to me as if it had the same magic as before, and I believed that along with everything else that was happening for me, this would be the project that took my music to a larger audience.

AFTER THE EXPERIENCE of my first album back in the late 1970's, when I was told the proper way to do a recording was to add the vocal track after all the backing tracks had already been laid down, I had always insisted on the takes being "live on the

The Boardwalk at Skagway: The Omaha Symphony, Haines and Napa Valley

floor." In other words, I would record the vocals, guitar, percussion and bass all at once, adding other voices or instrumental overdubs later. I had come to believe that, in addition to it being a much more honest way to lay down the music, it also gave the songs a verve that didn't exist using a strictly segmented method.

Using this method as a blueprint, we began this new recording on January 8th, 1994. This technique again worked well on the album, which would wind up being called "River and the Road."

The title song I adapted from a poem written by my then father-in-law, the prolific Bob Reilly. I had added some additional lyrics and composed the melody, and it wound up having a haunting, melancholy feeling to it, supplemented by Neil Johnsen's bluesy guitar work.

Almost all the tracks would include the ensemble I had come to rely up for not only recording, but also for live shows. Avery Grimes took the keyboard duties, Cliff Jones played his acoustic upright bass and Debbie Greenblatt filled in with her evocative fiddle work. In addition to my rhythm guitar, Neil Johnsen added lead guitar lines. Mark and Judy Moebeck from St. Louis generously traveled to Omaha to add harmony vocals.

Other songs on that album that I still enjoy the arrangements of are "The Boardwalk at Skagway," "The Fiddle and the Rose," and probably the most romantic song I have ever written, "Weaver and the Loom." I was quite proud of the melody lines I wrote for Avery's keyboard to accompany that latter piece. They would later be used as a blueprint for the arranger when he wrote the symphony orchestration of that song.

I also included the television version of the instrumental "Cliff's Whiskers," the theme for River City Folk, and a solo version of the song I had written for the rancher in Gordon, Nebraska, "Silence in the Wind." Added to the mix was a David Mallett song and a Jack Gladstone song I was performing regularly at that time, "The Valley of the Little Bighorn."

Sadly, Clete Baker could not fully participate because of a

potential conflict of interest between his employer, American Gramophone, and the studio where I was doing the work. So I again functioned as producer as well as artist on this project, and Dave Cwirko and Tom Ware did a fine job recording it and mixing it with me. Clete did provide advice and assistance however he could.

I obtained permission from the Manhattan, Kansas, newspaper to use the photo they had run of me on the cover of that Sunday paper the summer before. Kathy Gallagher, a friend from the Pacific Northwest, designed the cover art and hand-painted the background. We finished mixing the project in late January, working in the evenings and on the weekends, all the while recording both radio and television programs at the university during business hours.

Even before I started work on "River and the Road," I had a verbal commitment from a record label in Chicago to carry and distribute the album when it was done. Folk Era was a record company that had developed from the owner, Alan Shaw's, devotion to the music of the Kingston Trio. He had gone on to diversify to other styles of folk music and thought my project would be a good fit.

Folk Era's offices were in a cemetery outbuilding in Naperville, Illinois, just outside of Chicago. I suppose Alan Shaw got a good deal on that property. At least it was very quiet there, not a lot of noisy disruptions when you were meeting with him.

NO SOONER WAS I finished with "River and the Road" than I was off to the Pacific Northwest again for another Winterfolk in Portland and some attendant gigs to make it feasible to travel there. That year, Winterfolk was held at Kells Pub, which proved to be a very bad idea. It was larger than the Horse Brass and had a PA built in, so I had thought it might work out well – but it was a disaster. Not much money was raised, and I worried about the event surviving after that debacle.

After I returned from Portland, I spent the rest of February recording numerous radio and television programs. I also journeyed to do some arts council concerts in Kansas and Nebraska. The fine singer/songwriter Anne Hills traveled from Pennsylvania to tape both a radio and television program, and as often was the case when an artist had come so far, Michaela and I sponsored a house concert for her.

Anne has always been on of my favorites. She has the voice of an angel and is very judicious in the songs she chooses to play, whether her own or others. The topics of her music range from workers in the mills of the Eastern Seaboard to women's rights to traditional folksong themes, all delivered with conviction, wit and compassion. She is a sweet and caring person, in a sincere, not cloying or phony fashion, and I greatly respect her work.

After the annual St. Patrick's bacchanal in Portland in mid-March, I was hard at work back in Omaha on the TV/ radio schedule. The colorful Texan Alan Damron, who I mentioned earlier, was one of my scheduled guests for the television show.

He and his girlfriend at the time had arranged to stay in our guest bedroom while he was there. He pulled up in a huge, late-70's Cadillac decked out with bells, whistles and cowboy ornamentation – longhorns on the hood and such. He was an outsized character but also an engaging conversationalist, intelligent and a fun-to-be-around guy. Just stay away from politics!

He would regale you with funny stories and tales about his Texas pals such as Willie Nelson, Townes Van Zandt, etc., the beginnings of the Kerrville Folk Festival, appearing in a movie about the Alamo, and what it was like to perform on the mainstage of the Newport Folk Festival in 1965 – the year Dylan went electric.

After an evening when he kept me up way too late spinning those yarns and drinking whiskey, it was time to head to the

"I WOULDN'T COUNT ON IT" — CONFESSIONS OF AN UNLIKELY FOLKSINGER

television studio. He said his asthma had been bothering him, though I suspect the previous night's activities didn't help much, either, and he asked if we had some cough syrup he could use for the taping. We did, and he proceeded to swig the entire large bottle down before and during the numerous takes the program required. He must have had a pretty good buzz from the alcohol in it, too. When you watch that episode, you'll see that Alan Damron's tongue is as red as a Santa Claus suit.

Alan passed away a couple of years ago. I miss his laughter, bad jokes and outrageous stories. He was a dear man and such a memorable character.

IN THE SPRINGTIME that year, I didn't travel all the way to the East Coast but rather to Chicago, St. Louis, and other points closer to home. I auditioned the new album for the Folk Era staff and signed a formal contract with them. It would be released nationally on May 1.

I also had a new vehicle. The Ford van had begun to give me trouble, so I traded it for a 1992 short wheel base Chevy van with a V-6. It was white with gray highlights – very handsome. It had a power bed in the back (a seat that turned into a queen size bed when you hit a button), that was a comfortable place to sleep. The van would turn out to be the best transportation I ever owned, and I would put almost 400,000 miles on it. I called her Maggie, and I ran the wheels off her.

One of the stops during that beautiful April consisted of a couple of nights in Branson, Missouri. One of the sponsors behind my television show, Stan Hitchcock, had arranged for me to appear on his program on the Americana Cable Network. I also had the very weird experience of performing a couple of those dreadful breakfast shows I mentioned earlier. The senior

The Boardwalk at Skagway: The Omaha Symphony, Haines and Napa Valley

citizens would pile in, and you did a 60-minute set as they had a buffet style meal of waffles, eggs, etc.

They were an attentive bunch, I must say, but I think I was a little too counterculture for them, with my long hair, beard and songs about injustice towards American Indians, etc. They were marginally polite but extremely reserved – or maybe that's the way they always were at 9 in the morning. For me, I know it was about 11 hours too early in the day to be singing for a crowd, particularly for an audience that wasn't drinking anything but orange juice. But I made the best of it.

On Stan Hitchcock's television program, my fellow guest was the enormously popular, hit-making country singer Don Williams. Stan had suggested I might join Don for a song on the show, as I typically did on my own broadcast. Don walks in with his trademark slouch hat, with the two tassels on the brim, and Stan said, "We thought it would be nice to have Tom join you on a number."

Don looks askance at me, and says, "Sorry Stan, I don't go in for any of that circle jerk stuff." I had to stifle a laugh. So, I just played a song or two of my own, Don sang one of his bazillion-selling songs, and that was that. I filed away his quote for future reference, though. You just can't buy stories like that.

Someone should really write a satirical novel, or at least a short story, about Branson, Missouri. The combination of the god-and-country culture, aging country, gospel and pop music stars, and the Fox News-watching, massive-RV-driving, gun-glorifying middle America out in force – usually in a terrible traffic jam on the main drag – could be a potent theme for a talented author or film maker. I wish Mark Twain could have seen it and commented on it.

"I WOULDN'T COUNT ON IT" — CONFESSIONS OF AN UNLIKELY FOLKSINGER

ON MAY 1, I had the album reception party for "River and the Road" at the Storz Mansion in Omaha, which had been kindly lent to me by its owner for the festivities. It was an uncharacteristically cool and cloudy Nebraska afternoon, but it still was a success and well attended.

Later in the month I would have eye surgery (RK, or radial keratotomy) to correct my vision to 20-20. There was a short window where it was covered by Michaela's insurance, so I figured, "Why not?" It turned out to be a dumb move. I was able to go without glasses for just a couple of years before my eyes overcorrected. Instead of being near-sighted, I was extremely far-sighted with terrible night time glare problems that impacted my driving while I was touring. I vowed to never go down the elective surgery route again, and I have kept my promise in that regard.

Also during that month, we taped what I think are the two best River City Folk television shows we ever produced. One was with Doug Smith, who would eventually go on to win a Grammy Award for his work on an instrumental CD of Henry Mancini music. The other was with the ever-traveling Bill Staines from New Hampshire, who had written such enduring folk classics as "The Roseville Fair" and "All God's Critters" (got a place in the choir).

The set had become more interesting and colorful, and I had become a little more comfortable on camera. When I go back and watch the first couple of shows we recorded, I was just stiff as a board and looked like a grinning salesman about to sell you a lemon of a used car, whether you wanted it or not. I had improved, at least a little, since those early efforts.

The night before the Bill Staines taping, we both got way too far into our cups at my house, bemoaning the lack of traditional sensibilities in modern folk music and other earth-shaking matters. We look a bit peaked on camera.

I was wearing a blue shirt and my usual vest that day. We played Bill's song, "The Roseville Fair," together on the broadcast and every time he sang the line, "You were dressed in blue, and

The Boardwalk at Skagway: The Omaha Symphony, Haines and Napa Valley

you looked so lovely," one or the other of us would crack up and ruin the take. Took us forever to get that damn song done. It was like a Marx brothers routine. The camera people and director were less than amused, but we thought it was hilarious.

As I moved into the charmed summer of that special year, I would do a large outdoor concert at an Amphitheatre in Glenwood, Iowa, travel up to Canada to do some shows, do some regular stops in Iowa City at the Mill and in Minneapolis, and make the annual trek to Grand Lake, Colorado, with Michaela and Dylan.

At the end of July, I had the unique experience of hearing what the Omaha orchestra arranger had come up with for my songs. He played me a synthesized cassette version of approximately how the orchestration would sound on my compositions when the symphony joined me in September. I was able to make a few suggestions that he promised he would implement. I still treasure the preliminary tape of that session.

August was full of work, as I recorded both Jack Gladstone and my old friend, the gifted poet and composer Bill Morrissey, for the television program. I was particularly pleased with both efforts. Then it was time to be off on another adventure up north.

I had heard that the state fairs in Alaska (each region had one) were fun events and had good budgets for music. Since my radio program was so popular at that time in Southeast Alaska, I had proposed that the Southeast Alaska State Fair in Haines bring me up for a week both to do some performances of my own and to capture some of the unique songs and artists of that area for the national radio audience.

The management of the fair agreed to my proposal and paid for my airfare to Haines, accommodations at the Halsingland Hotel, and a performance honorarium for my concerts. KVNO used part of our NPPAG budget to send Jim Payne with me to record the artists there. Cliff Jones decided, "What the hell, I've never been to Alaska before, and this is a good excuse to go," so he joined our Nebraska contingent, too. I don't recall how in the world we found a full sized acoustic bass for him to play with me up there, but we somehow did.

Haines is situated among some of the most glorious scenery on the planet. Surrounded by the Chilkat and Coast Ranges and bordered by the impossibly blue waters of the Lynn Canal, it is a truly a magnificent setting. The Southeast Alaska State Fair was a medium sized but lively gathering, assembled on one of the verdant meadows right next to the Halsingland Hotel. Folks from all over the region, from towns with beckoning names like Yakutat, Elfin Cove, Gustavus and Wrangell, would hop on the ferries to mingle with their friends and neighbors. Though Southeast Alaska is huge in area, it is relatively small in population. I was always amazed at how many people from different sections of that archipelago region knew each other.

Just a few weeks before the fair was due to begin, a cancellation left a big hole in the fair's schedule. I had suggested David Mallett as a replacement, and they flew him all the way from Maine to sing there. The weather was perfect, and there were still almost 19 hours of sunlight each day in Haines at that time of year.

The concerts and radio show tapings all went well. I particularly remember a young native Inuit woman who incorporated traditional styles of singing into her hard hitting, contemporary accounts of what life is like in some of those remote villages. I sang " The Garden Song" with David, did my own shows, and just generally had an idyllic week of work and fun.

Cliff and I even arranged to go on a guided fishing boat expedition one day, and we both caught our limit of beautiful king salmon. I had all our fish smoked in Haines before returning to Nebraska.

The small airplane flying me back to Juneau, where I would catch a flight to Seattle and then on to Omaha, almost didn't take off that morning. Fog in the Lynn Canal was heavy and there wound up being serious delays. I was on a tight schedule with those connections, and I was worried I wouldn't make it back home before my next obligation – The Festival at the Fort.

The Boardwalk at Skagway: The Omaha Symphony, Haines and Napa Valley

I did make the connection in time, though the plane from Juneau to Seattle was overbooked, and I didn't think I was going to get on that aircraft. I was still under the spell of Alaska and the influence of Arnie Olafsen's powerful Bloody Mary's to reduce the worry and stress – and it all turned out okay.

It was a long flight home, and I arrived extremely early in the morning to Omaha. I didn't want to wake Michaela, as she had to teach that day, so I took a cab home from the airport. I have a clear memory that morning of the largest bunch of raccoons I ever saw crossing the road in front of the cab, just a few blocks from our house. They reminded me of the Haines folks festival folks heading for the bars in town after the music for the night was done. It was a weird apparition after a tiring, but productive, journey.

Immediately after I returned, I had numerous radio and television interviews scheduled to promote that year's Festival at the Fort. It took place that following weekend and was even more successful than the original effort in 1993. It seemed we were really building something there. Bill Staines from New Hampshire came out to join us, as did my pal Chris Kennedy from Wyoming and the Native American recording artist Joanne Shenandoah.

The month would end with more radio and television tapings (of course) and a presentation I had been engaged to produce at the Nebraska State Fair in Lincoln. The fair had allowed me a generous budget for the event, "Tom May presents River City Folk at the Nebraska State Fair."

I was able to fly in both Anne Hills and Michael Johnson, the extremely successful folk performer who had hits on the radio with "Bluer than Blue" and "Give me Wings," to be part of the stage show. We taped it all for eventual broadcast, as well. Cliff, Avery and Debbie Greenblatt joined me on some of my new songs from "River and the Road."

The show was held in a large hall with another of those revolving stages. Thank goodness it didn't revolve that night. I was very skeptical we would have a decent crowd in that kind of setting, but it turned out very well – we had about 1,000 people in attendance that evening. It was a terrific end to what had been a whirlwind of a month.

THROUGHOUT SEPTEMBER, I rehearsed with Avery and Cliff almost every day so the songs would be as tight as possible for the symphony appearances. There were two nights of rehearsals with the orchestra too, but I recall not actually getting much time with them to go over things. The publicity mill for the symphony had done its work, and it looked like there would be good crowds.

I think I counted somewhere around 60 orchestra musicians onstage at those shows, each of them thoroughly knowledgeable about theory and more trained than myself. I didn't let it put me in a panic, though. As before other important performances in my career, I just took a big breath, walked out onto the cavernous stage, and after a flattering introduction by conductor Bruce Hangen, kicked off the first song, "Blue Northern."

On that first night, a Thursday, over 2,000 people attended the concert. The horns, strings, and percussion all triumphantly joined the instrumental line I had written to begin the song. That introduction was inspired by themes from old western movies, particularly The Magnificent 7.

Cliff and Avery were right next to me, but so was a drum set which was a little distracting, particularly on that first number. Still, the first song received thunderous applause. Despite the fact that it was a concert celebrating Nebraska Heritage, I was the only one on the program who did music that was at all western or historically themed. I think the audience really appreciated my subject matter, particularly in context with River City Roundup.

The next piece, however, was a love song. "Weaver and the

The Boardwalk at Skagway: The Omaha Symphony, Haines and Napa Valley

Loom" (Chris Kennedy calls it "The Weaver and The Lunatic," a title that deserves to be remembered) is set in the Pacific Northwest and is very pensive and emotional. I did a solo introduction with just a hint of harp added. Toward the end of the first verse, the violins came in, and I have to confess to tearing up – it sounded so beautiful.

Chills ran up and down my spine as I felt the crowd responding to my lyrics and melody, so tenderly accented by the orchestra. That song does not resolve to the base chord, and I heard the audience collectively sigh as it ended. Then, again, massive applause.

The rest of the set – six more songs – went by all too quickly. After a standing ovation, I welcomed the three acts that had preceded us onto the stage, and they joined me on the classic "Four Strong Winds," by Ian Tyson. I had needed to teach it to everyone, and the symphony put together a chart for that one, too.

The Thursday night presentation was such a rush, and the next two nights would be even better as the symphony became more familiar with my material and the pace of the concert improved. The Saturday night show was sold out, the Friday night one nearly so. The last one was taped for public radio and was broadcast live statewide, and I was able to use those recordings on some of my albums farther down the road.

After the Saturday night concert, Michaela and I welcomed conductor and musical director Bruce Hangen, Avery, Cliff, and a few other close friends for a reception. We served the smoked salmon Cliff and I had caught in Alaska, along with the very best wine I could afford.

One of the sweetest aspects of the event was the opportunity for Michaela and Dylan to bask in the limelight. Michaela had always been a devoted fan of classical music, so for her to be able to go backstage, hobnob with the conductor and others was a deserved treat for her.

I was aware of how much she had sacrificed for me to reach that plateau. She attended each night's show. Dylan was 12 at the

"I WOULDN'T COUNT ON IT" — CONFESSIONS OF AN UNLIKELY FOLKSINGER

time, just the right age to fully appreciate the experience, and I know he enjoyed himself, too.

On the Friday night, my parents agreed they would attend. I made sure they had complimentary seats in the front row. Right after I began my first song, my mother asked my father to escort her to the restroom. They didn't return for more than 35 minutes, until just before the end of the concert. I don't know if it was a deliberate slight or not. It surely hurt my feelings at that time, though must say I wasn't surprised. Ah well.

Other than that little incident, those shows were among of the supreme highlights of my performing life. I hired one of the KVNO staff to sell my new CD, "River and the Road," in the lobby, and we had success with that endeavor, too. The glow from that weekend would last until the next journey was undertaken, soon after those concerts concluded.

NO TIME TO bask in glory. It was time to head the van west again, and this time a new festival would be on the agenda. After shows in Evanston and Rock Springs, Wyoming, I was due to perform and record some River City Folk radio programs at the Napa Valley Music Festival in California.

The Napa Valley Festival had been founded by Rod Kennedy from Kerrville, Texas, along with other local California music types. Set as it was in the most famous wine region in North America, I was looking forward to being a part of it – for the wine, as well as the music.

I had lobbied David Maloney, who I knew well from Boston and Kerrville, and who was also one of the directors there, to see if I could insert myself into the lineup. Bless David's heart, he strongly recommended to festival producer Alan Arnapole that I be invited to Napa Valley to both record radio programs and to perform.

The Boardwalk at Skagway: The Omaha Symphony, Haines and Napa Valley

I arrived in Northern California and checked into the plush accommodations they had arranged for me – quite a change from my usual digs on the road. There was an opening reception at the historic Freemark Abbey Winery, which had been built in Napa Valley before prohibition. I was looking forward to the party, to the wine (and indeed, Freemark Abbey wine was and is fabulous stuff) and to meeting some of the legendary names that had been booked for the festival.

Among those were Hamilton Camp, who had performed with folk legend Bob Gibson at the Gate of Horn and elsewhere in the early 60's, and who then segued into a successful acting career on shows like " Mash" and "Cheers." He turned out to be an exuberant, timeless soul with a wicked sense of humor. He could also sing well and had a restless, enthusiastic guitar style and stage presence. Along with appreciating the fantastic cabernet at Freemark Abbey, I enjoyed playing a few songs with Hamilton immensely. He was small in stature but had an outsized, joyful personality.

There were lots of other fine musicians there that I had not met before, who I appreciated hearing – Al Grierson, Evan Marshall and many more. I was especially anticipating reconnecting with an old acquaintance from my Toronto days, David Rea.

David Rea was one of the most memorable, talented, and eccentric people I have ever known. He was a great picker and an even better songwriter, and I loved the guy. If you are not familiar with his name, he played guitar on Gordon Lightfoot's first album and on many of Lightfoot's early gigs. David went on to record and tour with Canada's legendary Ian and Sylvia Tyson. He also recorded his signature filigree guitar style accompanying Judy Collins, The Clancy Brothers and Jessie Winchester. For a brief time, he replaced Richard Thompson in the popular folk-rock group Fairport Convention.

Though I had met him and gotten to know him in Toronto during the 70's, I did not encounter him again until I performed at the festival that year. David was living with his wife and young children in Calistoga, California, at the north end of the Napa Valley. He came into that reception, sat down at the big grand piano, and began to play. Soon some folks joined him on guitars. The next day, we got to visiting, and he and I would pick together on our guitars a song he had accompanied Lightfoot with on that first album, a beauty called "The Long River." It would be the first of hundreds of songs we would eventually perform together.

David and I really got to know each other well and share more music when he relocated to Bainbridge Island, Washington, a couple of years later, after he had fallen in love with a woman there during a tour with Ramblin' Jack Elliot. We did many shows and festivals together in the following years and even a tour in Ontario in 1999, with my son playing bass with us. David Rea was a relentlessly interesting – and sometimes maddening – character to hang out, play songs and swap tall tales with.

IN OMAHA, I was a regular purchaser of wines at a store not far from our house, run by a fellow who had been in that business in California before he moved back to Nebraska. He gave me two of his business cards to show at the wineries when I got out to the Napa Valley, which he said would allow me to avoid any tasting fees.

Steve O'Gorman was now my engineer and co-producer of the radio program, so KVNO bought him a plane ticket to California to record the stage shows at Napa Valley for us. I took Steve for a tour of wineries in my van, and those calling cards my friend back in Omaha had given me worked superbly. At Behringer, we even had free admission to the reserve room, where they pour their finest. And they gave each one of us a case of wine when we left. What a deal. It was my first trip to the Napa Valley, and I fell in love with the vino and the landscape.

One of my favorite vintners there was Peju Province, where

The Boardwalk at Skagway: The Omaha Symphony, Haines and Napa Valley

Alan Arnapole, director of the festival, worked. Located at the edge of the famous Rutherford Bench region of Napa, it is renowned for its cabernet sauvignons. Another was Silver Oak, one of the sponsors of the festival – not that I could afford their wines, but Justin, the owner, sent some complimentary bottles to the event. Another was Ehler's Grove, as well as oh so many others. Both 1994 and '95 were terrific years for the vines and produced some collectible vintages.

The first year I performed there, the festival was at the Napa County Fairgrounds, which was a pleasant setting.

I had a good reception from the crowd, both on the mainstage for my solo set and for the River City Folk tapings, which took place on a different stage later in the evening. It was a little chilly that first year though, and they would eventually move the event to an earlier date, hoping for warmer weather.

After the pleasure of spending five days in Napa, it was north to Portland, Seattle and other Northwest locations.

Coming from Nebraska, I had never even seen the ocean until I was grown and away. So, I always took advantage of opportunities to do a gig close to the beach. I had met Rob Royster, who had once tended bar at The Horse Brass. He had opened a tavern on the spectacular Oregon coast, in the then-undiscovered gem of a town, Pacific City. He and I had kept in touch, and I always stopped into his pub, The Sportsman, for a brew when I was anywhere close.

He built an addition to the place, and I began doing one or two weekends a year for him in that autumn of 1994, right up until the present day. It is not a concert hall. It's a tavern with a couple of pool tables and gambling machines on the back walls. But folks there have always been kind and receptive toward me and my songs, and Pacific City is a very picturesque destination I have always enjoyed immensely.

When you play a venue that often, you get to know some of the regulars. An older woman by the name of Norma frequented the bar, drinking her Heidelberg beer and chain-smoking Pall Malls. She was an entertaining gal. I learned the old country song, "Life is like a Mountain Railroad" to sing for her. She had been married seven times and always threatened to make me her eighth.

I have noticed in recent years much of that bar culture disappearing, as cigarette smoking in public is forbidden and stricter drunk driving rules are in effect. These are all good ideas, to be sure, but they have also cut down on some of the colorful souls like Norma, who contributed mightily in keeping this job so interesting. She once knit me a stocking cap with my entire name on it. She passed away a few years ago, and whenever I go back to The Sportsman now, I play Ian Tyson's "Navajo Rug" song in her honor, substituting the name "Norma" for the "Katie" in the chorus.

After that Pacific City weekend, it was time to once again turn the Maggie, the van, back toward Nebraska. I played a packed concert in the small town of Whitehall, Montana, on the way home, and also a memorable date at Dornan's in Moose, Wyoming, close to Jackson Hole. It had been a tumultuous few months, full of once-in-a-lifetime kinds of experiences, abundant music, travel, wine and good friends. It seemed as if all kinds of horizons were opening up for the future.

YOU MIGHT REMEMBER all my prattling on in earlier chapters about most agents being worthless. It's a pity I didn't listen to my own advice. This instance was not the first – nor last—time this would be true.

I had been approached by a company that purported to work with "rising stars" (his words, not mine) like myself to book more lucrative concerts. If I paid for $150 worth of promotion each month, the company would guarantee me 20 concerts a year at

The Boardwalk at Skagway: The Omaha Symphony, Haines and Napa Valley

a minimum of $1,500 each. It would also take 10 percent of that amount, which seemed fair.

When you did the math, it seemed like an attractive offer. I did all the research I could do on them. They were located in the state of Ohio, and they had no Better Business Bureau complaints against them when I checked up. It was much tougher to get accurate information on firms in those pre-internet days.

It's too bad the contract wasn't worth the paper it was written on. I was bilked out of over $2,000 and never got one concert, at any price. The company and agent kept stringing me along with talk of a complete tour for me "almost complete." I was gullible and greedy, and I got my comeuppance – the agent eventually wound up going to jail for fraud from a lawsuit another of his clients had filed. I wish I could have said, "easy come, easy go," but money really wasn't that painless to come by in this profession. I had learned another lesson though, albeit an expensive one.

CLIFF'S WHISKERS, FESTIVAL AT THE FORT

BY THE FIRST OF THE YEAR IN 1995, THE TELEVIsion version of River City Folk had been airing for a few months, and it seemed to be very popular, both locally and around the country. There was talk at the Americana Network in Branson of renewing it for another season. It certainly wasn't the most fun thing I had ever done in the music business, but I agreed I would again host it if the series was renewed.

The Americana Network did eventually pick up the option for another 16 episodes of River City Folk, so I still had that responsibility to tend to. After only eight more episodes, however, they encountered some kind of rough financial waters and reneged on their contract with University Television. I had cleared my calendar so I would have time to do the programs, so when it all fell through, I was quite miffed. But KYNE's Howard Rowe, to his credit, gave me a cash settlement that amounted to most of what I would have made had I actually labored through all those tapings.

I was fine with that, because as I mentioned, I was somewhat ambivalent about the work. We wound up producing 24 television shows total. It is now more than 20 years since the last TV program was produced, and it still airs frequently, by request (for some reason!) on University Television in Omaha.

Here is a reprint of an unedited letter posted to a television website about River City Folk, written back in 2006. Responses like this reassured me someone was watching and listening-

> Does anyone else out there ever watch River City Folk? You know, that glorious series of about 32 episodes of folk music ecstasy recorded at the UNO TV studios from 1994 to 1995? Some of the best moments of my TV-watching life have come about thanks to great friends, great rum, and great music courtesy of Tom May and the gang. Every week, a different folk singer comes in and struts his or her (or their) stuff while May smiles, taps his toe, and sometimes sings/plays along. There was this one episode that featured this nautical sailor-type guy singing sea shanties and drinking songs while accompanying himself on the concertina and ukulele…I can't think of what his name was. I want to say Tom Lewis. Anyways, he was supposedly in the British Navy for a while and his show was a rollicking good time. I'm going to tape it next time it's on. He played one of the most bad-ass drinking songs I've ever heard…It goes something like this: "Don't pull on the ropes, don't climb up the mast, 'cuz if you see a sailing ship it might be your last, so get your civvies ready for another run ashore, a sailor ain't a sailor ain't a sailor anymore." HOTT SHITT, I TELLS YA. That man is a musical and cultural genius of the highest order.
>
> What I really want to know is why the hell aren't they making any more episodes of the TV show? They are still doing new radio shows every week, but that doesn't do me a bit of good because when I'm all tanked at 3 AM I don't want to listen to the damn radio, and even if I did, River City Folk would definitely not be on. I want to turn to Viewer's Choice and call up and request an episode of the show that I haven't

"I WOULDN'T COUNT ON IT" — CONFESSIONS OF AN UNLIKELY FOLKSINGER

already seen at least five times. Unfortunately, there aren't any, as I have seen every episode enough times to pretty much know all of the songs on most of the shows and most of the songs on all of the shows. Except, there was this one show that I only saw part of once and it featured a husband and wife cello duet playing some really wonderful stuff. I'd really like to see that one a few more times instead of seeing Bill Staines or Armour & Sturtevant for the 50 millionth time. But, what can I do? That episode seems to have been taken out of the rotation for some reason. It's not a perfect world, so I'll have to be happy that the show is even still on the air...

Thanks, buddy! I laughed for 10 minutes, and you made my day!

THE COMBINATION OF the radio show playing in so many markets as well as the television broadcast's success, gave me a chance to play some other larger venues I had not done before.

In January, I was invited to be the featured performer at a national historian's convention at the prestigious Newberry Library in Chicago. The theme of that year's conference was Frederick Jackson Turner's controversial, but celebrated, treatise on the closing of the American Frontier in 1890. It was a plum gig, and I was so pleased to be recognized for the kind of songs I was writing and performing, different sorts of material from what most folksingers were doing then – and now.

The Newberry Library is an impressive, massive stone edifice that coincidentally was just across the street from what had been Universal Recording Studios, where I had recorded my first demo tapes in 1974. It was a measure of how far I had come in the business. Though sometimes it didn't feel like it, I really had made progress and had managed to make a living – all the while doing something I believed in and also having a lot of fun in a tough field. For me, those rewards were so much more valuable than a new car, a fancy house or even a gold record.

Later that winter I was back in Portland, where I would produce the first Winterfolk to take place at the Aladdin Theatre. The National Folk Alliance Conference also was in Portland that year. That event is the largest gathering of professionals and wanna-bes in the Acoustic Music World, attracting agents, performers, record labels, etc. Utah Phillips aptly named it "Folk Annoyance."

I scheduled Winterfolk to fall on the Sunday after the conference ended, and consequently I was able to recruit Tom Paxton, Neal and Leandra, Jack Gladstone and others to be part of that year's benefit for Sisters of the Road. Chris Kennedy and Avery Grimes also joined me for some songs on stage, and Utah Phillips again headlined the event with his stories, songs and insight.

At the Folk Alliance conference, I appeared numerous times at the Folk Era-sponsored showcase, playing songs off my album that had been released on their label. The noted folksinger Bob Gibson attended one of my daytime sets, and I had a chance to meet him and visit with him. Bob Gibson was one of the most important and influential people in the folk revival of the 1960's, but he does not get the credit he deserves.

He was a dynamic performer who jump-started Joan Baez's career by inviting her to share his set at the Newport Folk Festival. His performances with Hamilton Camp inspired thousands of young folks to pick up guitars and sing. His 12-string guitar technique greatly influenced people like Gordon Lightfoot, and Lightfoot also patterned his "Canadian Railroad Trilogy" structure on the template of Gibson's "Civil War Trilogy." A proclivity for illegal substances did much damage to him and sidetracked the great success he had early on, but he had gotten beyond that and rebuilt a solid career. He really was a living legend.

By 1995 however, he was in ill health and confined to a wheelchair.

"I WOULDN'T COUNT ON IT" — CONFESSIONS OF AN UNLIKELY FOLKSINGER

One of my sets at the Folk Era stage was scheduled for one in the morning. I was convinced no one would be there at that hour. A few tired souls staggered in, and then who rolls down the aisle but bright-eyed Bob Gibson and his daughter, who listened intently and applauded again enthusiastically for my songs. After the set, I thanked Bob profusely for staying up so late and making the effort to come see me again. He replied, "Tom, I would *never* miss hearing you play and sing when I had the opportunity."

It was a generous validation of all I had been working toward to have him say that, and it meant the world to me. We lost Bob in 1996, but I still see his daughter, Meridian, in the Portland Oregon area. She has worked relentlessly at keeping his musical legacy heard and accessible.

AFTER WINTERFOLK AND the Folk Alliance conference, back to Omaha – only to depart for the Pacific Northwest again a month later for the annual St. Patrick's Day Festival at Kells. After my return from Portland, I was just home a couple of days when I drove back out to western Nebraska for some arts council dates there.

Time to stress once again that I could never have made all of this traveling pay, had not there been my dear friends, generous souls all, who welcomed me into their homes when I was on the road: Tom Bryson and Claire Levine in Portland, Don Younger in Portland, Chris Kennedy in Rock Springs, Wyoming, Al and Anita Avery in Baltimore, Jeff McLaughlin in Boston, Mike Donovan in Chicago, as well as all my other friends throughout North America. They were angels without which this profession would have been impossible. Only occasional concerts and gigs provided hotel rooms. Much of the time you had to sort out sleeping arrangements yourself.

Cliff's Whiskers, Festival at the Fort

Though I was fortunate to have a decent income from the radio and television broadcasts of River City Folk, other gigs in the Omaha area seemed like they were drying up. This kind of created a feast or famine scenario, where I would either be making a lot of dough doing arts council concerts and other shows on the road or playing in dismal venues for almost nothing at home. This was a major concern moving forward.

On the other hand, the Folkfest at the Fort in 1995 had the best turnout ever. The legendary Odetta was the headliner, and David Mallet came from Maine for the festivities. We also were blessed by the angelic voice of Anne Hills form Pennsylvania and the traditional folk sounds of Dave Para and Cathy Barton from Missouri.

I had very competent assistance and invaluable input from Jim and Kathy Wood of the Omaha Folklore Society and tireless work and willingness to please from the college's staff. The president of the Metro Community College, Richard Gilliland, had worked hard to establish and fund the festival as one of the institution's signature events, and it was really paying off in attendance and overall quality.

In the autumn I turned Maggie toward my beloved western landscapes again. Chris Kennedy and I had schemed that he would join me in Alaska for some performing dates during his teaching sabbatical from Western Wyoming Community College. So, I had some company to look forward to on this journey.

But first, I had again been booked at the Napa Valley Folk Festival. I performed a night at a place called Kate's in Evanston, Wyoming. I drove off immediately after the gig, traversing the Utah and Nevada deserts on the way to California. I pulled over and took a little nap in the Sierra Nevada mountains and arrived at Napa in time for the opening party the following day. I didn't want to miss that party – it had been such a memorable bash the year before.

And, just as the year before, the entire festival was a delight. A highlight was singing Kate Wolf's anthem, "Give Yourself to

Love" with country star Kathy Mattea on the closing night. Festival director Alan Arnapole had me do a verse myself, and then Kathy and I sang the choruses. It was magic.

I also had the opportunity to spend a good bit of time with Lou Gottlieb, one of the principal performers in the renowned folk revival group The Limeliters. I had first met Lou in Kerrville, and he and his wife expressed how much they appreciated and enjoyed my "Bessie and Me" song. That topic led to conversations full of priceless stories he related about his life and times in music.

In his droll fashion, he was one of the funniest people I ever saw on stage, as well as being a talented musician and singer. Lou had even been the guru of a California nudist ranch in the swingin' sixties, which spawned a whole other list of escapades he would regale you with. The Limeliter's version of "A Little Madeira, My Dear?" with all of Lou's winks, asides and innuendo, was hilarious.

That year, Glenn Yarborough was also booked at the festival. Back in the day before he established his solo career, he had been the Limeliter's lead singer. He had an unforgettable rich baritone voice – and he'd had a top-10 hit in the 50's with "Baby, the Rain must Fall." But he had become somewhat of a recluse on his sailboat in the San Juan Islands. I talked to him about possibly appearing on my radio and television program, and he was very interested, but it never worked out. After kind of a disappointing set where he sang with canned music backing him, he did an impromptu reunion with the Limeliters that brought the house down.

After the festival, I drove to Portland, where I left the van and flew to Alaska. Chris and I had made plans to meet in Skagway, where my dear friends Don and Sue Plummer agreed to provide us with gratis accommodations at the Skagway Bed and Breakfast.

It was a beautiful, blue-sky day flying into Juneau, then boarding the small four-seater airplane to Skagway. Someone had mentioned to me that on occasion, if you asked and the weather was good, the pilot might fly over the 165-mile-long Juneau icecap, a massive glacier, on the way to Skagway, instead of flying up the Lynn Canal. That September 19, the weather was perfect. The plane was flown by a woman pilot, and she gladly granted my wish to take that route. I was her only passenger.

You climbed, climbed, climbed over the enormous wind and rain-etched ice sheet, until you crested a final ridge, and the deep green valley Skagway occupied was laid out before you. It was a panoramic, unforgettable flight: Every color of the rainbow reflecting in the chasms of the ancient ice as the autumn sun hit them, and the impossibly high peaks of the Canadian coast range so close it seemed you could reach out and touch them.

When I arrived, Chris was already there, having come in on an earlier plane. Coincidentally, it turned out Chris's pilot had also taken him over the glacier route that day! We were both extremely lucky to have that experience when we did. Not two weeks after we had been there, one of the small airplanes that plied that route to Skagway crashed on the Juneau icecap, with everyone aboard the flight perishing. The FAA prohibited future passenger planes from traversing the glacier route on the way to Skagway.

I personally got a kick out of traveling on those single-engine Cessna aircraft around Alaska, but it wasn't without risk. I often selected LAB as my airline of choice for those puddle jumps in Southeast. They employed just-graduated pilots from a flight school in Texas who were receiving their first commercial experience behind the control yoke in that challenging Alaska landscape.

One 1990's autumn on a tourist flight close to Haines, the patrons on an LAB Cessna requested the pilot descend so they could get a better look at a grizzly they had spotted at the edge of the forest. When the pilot acquiesced, he dropped a little too much, clipped a wingtip and crashed. There were no survivors.

For a while after that, and before they wound up going out of business, LAB was known as "Look, a Bear!" airline – a little northern black humor.

Our first concert together on that mini-tour was in Skagway, again hosted by Barbra Kallen at the Gold Rush Presbyterian Church. It was a good turn out, and it was always a pleasure to do a show with Chris. In addition to being such a fine guitarist and songwriter, Chris always made me laugh with his jokes, stories and puns.

The following night we were booked in Haines, at the Chilkat Center. We flew over there the next day, where I was informed by my contact that some kind of monumental screw-up had occurred. Despite the fact I had just checked on the arrangements the week before by phone and that I had a signed contract, somehow the gig had evaporated. The substantial funding, the promotion, the availability of the hall had all unexplainably vanished, and no one had informed me.

Chris and I were both disgusted, but there was not much we could do short of filing a lawsuit, which would have been an idiotic move, as the attorney fees would cost as much as the gig would have paid.

At least we had free accommodations from Arnie Olafsen at the Halsingland Hotel, who sympathized with our plight and was also upset with the organizers. He said that had he known, he would have made something happen in Haines himself. He proceeded to buy Chris and me drinks in his cozy bar, but Chris was just not in the mood to do much socializing. He was rightly pissed off about the whole episode and was done rehashing the gory details of the disappointment.

I was a little more philosophical that evening than Chris and figured I might as well linger and enjoy Haines and Arnie's company, hospitality and his cozy pub. He broke out a bottle of Napa Silver Oak (I couldn't believe he carried wine of that caliber and price), opened it, and sat it in front of me to drink as a "town apology" as he put it, though certainly none of it was Arnie's fault. I enjoyed myself thoroughly, and he and I traded stories and lies until the wee hours. The next morning, Chris and I flew back down to Juneau for a weekend of gigs at a restaurant called Fiddleheads.

That establishment had arranged for two comfortable rooms

for us at a motel right next to the gig. It was set up as two nights of concerts, but it turned out a little differently than that. They were more like evenings during which we were playing for folks who had come out to dine. Still, we had a good time singing together and hiking around the Mendenhall Glacier in between shows.

TOM AND CHRIS KENNEDY (SCOTT DOCHERTY)

Chris flew back home to Wyoming after Juneau, and I continued north to Cordova and Talkeetna – both fascinating towns. After those adventures, back to the Pacific Northwest, where I did my usual fall stops, adding Anacortes, Washington, and Newport, Oregon. As I made my way back toward Nebraska, I did a Montana swing that included Ronan, Polson, and St. Ignatius, tucked in the valley of the steep, remote Mission Mountain range, as well as the intimate Myrna Loy Theatre in the state capitol of Helena.

Then, a Monday night, last-minute booking in Cody, Wyoming. I had great affection for the town of Cody, with its proximity to Yellowstone Park, its world-class western museum, the nightly rodeos during the summer season, and the historic

"I WOULDN'T COUNT ON IT" — CONFESSIONS OF AN UNLIKELY FOLKSINGER

Irma Hotel, which Buffalo Bill Cody built and named after his daughter in 1902.

The Irma Hotel restaurant has a back bar that was gifted to Buffalo Bill by Queen Victoria, in appreciation of the many performances of his Wild West Show he put on in London. It was freighted "round the horn" of South America by sailing ship and installed in the hotel. The hotel also has one of Bill Cody's famous silver saddles in the window, as well as other artifacts from his life and times. The Irma also had a delicious appetizer of prairie oysters on the menu that I enjoyed ordering – bovine testicles breaded and deep fried. Yum.

To be back in that friendly town with folks who had enjoyed my music on previous stops, I had consented to do a show on a Monday night with no guaranteed fee at a local coffee shop. I knew it was a crapshoot as to whether it would even be a break-even night, by the time I paid for a room at the Irma.

This was a perfect illustration, however, of how important it was to take what gigs you are offered and keep busy performing on the road. An offer would be worth accepting if you thought there might be a listening audience or a good fee is involved or if it might garner press or a review, if you just have friends there – or any combination of the above.

As I expected, the crowd was small, it being a weekday night. I may have covered my expenses when you include album sales, but I doubt it. However, in the crowd was my old acquaintance from Sitka, Frank Howes. After the show, he asked me if I recognized him and remembered his question about what I would charge per show for the Alaska/Yukon/ Northwest Territories annual tour that he booked. I replied that indeed I did remember him, and we made a date for breakfast the next morning to come to a final agreement. He said he definitely wanted me to be the touring artist for his series in February 1997. By coincidence, he was in town doing presales for his Cody concert, which he also put on most years.

I was overjoyed. Not only did I really want to do that tour and see those remote places, but the money was decent and all expenses were paid. I also got to choose an opening act, if I desired, that would receive a much smaller fee but have all expenses covered. It seemed too good to be true, but in this case it actually was a bona fide offer.

I engaged my old pal from St. Louis, Mark Moebeck, as my opening act, sent Frank the contracts which he signed and had notarized, and inked it in on the calendar.

Chris Kennedy then drove up from Rock Springs to join me again in a KEMC radio-sponsored concert in Billings, Montana, at Cecil Hall, and also for a delightful evening at Dornan's in scenic Moose, Wyoming, while he had the time off for his sabbatical from teaching. It had been such an enjoyable autumn having the musical company and comradeship of Chris at many of the shows before he went back to his real gig as communications professor.

Finally, back to Nebraska and the performing wasteland that Omaha was becoming. And on into 1996, where I would make far more bad decisions than good ones.

THE WEAVER AND THE LOOM

THE WINTER OF 1996 WAS A ROUGH ONE ALL around the country – a harbinger of the rest of my year.

After repeated snowstorms in Omaha in January that thwarted a number of my gigs, I flew to Washington, D. C. for the annual national Folk Alliance conference. There I was nominated and elected to the board of directors.

This would require more travel, at least two trips a year. But I figured since the genre had been so good to me, it was a way I could pay back some of my good fortune.

Michaela flew out to the East Coast to join me, and we spent some nice time at the Renaissance Hotel in D. C., and at Al and Anita Avery's home in Baltimore.

Michaela then flew home, and I boarded a flight for the West Coast for that year's Winterfolk concert at the Aladdin Theatre. I had convinced Michael Johnson from Nashville to contribute his time and talent to that year's benefit.

It turned out Winterfolk that year nearly did not happen at all, as the worst flooding in 100 years came close to inundating the downtown core of Portland. It was nearly a major natural disaster, but the water stopped just an inch or two from the top of the seawall.

So, the concert went on, but it wasn't particularly well attended. Michael Johnson was doing gigs in the Seattle area before the show and almost had to cancel because washed out roads were blocking him from driving south. There was great anxiety throughout Portland. People just weren't leaving their houses.

Returning to Nebraska from that near-fiasco, I headed east for concerts in Nashville, at the Bluebird; to Roanoke, Virginia; to a really memorable, packed show in Little Rock, Arkansas; and to other stops, including Memphis and St. Louis.

I always worked hard at trying to remember people's names I had met previously when I was on the road. I also used tactics to get folks to tell me their names when I drew a blank. The PA guy in Little Rock had done my sound a couple of times before and was very friendly and enthusiastic about my music. He also bought a couple of my CD's, and I gave him another couple in gratitude for his work.

I had been trying to finesse all evening the fact that I didn't remember his name. I did what I often do when I had forgotten people's name's I should know, when they bought a recording: I asked how to spell his name when I signed his CD.

He smiled and replied, "BOB. B-O-B." Boy, did I feel like a putz. So much for thinking I could wriggle my way out of that embarrassing situation. He didn't seem too upset, but I sure felt like a fool. Another lesson learned.

In March, I was beginning to feel again like that traveling salesman as I boarded the plane in Omaha bound for Portland and that year's Celtic festival at Kells. At least I had the musical company and friendship of Mark Moebeck, who again journeyed from St. Louis to join me.

It seemed I was spinning like a top. Right after I returned from Portland I would drive to western Nebraska for arts council concerts in North Platte and McCook. The next week I was on a plane to Toronto for a Folk Alliance board meeting and attendant performances. I can tell you that all this traveling was less romantic than it might sound.

I was needing to book more and more dates away from home

though, as the gig situation in Omaha itself was becoming dire. I was also very unhappy with the few shows I did have when I was back there. In April I did some concerts in the Chicago area, and in May I went west again, performing in Casper, Billings, Sheridan, Red Lodge, and again in Cody, Wyoming.

Rod Kennedy from the Kerrville Folk Festival had invited me to join the festival's 25th anniversary celebration in June. For that landmark, Rod had extended the festival duration to 25 days. (Some people would camp out in the Texas heat, monsoons and with the fire ants for that entire period!) He offered me a decent honorarium and seven nights of accommodations in the town located nine miles from the festival site to do a couple performances and tape some segments for my radio broadcast.

I was flattered to be invited, and looked forward to the event for many reasons – not all of them admirable ones.

For four years I had been having an increasingly torrid affair with a woman named Rebecca back in the Pacific Northwest. I had written the song "Weaver and the Loom" for her. She had come to visit me at many of the more far-flung gigs and was planning to fly to Texas for a rendezvous.

Ever since I had been doing extensive touring, I had wrestled with the temptations of women while on the road. Though I truly loved Michaela and Dylan, saying "no" wasn't easy for me. Not to pardon my behavior, but you were by yourself, pouring out your guts on stage, drinking in the applause and adulation. Then, you had to gather yourself up and retire in solitude if you were behaving in a responsible way towards your family.

I had occasional transgressions of infidelity through the years of my marriage to Michaela, but I had always sworn I would not fall in love with another woman. At the time, I forgave myself those faults and justified them with the knowledge that no man I ever knew who was traveling and performing extensively had been true to his marriage – the "boys will be boys defense." Feeble, I know.

Still, I realized my actions were wrong and felt terrible guilt

The Weaver and the Loom

about it. I would resolve to do better, and for long periods of time, I would indeed be faithful. Then I would slip again.

I did not want to lose my wife and son. Michaela had once found out about another of my indiscretions a few years before, and we had worked our way through it, but I could hardly expect her to endure that heartache again.

Then, I met Rebecca. She had a strange hold over me. I was not immediately in love with her, but she grew to be an obsession over a long period of time, fueled by romantic letters and enforced distance. She had been married for many years and had five mostly grown children, but by the mid 1990's she was in the process of getting divorced.

She had flown to Kerrville to spend time with me, as she had occasionally done at other festivals I had performed at. It was at Kerrville that year, however, that we agreed I would leave my home in Omaha and move to be with her in the Pacific Northwest. She had put the idea into my head previously, and it burrowed into my being like a bad virus.

It was a decision I struggled with all through that difficult summer. I went with my family to Grand Lake, Colorado, and to Wyoming, arguing with myself the entire time on one side of the fence or another. The truth is I was in love, or maybe lust – as I look back now I can't honestly say which it was, probably a little of both – and my vision was terribly clouded.

Hell, I'll just say it: I was nuts at the time and living out the classic male mid-life crisis scenario, though I'm sure I painted it in nobler terms at the time. As Michaela put it later, I was becoming a cliché of a dissatisfied older, privileged man – and she was right.

In August came the annual Festival at the Fort, and Richard Gilliland named the main stage for me, which was actually pretty embarrassing. The festival was again a great success despite that stage's name change.

Sometime that September of 1996, after having a few glasses of wine with Michaela at La Buvette, I told her I was going to leave my home and move to the Pacific Northwest. To that point, it was the worst night of my life. She had offered to come with me and try to live in Portland if I was that restless, but I rejected that option.

Yes, increasingly being unhappy with the provincialism of Omaha was part of it, and the great appeal of the part of the continent that I loved the best, the Oregon/Washington area, was another consideration. But I also wanted to be with Rebecca. I imagined her to be this bohemian artist and free spirit who was so in love with me, unlike my schoolteacher wife, who I had put into a little box of conventionality and dullness – neither of which was fair or accurate.

I had figured I would need to come back to Omaha frequently to work on the radio broadcast, so I would still see Dylan a lot – and hopefully get him out to the Northwest often, too.

I was a fool. Michaela had never done anything but love me and stand by me, and Dylan didn't deserve to have his father move almost 2,000 miles away. This inane decision also minimized the love and acceptance of the Reilly family, her parents and brothers and sisters, who had been the only real family I had ever known. I was quite removed, if still friendly, with my parents and sister, but the Reilly's had always treated me like their own son or sibling.

Looking back, I don't know how I could have so hurt the ones who had been abundantly kind and supportive to me. But that is indeed what I did. Time moves on and heals some wounds, but looking back on it all it is difficult to forgive myself for inflicting such pain on those I loved the most.

As perverse as it sounds now, I think in the back of my mind I realized none of this was going to end well. But I felt pushed forward as if by a dark, malevolent wind. After a river of tears, bitter words and sad goodbyes, I would load up my van and head west. I arranged to be back by Thanksgiving to pick up more of my belongings, to see Dylan and to work on the radio broadcast.

The Weaver and the Loom

THIS ILL-CONCEIVED CHANGE of life meant I was going to be driving and flying that distance between Eastern Nebraska and the West Coast even more frequently than I had been making that journey in recent years. The radio program had become a vital source of income for me, and I was determined to keep it going. Plus it meant I could spend time with Dylan frequently as I made that pilgrimage back to Omaha.

There is not much to be proud of in those jumbled times, but I did keep the radio program on the air, with the invaluable help of my engineer Steve O'Gorman. Through the income I derived from that, I was able to meet my child support obligations and pay my expenses. I knew a number of other performers who had reneged on their responsibilities to their children. But though it was always a stretch, I never missed a support payment.

Mothers who read this would say you should not get credit for something you are obligated to do, but given my profession, it was never easy. Still, with hard work, incessant driving and travel, and good luck, I was able to keep it all together. I was extremely fortunate that KVNO was willing to keep its commitment to me and continue to pay me, even though I had moved away from Omaha. As long as I got the work done and folks continued to enjoy it and listen, KVNO didn't care where I lived.

The rest of that fateful autumn, I would do concerts in Wyoming, then head back to the Pacific Northwest, where I would do the first of many shows I would perform over the years for the Seattle Folklore Society. Then off again to dates in Montana and Nebraska to spend a few weeks around Thanksgiving. There were notable shows along the way in Chadron and Hastings, Nebraska, for the arts council, as well as other Midwest performances in Rockford, Milwaukee and other Chicago area venues, before the long, snowy drive back to Eatonville, Washington, where I was living with Rebecca.

Eatonville lies in the shadow of magnificent Mt. Rainier, about 25 miles from Tacoma and 35 miles from Seattle. It is a small town of about 2,000 folks, with a history of being a timber town. It seemed a romantic, idyllic spot to put down roots, though it never turned out to be the welcome, comfortable nest I supposed.

I had many clues to Rebecca's bipolar nature in our brief times together, the previous few years, but I had chosen to ignore them. It seems I had also forgotten the hard truth I encountered when I was with Jennifer, my first wife: no matter how much you love someone, you can never fully remedy another's heartache, pain and history.

It was all too apparent within a short time of me being in Eatonville that our relationship was not going to be quite the bliss that I had imagined. I had lived there less than a month when I wrote to Michaela and asked if she wanted to try to patch things up and get together again. To her credit, this time she gently but firmly, declined.

I was on my own to try to sort things out as best I could. I resolved to make the best of the situation and determinably play out this chapter in my life.

Michaela flew Dylan out to visit me at Christmastime, an extremely generous gesture considering her hurt and anger at our break up. I took him up to Mt. Rainier National Park, and we spent a lovely holiday together, especially given the pain of our parting. Rebecca was kind to him, as well she should have been. She was a great cook, and he always immensely enjoyed her culinary skills.

DYLAN FLEW HOME shortly after the New Year in 1997, and a couple of weeks later I would follow him to Nebraska, to work on the syndicated radio program and spend time with him. I was beginning to fill in dates in the Northwest with numerous gigs at Kells in Portland and other area venues.

Portland was just about two and a half hours from Eatonville. On many days, with traffic, it was nearly as quick to get there as it was to drive the much shorter distance to Seattle. Tom Bryson and Claire Levine in the Rose City, as well as Don Younger, were always happy to have me as their houseguest, which was again so fortuitous. Without their loving generosity, I don't know how I would have made it. They all non-judgmentally nurtured me both in body and spirit, and patiently listened to my relational tales of woe.

YUKON JOURNEY, 45 BELOW

AS FEBRUARY BEGAN, IT WAS TIME TO EMBARK on what was probably the most interesting, challenging, and colorful journey of my life: the tour that Frank Howes had booked to do the concert dates in Alaska, the Yukon, northern British Columbia and the Northwest Territories.

Rebecca had purchased air tickets to join me on this foray and brought large numbers of her handmade woolen goods to sell at the shows. She would also sell CDs for Mark and me. The trip would begin by heading the wrong direction – driving to the east, over snowy and slick White Pass in the Cascades to Yakima, Washington. I performed at a folk society concert in a history museum there, surrounded by covered wagons and other pioneer paraphernalia, an appropriate setting for my songs about American history.

After that enjoyable show in front of a good house, it was south over Satus Pass to I-84, then west into Portland for Winterfolk XIV. Anne Hills consented to come in from Pennsylvania to be the headliner that year. Her entire performing career had been built around willingness to use her music to make a positive difference in the world. She did a marvelous set, even though much of it wound up being totally acoustic when the PA malfunctioned. She handled that misfortune with grace and humor, and with her crystalline contralto she reached all 500 or so folks there in an endearingly intimate fashion.

I knew Anne well, of course, from other productions of mine I had involved her in. She was personally disapproving of the marital decision I had made but was still courteous to myself and Rebecca at the event and the party afterwards. I loved her for that. In addition to her great talent, Anne has always been the very embodiment of tolerance and respect.

THE NEXT DAY, Rebecca and I were on the Alaska Airlines shuttle to Seattle, where we would meet up with Mark Moebeck, coming in from St. Louis. From there it was on to the first show, which was to take place in Ketchikan – gateway to Alaska.

In Ketchikan we were quartered at a couple's very comfortable home that Frank, the promoter, knew. The town was going through a difficult time as the pulp mill, the major employer in the community, was in the process of closing. The radio station sponsored the event, and I remember the turnout being good.

These concerts were all a strange concoction put together by this eccentric fellow, Frank Howes. His modus operandi was to partner with a local non-profit organization – the Boy Scouts, the Rotary Club, whoever – and agree to split in half the proceeds of the event. He would arrange for the hall, print tickets and spend a week or two in each of the concert locations, living in a cheap motel and selling the $15 tickets in advance. The fees and expenses for the musicians came out of his half of the take, and the remainder of the money was his profit.

He would typically sell out the shows months in advance, and most times he didn't really care how many people actually showed up because he had already made his money. I must say he did honor every provision of my contract, not only paying myself and Mark, but also picking up all meals and any other incidentals as well as transportation costs.

That first stop in Ketchikan gave us all an idea of how things would actually work on the trip. He had intimated he would pick up Rebecca's meals too, but that did not prove to be the case – which right away made her quite testy. When I offered to pick up her meals, she just bit my head off. It was a preview of some uncomfortable moments to come.

Incidentally, that famous "bridge to nowhere" that the Republicans have always cited as a prime example of government waste? That was to be built in Ketchikan, from the mainland to the airport, and it was hardly a bridge to nowhere. Without it, if your plane came in too late, you were stuck sleeping in the little Quonset hut-like air terminal, on the floor, until the ferry began to run across the water again early the next morning.

Twice on the tour we very nearly suffered that fate. Flights in Alaska frequently run late because of weather conditions. Some Republican operative obviously seized on this red herring of an issue and used it effectively.

Their claim, however, was totally bogus: Ask anyone in Southeast Alaska, except for that lamebrain female ex-governor.

From Ketchikan we flew north to Wrangell, close to the mind-boggling Tongass National Forest – the largest remaining stand of virgin timber in North America. Wrangell was a rougher, less appealing town than Ketchikan. It was a working community of loggers and fishermen, many of whom lived way out on the edge of polite society. Alaska has always been known for the individuals trying to escape the law, or taxes, or an ex-wife, and it always seemed to me a lot of those folks had chosen Wrangell as their home and hideout. Frank put us all up in a perfectly lovely bed and breakfast.

I would have made more money on that trip had I not said I wanted Mark to be my opening act. It was fine with Frank if I had just done the shows solo. Having Mark along, however,

Yukon Journey, 45 Below

was the wisest move I could have made. (It was nice to know I still could make some of those, after all of my recent terrible decisions.) He helped diffuse Rebecca's unpredictable temper shifts, he always made me laugh, and we invariably had a fun time together. And because Rebecca and I were a couple, he more often than not was stuck keeping Frank company, which was not the easiest of duties.

Frank Howes was one of the most unique and odd characters I have ever met. He had not answered my letters or phone calls about this tour when I had written him back about it after our initial encounter in Sitka, because he only checked his mail once every few months and did not actually have a phone. He had no fixed address, save a storage space in Whitehorse, Yukon, and that mailing address in Las Vegas.

He didn't have a credit card, so when we needed to rent a car we used my card, and he would reimburse me in cash. I am quite sure he had not paid taxes, on either side of the border, for decades. These concerts were his living, and he also promoted shows in other towns in the western U.S., like Lander and Cody, Wyoming. But the annual Alaska/Yukon/NW Territories tour was his big score for the year.

Frank would pay for the meals in restaurants for myself and Mark, but he did not believe in tipping. So, Mark and I would slip back into every establishment we ate in after the bill was paid, apologize, and leave an appropriate gratuity. Frank's rationale was his life would cost him 10 percent more if he tipped, since he ate out all the time, and he said he simply could not afford it. All our efforts to convince him otherwise were futile.

In any case, after Wrangell, our little entourage flew on to Sitka, which would be the high water mark of that entire trip. The concert was scheduled for Valentines Day, 1997, at beautiful Centennial Hall. The hall has stunning panoramic floor to ceiling views behind the stage looking out over the expansive northern Pacific Ocean. As with most of Frank's shows, it was sold out. But for this one, all the folks who had bought the tickets actually attended.

It was a wonderful affair, set up in cabaret seating with Valentine's Day favors decorating the tables. Our accommodations were at a local Ramada Inn style hotel, and we had a little party afterwards with lots of good red wine. Romance – or something – was in the air, and it seemed all was well.

The next day we were to fly to Juneau, where we would have a couple of days off before our concert. Juneau is only a 20-minute flight from Sitka, on one of the ubiquitous Alaska Airlines 737's that carry cargo and passengers throughout the 49th state. It was destined to take a whole lot longer than that to get there.

Juneau has the distinct challenge for a pilot of being surrounded by precipitous mountain ranges and having a dog-leg on the final approach pattern before landing, narrowly avoiding some rather prominent peaks. The airport has more sophisticated radar now, but back in 1997 the airport was inaccessible at least a quarter of the year due to fog, impaired visibility and ever-changing weather conditions – plus a large glacier close to the airport, which creates its own problems.

This day we made two unsuccessful approaches into Juneau, then diverted north to the small Tlingit Native American town of Yakutat. We lingered on the runway in Yakutat, waiting for word that the weather in Juneau had improved. Finally, we were told to board the plane again. We were going to the aircraft's final destination (I always thought that sounded a little ominous), Anchorage, where we would catch a different Alaska airlines jet south and attempt the Juneau approach again.

All our baggage was transferred to the flight heading south from Anchorage. We four people, between our three guitars, personal luggage, boxes of CD's and Rebecca's wool products for sale, had around 20 bags. They didn't charge by piece for luggage on Alaska Airlines in those days, and you could bring as many articles for free as you liked, within reason, as long as none of them were oversize or overweight.

The new flight from Anchorage departed for Juneau, and we were hopeful this time it would be able to land.

After two harrowing approaches, however (even the stewardesses were fearful and nauseous), the pilot gave it up and headed for the final destination of that flight – all the way back to Seattle!

When we finally arrived in Seattle, frustrated and disheveled, Frank secured a hotel room with two queen beds for us, to sleep a few hours before we returned to Sea-Tac Airport and headed north again. He had made an early morning reservation for us on the Alaska Airlines milk run north, stopping again at Ketchikan, Wrangell, and Petersburg on its way to Juneau.

No one was very happy about lugging those 20 bags into that little room and sleeping those few hours in two queen sized beds. (At least I had Rebecca in mine; Mark had Frank in his.) We were back at Sea-Tac bright and early, if not bushy-tailed.

As this 737 stopped at the smaller towns on the way north, Frank would get updates from the pilot on the situation in Juneau. It wasn't looking good. He made the command decision, since it was his role to make sure we made the concert in Juneau the next day, that we would get off the plane in Petersburg and catch the Alaskan state ferry to Juneau – about an eight-hour overnight ride.

So, we disembarked at Petersburg, and Alaska Airlines consented to take all of our luggage off that flight for us. Unfortunately, none of it was on that flight! Alaska Airlines had mistakenly put all 20 bags on the other flight to Juneau that morning, the nonstop direct plane.

Well, this was a real problem. Frank still figured we should get off and take the ferry to Juneau and hope the direct flight was able to land and that our bags would be there when we arrived. Mark and I were cracking jokes this whole time, while Rebecca was seething. Still, there was nothing to be done about it but roll with

"I WOULDN'T COUNT ON IT" — CONFESSIONS OF AN UNLIKELY FOLKSINGER

the adversity. Frank got Rebecca and me a separate sleeping room on the ferry, and poor Mark once again had to share with Frank.

We arrived by water in Juneau the next morning and took a taxi to the airport, which is outside of town a few miles. There we discovered that our flight, without our luggage, had actually been able to land the evening before. The direct flight, with our 20 bags had not been able to land and had been diverted again to Anchorage.

This was certainly Alaska Airlines' fault, at least the fact that the bags had not been on the same aircraft we had been traveling on. After an animated, vigorous discussion Frank and I had with an airline employee, who told us he was an ex-Marine and who was not easily cowed, we each were issued a voucher for $200 to purchase toiletries, clothes, rent instruments for the show, etc.

Mark and I went to a thrift shop close to the airport to get clothes, and the MUZAK on the sound system in the place was playing my song, "The Boardwalk at Skagway." We both laughed heartily at the improbability of hearing that tune (Mark had sung harmony on the recording, back in Nebraska) as we shopped for cast-off clothing in Juneau, Alaska. (Regional Northwest MUZAK was playing many of the tunes from "River and the Road" at that time – one of the side benefits of being on an established record label.)

By now it was already the day of the show, and Frank arranged for us to bunk at a comfortable bed and breakfast just across the Douglas Channel, by the name of the Blueberry Inn. The proprietors were a kind, sociable couple whose hospitality and good cheer helped take our minds off our travails. If our bags did not arrive within the next day or two, we were in a real jam, as from there we were headed into the Canadian driving part of the tour.

Somehow the plane from Anchorage, with our excessive amount of luggage, got into the Juneau airport later that day, and the bags were delivered to the bed and breakfast just an hour or so before we left for the concert hall. Thus ended the longest 20-minute journey (the quoted flight time from Sitka to Juneau) of my life. I recall a woman on that flight who had just been going to the dentist in Juneau. In the end, she would have flown more than 4,000 miles to get her filling replaced!

AFTER THE CONCERT in Juneau, we made a successful flight roundtrip back to charming little Petersburg for a performance, then had another ferry trip scheduled to get to Skagway for a show. No way you could put us and all those bags on a small plane, the only kind of aircraft that flew into Skagway, even if it was able to land there.

The Alaska ferry system runs an abbreviated schedule through the winter, and the lone option was again an overnight journey. Rebecca was not pleased about this, but she was even less happy when she found out that this small boat was filled with high school wrestling teams on their way to a tournament in Skagway. Loud, rambunctious, excited teenagers filled every chair and most of the floor space, too.

The weather was icy outside, which caused the captain to seal the doors to the deck, often done in bad weather so folks wouldn't slip and fall off the ferry. You couldn't even get fresh air, and the atmosphere got kind of close in the enclosed space. Nothing like the fragrance of large groups of adolescent boys.

Again, Mark and I thought it was all kind of funny, weird and a great adventure. But Rebecca didn't see it that way. She sat in the cafeteria angry all night and refused to speak to me. She looked mad enough to spit. I kept my distance.

When we arrived at Skagway, my friends Don and Sue from the Skagway Bed and Breakfast were there to meet us, to help with our bags and give us a ride from the dock to their inn. Rebecca still refused to talk and didn't come out of her room until the next day. I did a concert in Skagway for Barbra Kallen again that night (this was an extra performance, apart from Frank's scheduled tour shows), and Frank had arranged for Mark to ferry over to Haines to do a concert on his own.

It all worked out like clockwork, and Mark was back early the next day. Mark had a fine time in Haines with a good crowd, and I was happy he had the opportunity to do a full show solo.

The next part of the tour was by car. Frank had bought a rusted, dented, roughly used 1992 Plymouth Voyager that had seen better days for $2,000. This was to be the vehicle we took into the northern wilderness. If I had given it too much thought, I would have been terrified. Refusing to worry (I was too busy trying to keep peace with Rebecca), we stuffed the menagerie of bags and ourselves into the Plymouth mini-van and drove up the highway that followed the 1897 White Pass route, headed for the Canadian border.

FRANK HAD TAKEN care of all the necessary paperwork and fees (this was before you needed your passport to cross into Canada, as you do now). The border guard was a fellow I knew pretty well who lived in Skagway and had seen me perform numerous times, and we had shared a couple of beers together on occasion, too. Such were the connections you make in a small community.

In those pre-9/11 days, the border crossing at Fraser wasn't staffed overnight. You were simply instructed to get out of your car so they could take a picture of you and your vehicle. It was easy for the powers that be to nab you in the little village of Skagway, where the only ways out were by single engine plane, ferry or small boat, if, when they checked the records the following morning, they found out they didn't want you in the U.S.

However, we were crossing the border in the other direction, toward Whitehorse into Canada. Though the papers Frank had filed took care of the immigration issues and work permits, they sure didn't cover all that luggage we had jammed in that van. Somehow the Canadian customs folks let us through, without even a question about all those bags. I still can't figure out exactly how we got away with that.

It was fortunately a mild winter, as we covered enormous distances in that rattle-trap jalopy. Whitehorse, Yukon, was a balmy 32 degrees when we performed there. We had a decent turnout for that show and an enthusiastic crowd. From Whitehorse, it was a long drive up the Alaska Highway to Fort Nelson, British Columbia, the next concert stop.

We were to pass through Watson Lake, where the famous "signpost forest" was located. Just outside of town, we had a flat tire – close enough that we were able to push the mini-van into the service station. The attendant tried to talk Frank into buying a new tire or at the very least putting on the spare rather than just repairing the worn tire that we were running on.

Frank didn't want to buy a new tire, and his reply regarding the spare was, "Just fix the tire that's on there – the spare's no damn good either. It's actually more bald than the one on the wheel." It made me wonder what I had gotten us all into. I volunteered to buy a new tire myself for the van, but Frank adamantly declined. Away the circus went again rolling towards the arctic circle, in a dented steel box with bad rubber.

Frank was driving, but he had the unnerving manner of turning the steering wheel hard to the right when he talked to whoever was sitting in the back seat. He also alternatively drove either very slowly or crazily fast. Both these behaviors nearly brought us to catastrophe on that early leg of the trip.

Mark and I staged a mutiny after we got to Fort Nelson and insisted that either I drive from now on or he would not have an act to present. He caved in to our demands, and at least the rest of the driving journey was more sanely accomplished.

Fort Nelson, British Columbia, was just a wide spot on the

road, but it was an important junction – and very surprisingly it had a lovely, 300-seat theatre. We had a successful show there before heading due north to the most remote stop on the tour – Yellowknife, Northwest Territories.

You turned left and headed straight north from Fort Nelson up the Liard Highway – more than 200 miles of dirt and gravel road with no towns, no houses, no telephone poles, no signs of civilization whatsoever. Eventually, you arrived at what was referred to as a checkpoint. It was a place to fuel up, get a bite to eat, do laundry if you needed to, and see another living human being. Turns out winter was the preferred time to travel many of the northern roads like the Liard Highway. The dirt and loose gravel made the visibility terrible in summer, what with all the dust. The snow and cold kept the dust down and made an easier go of it.

And boy, it was getting colder, all right. It had dropped down to below zero at Fort Nelson, and as we headed north from there, you could feel the temperature quickly retreating even further. That Plymouth's defroster just barely kept the condensation on the windows from totally freezing up. I drove looking through a couple of partially defrosted spots in the windshield. In the rear seat, Mark and Rebecca drew panicked-looking cartoon characters in the frost on the windows.

After a turn back again to the east, you hit the cutoff for Yellowknife. The only road access is a maintained ice bridge across the wide, imposing McKenzie River, almost three miles across. All kinds of vehicles, including 18-wheeler semi-trucks with trailers, use this road, which is Yellowknife's principal access to the outside world.

During breakup of the ice in the spring (June), nothing gets through that can't be flown there. A ferry runs throughout the summer.

Driving across that ice bridge was an odd, unsettling experience. You come up over a low berm and then you're out on the river, on a two-lane course slightly elevated and well marked. We stopped in the middle, and everyone took photographs of each other framed against the open, white desolation. After you cross, it is another hour or so to Yellowknife.

For such a remote place, Yellowknife was a surprisingly active, artistic and progressive community. It is the capital of the Northwest Territories and thus has lots of government agencies headquartered there. Frank had us lodged in the nicest hotel in the central part of town, The Yellowknife Inn, which was connected via sky bridges to most of the other shops and buildings in the district. Mark, Rebecca, and I went to a very rowdy bar the evening we arrived and had an entertaining time.

It was cold, all right. Every downtown parking space had a corresponding electrical outlet for the block heater on your car or truck to plug into.

Yellowknife had a large Inuit population, and many indigenous crafts and souvenirs for sale. I am sure Mark actually spent as much as he made on that trip on trinkets to take home to St. Louis. He really enjoyed picking up souvenirs for the folks back home. We all realized it was a once-in-a-lifetime trip to places we would probably never see again.

Yellowknife had an interesting museum, and many alternative artist types had decided this was the place to really get away from it all. Some of them bought houseboats and lived on the Great Slave Lake, which Yellowknife was on the shore of, so they wouldn't have to pay any municipal taxes. All in all, it was a fascinating, happening town, far different from what I expected.

The next evening's concert was at St. Patrick's Catholic School gymnasium. Gyms are notoriously difficult venues to get decent sound in, but the local PA company did a pretty good job, as I recall. A huge banner above the stage read, "St. Patrick's High School Welcomes Tom May," and the crowd numbered over 350 receptive folks – a significant percentage of the population. It was 45 degrees below zero that night, but after the show I drove us all north of town, to an abandoned gold mine to see a magnificent display of the northern lights.

It was still 45 degrees below zero, according to the bank next door, when we loaded all the bags into the van the next morning for the 17-hour drive through the Northwest Territories and Alberta back down to Dawson Creek, British Columbia.

We all liked Dawson Creek a lot. It was a vibrant town with a decent restaurant and some lively pubs. The night we arrived there, after that long drive through bands of heavy snow, we went to a tavern that had an enthusiastic Elvis impersonator doing his show. We were tired, but glad to be there, safe in a place that was a little warmer than Yellowknife, listening to an Elvis/Canadian version of "Suspicious Eyes."

Mark did have the unfortunate experience of once again having to share a room with Frank (at least he had his own bed this time), as Frank's preferred hotel was all booked up. When Mark left that morning, he found two soiled white socks by the door, left by a previous resident of the room – not exactly the kind of souvenirs he had been collecting. You also had to make a long leap up to get into the room he was in, as the steps had broken off, and the floor was all cracked and uneven from the continual freezing-thawing cycles. Ah, the glamour of the traveling concert musician's life.

After the next evening's show in Dawson Creek, we had a relatively short drive up the Alaska Highway to Fort St. John, which had an absolute gem of a theatre. That was another very successful night on the tour, with 270 people in attendance and a lot of CDs sold.

Things were beginning to wind down now. There was a somewhat funky concert at an Elk's Club in Chetwynd, British Columbia, on a snowy Sunday. I recall the town's sign, with a disgruntled looking grizzly bear pictured on it. He probably had lunch at the local diner, which was marginal at best. At least the Elks Club had a separate bar, and they were only too glad to slide

Mark and myself a couple of toddies. Frank didn't drink, but Mark and I whooped it up amidst the shows and the travel, and we generally had a great adventure.

From Chetwynd, it was a long, scenic drive through the mountains of Northwest British Columbia to the town of Kitimat, an old aluminum smelting town close to the coastline. After some car trouble (it was a miracle we didn't have more) that we got repaired in Terrace, British Columbia, we did our final concert of the tour in that hillside village, cozily nestled into the wild landscape. We departed Terrace immediately after the show and drove through the night to make it to Prince Rupert in time for the morning ferry back to Ketchikan,.

There was a great sense of relief on that ferry. The suspect Plymouth Voyager Van had survived the journey without having its transmission or suspension fail in some place where we could have frozen to death. Rebecca had calmed down considerably from earlier in the tour, and the last part of it was relatively peaceful. Mark and I had a great run of shows in places we would almost certainly never see again. And last but not least, we had cash in our pockets from the gigs.

We all said goodbye to Frank and flew home to Seattle via Portland. Mark came with us to Eatonville for a couple days before he returned to St. Louis. I don't know what Frank ever did with that Plymouth van. I sincerely doubt it successfully negotiated another tour.

Rebecca had a friend, Elizabeth, who I had previously met at Rebecca's house. Elizabeth had partnered up with the fellow she was living with at the time at one of our parties, and they were residing in a rough cabin close to Mt. Rainier. She decided to throw a welcome home gathering for us all after the tour, and it was a very pleasant evening with good food and wine. I mention it because of the part Elizabeth would come to play in my life a few years later.

I always thought I should write a song about that tour, but

it took me years to get it the way I wanted it. Finally, 10 years later, in 2007, I was able to relate the journey in a song form that worked. It is set to an upbeat, sprightly melody that fits the way I remember that memorable trip.

> **Yukon Journey, 45 Below**
>
> It was the best of times in the coldest place that I have even been
> I met the agent there in Sitka, as I had a drink with friends
> then in Cody, Wyoming, as the evening's show was done
> he walked in and asked if I'd play a tour in the land of the midnight sun
>
> Well, we started out in Ketchikan, got to Wrangell hours late
> Petersburg and Sitka, hard against Fairweather Straits
> the rough-hewn streets of Juneau, then on to Skagway town
> crossed the borderline at Frazier, we were Whitehorse, Yukon bound
>
> Chorus
>
> We crossed the McKenzie River on an ice bridge three miles wide
> seemed like 20 minutes 'til we reached the other side
> 18 wheelers rumblin' cross an ice bridge topped with snow
> it was a winter Yukon Journey, 45 below, 45 below
>
> We turned left at old Fort Nelson to head up the Liard road
> 200 miles of snow and dirt has seen many's the heavy load
> better watch for moose and caribou round every blind man's curve
> or in this rusty Plymouth voyager we might get what we deserve
>
> It's been a funny crooked highway, this old performing life
> taken me to New York City, and now to Yellowknife
> where the cars plug in at night, and the winter sun don't shine
> where the houseboats sit on nine-month ice just beyond the city line.
>
> Repeat chorus
>
> Then Chetwynd, Kitimat, Dawson Creek and on to Fort St. John

playing concert halls and Elks clubs in the outback of beyond
stuck two nights where frost heaves had buckled the motel floor
dirty white socks from a previous tenant still sit beside the door

Terrace B.C. is a lovely town, an Athens of the north
finish the show and take off late and drive for all we're worth
to catch the Rupert ferry, then back to Ketchikan
to wait for a late Alaska flight to right back where we began

Repeat chorus

There are places in this traveling life I hope never to go again
warmer climes where the breezes are kind, where I have made
    good friends
but I long for the sight of the northern lights where the arctic lands
    begin
where the only sound is sundown and the whine of the chilly winds

Repeat chorus

Tom May copyright 2007 Blue Vignette ASCAP
From the album "Blue Roads, Red Wine"

RETURNING TO THE Northwest, I was only in Eatonville briefly before it was time for another four day St. Patrick's festival at Kells, then a long drive back to Nebraska so I could be there when Dylan had his spring break. Omaha consisted of the usual round of very long days recording radio programs and pleasant evenings with my son.

    The second week I was back in the heartland, I had another festival booked that had been confirmed before I had made the big break from the Midwest. Dave Para and Kathy Barton were extraordinarily talented, traditionally-influenced singers and musicians from Boonville, Missouri, (close to Columbia), who had been hosting an annual festival for the previous few years.

"I WOULDN'T COUNT ON IT" — CONFESSIONS OF AN UNLIKELY FOLKSINGER

The event still continues and is called The Big Muddy Festival. They had booked me to do a set for the Saturday night show that early April, appearing just before the headline act, John Hartford.

John Hartford was one of my personal heroes in folk/country music. Originally from St. Louis, he had moved to Nashville as a young man and had great success. He was a renowned banjo and guitar picker and authored the song "Gentle on my Mind," a huge hit for Glen Campbell. He would go on to be a frequent feature on the Smothers Brothers TV show and then a regular on Glen Campbell's own series.

In the early 70's he had shaken up the good old boy network in Nashville with his "Steam Powered Aeroplane" album, still one of the most delightfully quirky and entertaining records ever made. He continued to perform and record relentlessly through the decades, but by 1997 he had been diagnosed with inoperable cancer.

His tour bus was parked outside of the pre-Civil War era hall the festival took place in, and it was an honor to be co-billed with him that night. My set was very well received, and I was even asked to do a couple of extra songs. Then, John Hartford took the stage with his trio. He looked thin and worn but still did a terrific show.

We had a chance to visit for a good while after he was done. Performing on that stage before him and meeting him remains one of my highlights in this crazy music business.

He died not long after that, and I felt very privileged to have shared a little time with him on that Missouri April evening.

From Boonville I made a big circle around the Midwest, performing in Chicago at the Old Town School, The Front Porch in Valparaiso, Indiana, the Lake County Folk Club, then down to St. Louis for Mark Moebeck's album release concert at the Sheldon Gallery. Back to Chicago for a couple of more concerts, then I once again made that tedious I-80 drive for the umpteenth time back to Omaha.

I had a good chance to spend more time with Dylan before

Yukon Journey, 45 Below

Rebecca flew to Omaha to join me for the return trip west, during which I would be stopping along the way to do a number of concerts. It was country she had never seen before, and I hoped she would love it as much as I did.

The first part of the journey is that interminable stretch on I-80 across the Platte River Valley of Nebraska, then up over the Rockies to Cheyenne and Laramie, Wyoming. From Laramie you cross over the continental divide many times until you arrive in the Rock Springs-Green River part of the state. We paused here to visit with Chris and Sue, neither of whom had met Rebecca previously. As true friends always are, they were welcoming and hospitable, despite the overwhelming evidence of my imprudence – if not outright insanity!

After a show in Kemmerer, Wyoming, at a history museum, we headed toward a truly unusual gig I had booked awhile back in the tiny town of Pony, Montana. Pony is located south of Interstate 90, over the continental divide from Butte. You pass through the town of Whitehall heading south, then you notice a small sign pointing up into the Tobacco Root Mountains that just says "Pony." It is a barely two-lane macadam path that dead ends at the tiny village.

The concert was sponsored by a fellow who had heard me in Butte, enjoyed the music and wanted to bring me to his town. He lived in a bottle house, constructed of recycled bottles with their bottoms turned towards the elements, then chinked to keep the drafts out. It was certainly an odd-looking structure. We stayed with him and his wife, as there was no hotel in town. I don't what the population of Pony was, but it certainly wasn't more than 50 to 75 people. There was a bank that had closed during the great depression and which had never opened its doors since that troubled time. You could look in the window and see the musty old furniture and even some ancient documents still sitting on the dust-covered desks.

The concert was in the school gym. I set up my PA and

"I WOULDN'T COUNT ON IT" — CONFESSIONS OF AN UNLIKELY FOLKSINGER

wondered who in the world was going to attend. By show time, there must have been close to 100 adults and kids in attendance – more than lived in the town.

It was a resounding success, and I felt good after the night's efforts.

Rebecca, however, was not happy about the accommodations. We slept in the only real bedroom in that house, but it was poorly sequestered by a waist high thin sheet used as a door. When we tried to go to sleep, the promoter and his brother were having a loud argument in the living room, only a few steps away.

I will say the argument was entertaining and interesting. A gold mining outfit had come to town, promising prosperity and jobs, and the opinions for and against had split the little community right down the middle. The company eventually got its permits and the town's approval and started mining. After less than a year, the mining outfit deserted the site in the dead of night – leaving the groundwater hopelessly polluted by arsenic, a by-product of the process. It was an old story in the west: exploitation, then environmental collapse. The brothers had been on diametrically opposite sides of the issue, and both were still angry.

Rebecca was less entertained than I by this garrulous discussion, and we were out of there at daybreak on virtually no sleep. It was May 1, and the snow was starting to fall. By the time we crested Bozeman Pass in my van, Maggie, there was a foot of the white stuff on the road. We had to make it all the way back to Lander, Wyoming, that night for one of those well-paying "extra" concerts that Frank Howes had booked for me.

Fortunately the roads improved as we dropped in elevation, and we made it all the way to Lander in time and without incident. I did concerts in Red Lodge, Montana, and another Frank Howes-promoted show in Cody, Wyoming, the fateful town where Frank had encountered me again and booked me for the Alaska/Yukon tour. Then, a concert in scenic Moose, Wyoming, and up to Ketchum, Idaho.

The Ketchum show was sparsely attended but memorable from a lodging standpoint. The guys who owned the bakery where the shows took place had access to a huge, mansion-like structure set in a plush subdivision outside of town. I had heard there was big money in that area, but I had no idea just how much. Down the street Arnold Schwarzenegger had one of his vacation homes. The entire subdivision was littered with unconscionable palaces, all used just a few times a year.

The place we were in had a full sized authentic Indian war canoe hanging in the entry way – that's how big that ridiculous foyer was. The house had been built by one of the premier "bundlers" (fundraisers) for Ronald Reagan. We slept in a massive circular bed next to a panel that, with just a touch, controlled the temperature, music, lights and security system.

The structure must have been 10,000 square feet. Dirty money had erected these walls, and I felt uncomfortable even being there. It was a restless night's sleep. I couldn't help but think of the patrons of Sisters of the Road Cafe back in Portland, who just looked for a simple meal and a dry place out of the weather. This kind of wealth was beyond obscene.

Breathing a sigh of relief as I left that disturbing place, we headed for the cool evergreen forests of Western Washington.

I TRIED TO settle into my new life in Eatonville. Despite my ability to communicate and make friends along the way in my travels, somehow I never made a close connection in that town, despite my efforts. Thank goodness for the regular Northwest gigs I had in places like Portland and Pacific City.

However, all of that was put on the back burner as Dylan made his first long trip to the Northwest to spend much of the summer with me. He arrived in mid-June, and I was so looking forward to showing him more of this incredible corner of the continent. We toured the Olympic Peninsula together and went to Mt. St. Helens, Mt. Rainier and the Columbia River Valley, among many other beauty spots.

I had been asked to perform concerts for the centennial of the Klondike Gold Rush, and I bought airline tickets for Dylan to join me up north. He and I had a grand time, flying into Juneau, then taking a small plane to Skagway for a concert, then hopping the historic steam train most of the way to Whitehorse, Yukon, (we had to transfer to buses for the remaining distance) where I also would also do a concert. At that time of year, the sun never set outside of our Whitehorse hotel.

A dear friend back in Skagway, Debbie Sanders, arranged to take us out on her partner's boat for a tour of the spectacular Lynn Canal while we were there. Dylan got to see a humpback whale in the wild, and I was pleased to have shared those experiences with him.

After Dylan departed in mid-July, I performed at an arts center in Newport, Oregon, then began to do a monthly, Sunday-through-Thursday gig at Kells in Portland, a very welcome bit of regular income.

Sometime that summer while I was back in the Northwest, David Rea came down and visited us in Eatonville for a weekend. He had divorced, remarried and moved to Bainbridge Island, Washington, just a short ferry ride from Seattle. The relocation cost him dearly, as he left behind his three children and had a very vengeful ex-wife on his trail.

He would tell the story of how Ian Tyson had given him the desk where Ian had written the classic song, "Summer Wages." When David got divorced and left California, his ex cut it up with a power saw and paneled her bathroom with it. David never was one to accomplish his separations gracefully (not that I was much better).

In any case, he drove down in his ancient Volvo wagon (at

that time I didn't realize he was actually as blind as a bat, even when he was sober), and we drank copious amounts of whisky and wine and picked and sang what must have been dozens of songs together. David was a chain smoker, and Rebecca's studio reeked of American Spirit cigarette exhaust for days after he departed.

That weekend, David and I made plans, reminisced and told tall tales until the wee hours each morning. It was the beginning of a sometimes-partnership with him that would last for years.

In August, I cheerfully got out of Eatonville and made the long trek to Grand Lake, Colorado, where Dylan would once again stay with me in cabin #42 while I performed at the lodge. Dylan and I would do a lot of hiking, and Avery and Cliff would join me for the gigs there, just like old times.

Avery had moved to a comfortable home in Denver, and Dylan and I spent a night with him there before continuing on to Garden City, Kansas, where I would perform at the Tumbleweed Festival for Willis Pracht. My old pal, autoharpist Bryan Bowers, was there, too, and it was an enjoyable time. I recall Dylan playing a few songs on acoustic bass with the ensemble at the closing party, which made me so proud.

After putting Dylan back on the plane to Omaha in Denver, it was time to point Maggie back in the direction of the Pacific Northwest. I had spent a memorable summer with my son, and it seemed things would work out – at least in that important part of my life.

For the last few years of the 20th century, my life devolved into a kind of predictable chaos. I would be in Omaha every autumn, early winter and springtime, where I would feverishly work on radio broadcasts and spend time with Dylan. Christmas time he would spend in the Northwest with Rebecca and me.

"I WOULDN'T COUNT ON IT" — CONFESSIONS OF AN UNLIKELY FOLKSINGER

Beginning with his high school sophomore summer, he would work at the Grand Lake Lodge summers, where I would visit him when I did my annual stint there. Reed James at the lodge was extremely kind in letting him start as a busboy at that age. Normally Reed hired no one who was not at least in college.

I had given Dylan a beginner's electric bass and amp, and like myself, the music he learned, wrote and played wound up being his ticket to ride through the rough waters of adolescence. He still loved folk music, but his interests were much more ecumenical than mine had been.

He immersed himself in funk and soul and began to listen, avidly collect and work diligently on perfecting that dynamic "slap" style on bass. I recall him going to a George Clinton concert in south Omaha, and that may have been where his lifelong passion for those evocative, hard-driving sounds really took root.

He was a kind enough kid, though, that he didn't mind accompanying his father on acoustic music, which he would do from his high school years right up to the present day.

In October of 1997, I was due to be back in Nebraska, and Dylan had noticed there would be a Gordon Lightfoot concert while I was in town. Michaela had met and hobnobbed with Gord, but Dylan had never had the opportunity – and Lightfoot's music remained an important part of his life. So, I called Gord's road manager, Barry Harvey, who had good tickets waiting for us at the door the night of the show.

Barry and Gord both knew I was going to be there with my son and put aside some very special time after the show for us to socialize in a private setting with Lightfoot. Dylan was thrilled. And I will never forget that Gordon Lightfoot told Dylan that night, "Your dad is a great musician and writer." It meant the world to me, and probably is one of the reasons I just won't countenance anyone saying unkind things about Lightfoot.

Gordon didn't have to say that – it was very sweet and gracious of him. Particularly at that time, when Dylan was going through adolescence and I was often so far away, it was an important moment for both Dylan and me.

TOM AND DYLAN MAY

MY PERFORMING ROUTINE was more or less that I would play at and manage Winterfolk in Portland and The Festival at the Fort in Omaha each year. I did five nights a month at Kells and would do even more nights when they opened a new outlet in Corvallis, Oregon. There was also the annual bacchanal of the St. Patrick's Irish Festival, which would run three to six days annually and was a much needed financial score for me.

I signed on for a Coffeyville, Kansas, tour every other year and played lots of stops between the Pacific Northwest and Nebraska. The radio program production was always a high priority, as that is how I was covering my basic monthly expenses. There were also the Horse Brass dates, Pacific City weekends and numerous assorted one-night-stand concerts. All of this combined to create what was a modest, but solid, living in the music business for me.

"I WOULDN'T COUNT ON IT" — CONFESSIONS OF AN UNLIKELY FOLKSINGER

In addition, I consistently seemed to be able to drum up some unusual, fun add-ons. In 1997, I did the Ozark Folk Festival in Eureka Springs, Arkansas. My old friend Iris Dement, who I had met when she recorded River City Folk, helped set that up for me. Every year I would do at least a couple well-paying concerts in Rock Springs and Green River, Wyoming, thanks to Chris Kennedy – who was more frequently joining me for those shows, when possible.

I also remember doing a show at the hoity-toity Omaha Press Club in the late 90's, too. Michaela was kind enough to not only bring Dylan but to stay for the presentation. Dylan joined me for a couple of songs on bass that night, which made her very proud.

In 1998, at Winterfolk X, Utah Phillips made the commitment to be my headliner each year as long as he was able to still travel and perform. He was such a strong supporter of social justice issues and Sisters of the Road Café – what an inspiration that man was. David Rea also played at Winterfolk for the first time that year and brought the house down with his songs, most of them from his tasteful "Brass Ring" album. We also made the first Winterfolk CD from that show. Utah had an incredible

WINTERFOLK 14

presence and following in Portland, and we would easily sell out each year's concert while he was on the bill.

Also in 1998, I began doing a gathering I would appear at for 17 years, the Juan De Fuca Music Festival in picturesque Port Angeles, Washington, just across the Strait of Juan De Fuca from Victoria, British Columbia.

I would do a couple of concert sets and be the primary emcee on the mainstage for the four-day event.

In addition to the wonderful folks I met who enjoyed my music there, I heard so many terrific acts that I would not have heard otherwise, some of whom became great friends: Tiller's Folly, a Celtic based kick-ass ensemble from B.C., featuring the evocative songs of Bruce Coughlin; Harry Manx, proponent of the Indian instrument the mohan veena, who combined blues with the musical traditions of India; and Hanz Araki, the eloquent flute virtuoso, with his dynamic take on Scottish, Irish and Breton tunes.

I also met the loveable bear of a man Rob Folsom, who was in charge of sound and would become very important to many of my later ventures. These are just a few of my solid musical compadres I first encountered at that gathering.

My relationship with Rebecca continued to flounder along. She could be the sweetest, kindest, most loving soul, then without warning become a hurtful, insulting, vindictive hellion. You never knew which personality was going to greet you at the door. I frequently reminded myself, "You left Omaha and Michaela and Dylan for this?"

In late summer of 1998 I had booked myself a lucrative series of appearances at the largest Alaska State Fair,

which took place in Palmer, north of Anchorage. When I had to fly out of Sea-Tac (between Tacoma and Seattle, just about 40 minutes from Eatonville) I generally obtained a room at the airport Super 8 and left my van in the complimentary, seven-day parking space that came with the room.

"I WOULDN'T COUNT ON IT" — CONFESSIONS OF AN UNLIKELY FOLKSINGER

On that journey, I paused and performed what was my second concert in the little fishing town of Cordova, Alaska. Cordova gets 240 annual inches of rainfall a year – more than 20 feet of rain, if you can imagine that – but oddly enough, both times I played there it was gloriously sunny. They should have me perform there more often!

I had an extra day before I continued on to Anchorage, and my generous hosts lent me their rusted-out old Subaru wagon to drive the 40 miles through the Copper River Basin, one of the greatest fish estuaries in the world, spawning grounds for millions of salmon, to the Child's Glacier. That feature is a large, high wall of ice, sitting just across the Chitina River, which regularly calved massive pieces of ancient ice into the water. What a spectacle that was.

Right on the side of the road, on the way back to the airport in Cordova, just a few miles outside of town I saw a massive grizzly bear fishing for his share of those salmon. The driver that the promoters had pick me up had been talking about his own fishing in the area and mentioned that he never dipped a hook in the rivers there without carrying a shotgun with him.

He told me a story of a college student on a summer job in Southeast Alaska counting fish, who was dropped off at his destination by a gregarious pilot. The inquisitive student asked the pilot if he should worry about bears. The pilot handed him a pistol and said, "Here, take this with you." The student asked, "Will this pistol bring down a grizzly bear?" The pilot replied, "Hell, no, but you can shoot yourself in the head with it if a brown bear attacks you." What a comforting thought.

Continuing on north from Cordova, the fair hospitality staff picked me up at the Anchorage airport and delivered me to my motel in Palmer, about 50 miles north.

The Alaska State Fair there was a big event. The agricultural component of the fair featured some of the gigantic vegetables from the nearby Matanuska Valley, where they receive almost 24 hours of sun during the long summer days. Also on the entertainment roster was Three Dog Night, who I had loved as a kid;

The Red Elvis's, a campy group from Russia doing a Presley routine; and Hobo Jim from Homer, Alaska, a fine songwriter I had met in Maryland, when McShane Glover had been working for us both doing some of our bookings.

My name was pretty well known in the north country, since River City Folk aired almost everywhere in Alaska in those days, and the crowds were enthusiastic and receptive to my songs. I also spent a fun night at a rough bar in Eagle River, where Hobo Jim and some of his local pals were doing a gig. I played a few tunes with them, drank too much and had an uproarious evening.

At the close of the fair, I flew back to Sea-Tac, picked up my van, and headed for Eatonville for one night. I planned to leave, driving, for the Festival at the Fort in Omaha the next day. I felt fine when I hit I-5 south of the airport, heading to Rebecca's, but by the time I arrived there I was feeling queasy. By 9 o'clock that night, I was flat on my back in bed with a high fever. There was a nasty, notorious strain of virus going around that late summer that actually became known as the Alaska/Yukon flu, and boy, did I have it. I couldn't even walk.

Rebecca never had an abundance of compassion for folks who were sick in her space, and this instance was no exception. I simply could not leave, however, the next day, since I could barely get out of bed without becoming dizzy. I had terrible congestion, fever, and chills – it turns out lots of people died from that bug.

I didn't know that at the time, however – not that it would have made any difference. I had to get to Omaha, except now I had only two days to drive the almost 2,000 miles to Nebraska. I departed at my usual leaving time of 5 AM after downing as much medicine as I thought I could handle and still drive.

I would frequently listen to books on tape as I traversed those long stretches. I had an appropriately named tome to listen to on that journey titled, 'The Agony and the Ecstasy," by Irving Stone, about the great artist Michelangelo, and I must say that helped. (The moral of that book is – don't work for Catholic Popes.)

I was so sick. As I reached the Blue Mountains of Oregon on I-84 outside Pendleton, a car next to me was honking and waving. It was my pal Terry Prohaska and his wife, Neva, heading to Pocatello, Idaho. I pulled over to the next rest area, as did they, and normally it would have been a fun chance meeting. I warned them, however, to keep their distance and continue down the road. I didn't want anyone getting this plague from me.

The first and only rest on that journey was at Chris Kennedy's house in Rock Springs, Wyoming. I had phoned him and told him not to stay awake for me, as I would be so late – and that he shouldn't come near me. Bless his heart, he got out of bed when I arrived after that 17-hour trek and welcomed me, from a safe distance across the room. I'll never forget that he had placed a book on the nightstand of the guest room, appropriately titled, "Bad Trips," in honor of that painful excursion I was right in the middle of.

I slept fitfully, took another handful of decongestion pills, and started for Omaha before the sun came up. Fortunately I had no car trouble. Maggie was as faithful as ever. I finally arrived in Omaha, where the festival put me up in one of the old barracks buildings with multiple bedrooms on Officers Row. I had arranged for David Rea to be flown in from the Northwest for the festival, too, and he was already ensconced in the house when I got there.

By this time I was starting to feel a bit better, and we went out and had some wine at the Old Market. Most importantly, I had survived the journey without passing out and running off the highway.

Bill Staines from New Hampshire was also one of my guests at that year's festival. The song Bill had been so influenced by that had really put him on the road as a young musician was Gordon Lightfoot's "Early Morning Rain," which Bill first heard Gord play at the Newport Folk Festival in 1965. David Rea was the very first guitarist to ever pick that song with Gordon shortly after it had been written. Of course, I had my own relationship with Lightfoot – and we decided all three of us would perform it, together, at the festival.

It was a special moment. By the time that evening of the event came around, I felt almost human again. I was lucky I hadn't killed myself, making that stressful drive while I was so ill.

AFTER STOPPING ON the way back to the Pacific Northwest for a few more concerts, I arrived home in Eatonville. Rebecca had consented to join me for another Napa Valley Folk Festival, and I rented a nice car for us to drive there. Napa was as much of a joy as it had always been for me. Steve O'Gorman came out from Omaha again to help me tape episodes for the program, and I chauffeured him to some winery destinations. We also rendezvoused with Clete Baker in San Francisco, who was attending a conference there.

That would unfortunately be the last Napa Valley Folk Festival I would be a part of. The folks who ran it disbanded it, but some of them would eventually move north and re-form a similar folk festival in Sisters, Oregon.

In the meantime, I had all those Kells gigs to do, and David Rea and I were performing more together, too.

Artichoke music in Portland had established a new, intimate concert hall space, and David and I would play there in November of 1998. We would also pick and sing together in Olympia, Washington; Salem, Oregon; and a number of other towns that year.

When David and I were in Salem, I had a terrible problem with one of my microphones. A fellow by the name of Don "Fuzzy" Purcell was at the gig, and he offered to go home and bring back some other equipment that might alleviate the difficulties we were having. Fuzzy was a fine musician, and he also had a stocked wine cellar and a passion for good red vino. We shared that predilection – and eventually dozens of gigs and great bottles of wine, in a friendship that lasted until Fuzzy's passing in 2019.

IN THE SPRING of 1999, I enlisted David to help me host a festival in the emerging tourist and wine growing country of Walla Walla, Washington. It took place at Merchant's Cafe there on the Main St., and I would co-ordinate that event for the next couple years. Walla Walla has now evolved into a high-falutin', upscale destination. I think I preferred the way it was back then.

That summer, before Dylan's senior year in high school, he and I made lots of plans for a memorable season. After he was done working at the lodge in Grand Lake, he would join me for a couple of concerts, then we would join Tom Bryson and Claire Levine on a sailboat trip we had concocted. Dylan accompanied me on bass at the prestigious Newport Performing Arts Center in Oregon, then we turned Maggie toward Anacortes, Washington. where we would board the chartered yacht for what I hoped would be a fond memory for him.

The trip was mostly grand. We played a lot of music together and the weather was fine, though we had a bit of a problem when one of the female crew members (no one I knew well) left a rope unsecured on the bow. It fell into the water and wrapped itself around the prop, bending the shaft. Tom Bryson had to pilot the boat into busy Friday Harbor totally under sail power. It may have been easy for George Vancouver back in the 18th century, but it was quite stressful for us.

A couple of weeks later I was back in the Cornhusker State for the Nebraska State Fair. Dylan was also back for his senior year. The manager of the fair, who had underwritten the successful gig there for me a few years before, decided he wanted me to be "the face and voice of the Nebraska State Fair." To that end, he offered me a 10-day contract at a generous fee per day, plus lodging and other expenses to perform and help out with emcee duties. Essentially, I would perform one set a day, do public service announcements, and open the evening concerts for the "stars" they had booked.

Aside from a rather large, welcome sum of money that this would garner me, I was tickled about doing those opening acts. I played my songs before Willie Nelson and a number of other country music luminaries who were well known at that time. Willie himself took the time to chat with me for a while after my set, before he went on, and he told me how much he enjoyed my songs. Very cool.

My final duty at the state fair I was to open the concert for the country superstars Alabama, who they tell me had 41 radio hits, many of them hitting number 1. This show began at 2 PM on Labor Day and was to take place in the Devaney sports arena. The concert was sold out, and 12,000 people would be there.

Dylan was spending the last few days of the fair with me, and I had asked him to join me on bass for that set. The size of the audience didn't faze me: Once you got beyond a thousand folks or so, it was all the same. You just had to determine to do your best and let the chips fall where they may. There was a problem, however.

Alabama was using what was a new innovation at that time, called "in the ear monitors." Instead of having big speakers in front of you, controlled by a separate engineer and mixing board, they just had little ear pieces. Those ear pieces were controlled by a much smaller board, specifically for their use. Alabama's crew had moved out the Devaney Center regular monitor amps, speakers, and mixing board, with the result that I would have no monitor while I performed.

Having no monitors in a house concert or a quiet hall is rarely a problem.

"I WOULDN'T COUNT ON IT" — CONFESSIONS OF AN UNLIKELY FOLKSINGER

Having no monitors in a sports arena, where the speakers are hanging off to your side 30 feet over your head, is another matter altogether.

Dylan didn't mind not performing with me (since he wouldn't have been able to hear himself or me, either one) but I was a little nervous on how this was going to work. The echo, or bounce back, from those curved rear walls of the arena was just horrendous when I did my short sound check. It was like hearing five of me – talk about cruel and unusual punishment – all slightly out of sync, and trying to decide which one I was going to concentrate on.

When the show started, however, I just focused and sang with what my fingers were feeling on the fretboard of my guitar. The echo was still terribly distracting, but the huge audience seemed to respond well and enjoy my set.

Listening to Alabama after I was done was also a little odd though, as they were the first group I had really seen that extensively used pre-programmed, time-fired band tracks to augment their sound. In other words, there are three singers and five musicians on stage, but you are often hearing five or six voices and 10 or more instruments in the mix. Give me the honesty, mistakes and the spontaneity that Willie Nelson's band displayed any day.

Hey, but the Nebraska State Fair was over, and I got my check. With a portion of it, I was able to pay off my van and also retire my child support obligations to Michaela early. Life was good.

♪ ♪ ♪ ♪ ♪ ♪

THE PERSON WHO had been responsible for the money that was pumped into each edition of The Festival at the Fort, Richard Gilliland, was going to be leaving his job. It looked like the 1999 version of this festival would be the final chapter. John McCutcheon and Christine Lavin were brought in from out of town, and of course I performed, too, but attendance was probably the smallest the event had ever attracted.

The booking of those headliners had primarily been done for that year's festival by others, since I now lived in Washington, but the musicians they engaged were fine artists. I just think that without the enthusiasm and drive of Richard Gilliland behind the event, and with me not living there to push things along, it just was not the same. It was a good run while it lasted, but 1999 was indeed the last year of that particular festival.

Before returning to the Pacific Northwest, I did concerts in Little Rock and Fayetteville, Arkansas, and an intimate house concert with Chris Kennedy and his dear friend, poet and photographer Mike Hensley, in Rock Springs, Wyoming.

Mike and his wife Marcia hosted Chris, Sue and me for many bucolic evenings at their ranch, where we would share a delicious meal Marcia had put together. And we would marvel at the ranchland nighttime sky afterwards as we sat around a campfire trading songs, stories and poems. There I had the clearest, most remarkable sight of the Milky Way Galaxy I have ever viewed.

Their ranch was close to "The Parting of the Ways," where wagon trains would separate and head either for Oregon or California. Mike drove us there in his jeep, to that spot where so many dreams branched off and continued. It was unmarked, only demarcated by the ancient wagon ruts of those pioneers – a very evocative spot, made even more so by its primitive state.

Back in Washington, I immediately had another festival to manage, close to Mt. Rainier. An acquaintance, John Sparrow, had asked me to organize, book and run an event that came to be called The Lark at the Mountain. That first year was actually the most successful, and we drew over 600 people on a perfect autumn day. It took place in a glorious meadow outside of Ashford, with incomparable views of Mt. Rainier and the Cascades.

"I WOULDN'T COUNT ON IT" — CONFESSIONS OF AN UNLIKELY FOLKSINGER

AS I KNEW had to happen sooner or later, there had been a change of management at KVNO in Omaha. Station manager Howard Lowe had moved on. The new folks in charge decided they wanted to use the NPPAG grant that had funded River City Folk for other purposes. I figured my run with the radio program was almost over.

But then, as always seems to happen with that broadcast, circumstances and friends came to the fore and made it possible to continue. Steve Robinson, from the Nebraska Public Radio network, was interested in taking over the syndicated part of River City Folk and doing the fundraising for it. My dear friend Clete Baker now had his own studio in a section of American Gramaphone's complex up in north Omaha and was open and amenable to doing the recording and production there. Back to Omaha I returned again for a whirlwind series of meetings that would secure River City Folk's future – at least for another year.

It was agreed that the first hour, the local and statewide record show, would be discontinued, but the syndicated one-hour broadcast would continue to be produced. Nebraska Public Radio would bear all the attendant costs, syndication fees and promotion, and Clete and I would be paid fairly for our time and expenses. Steve O'Gorman from KVNO continued to independently record many of those programs at Clete's Studio B, and of course, Steve was paid for his time, too.

So, somehow the broadcast had survived. A part of me was relieved about not doing the first local/statewide record hour, as it was so very time and material intensive. I would typically spend much of my tour of duty in Omaha working from 6 AM to 4 PM every day on those programs before we moved onto recording the live guest/nationally syndicated program in the evenings. This new arrangement would make my life much easier, though I would still be traveling back to Nebraska frequently.

Yukon Journey, 45 Below

THE LAST COUPLE of months before the millennium, I kept busy with the usual gigs, plus a memorable concert at historic Timberline Lodge at Mt. Hood, Oregon. John Tullis was the organizer of this series, and David Rea and I would share the spotlight that evening with Kate Power and Steve Einhorn, dear friends and talented musicians/songwriters who owned Artichoke Music in Portland. Also joining us was a couple I had judged and been so impressed by at the songwriting competition at the Napa Valley Folk Festival– Dave Carter and Tracy Grammer.

When I listened to Dave and Tracy's music at Napa, I knew I was hearing something special. The blend of their voices on Dave's stunningly literate, sometimes whimsical, occasionally genius songs was amazing. With his guitar and Tracy's fiddle and occasional guitar, they created a sound that was traditionally based, yet also unique and modern. I have never heard anything quite like Dave and Tracy, and their recordings still rank among my favorites in this genre.

It was kind of funny though. At the Timberline show, each duo would take turns playing a song and talking about their music throughout the concert. Listening quietly was never one of David Rea's great gifts. Dave and Tracy were singing one of Dave Carter's timeless songs – I think it was "When I Go." And David Rea started plinking along in the background on his guitar. If looks could kill, David would have been stone dead on the floor from the look Tracy cast his way. David was also usually not very swift on picking up hints, but he sure got that one. He remained quiet and respectful the rest of the night when it was not our turn to play.

I loved that cantankerous old cuss David Rea, though. We did a couple more memorable concerts together that winter, including well-attended shows at St. John's Pub in Portland and Traditions, in Olympia, Washington. Most of the time, however, I continued to perform solo.

"I WOULDN'T COUNT ON IT" — CONFESSIONS OF AN UNLIKELY FOLKSINGER

WITH MY ENCOURAGEMENT, Dylan was seriously considering attending university at Evergreen State in Olympia. Michaela was open to it, and since I was a resident of Washington, he could get in-state tuition. He and his mom resolved to come out and take a look at the campus. I picked them up at the airport and drove them to Olympia. Dylan would eventually get his bachelor's degree from that progressive institution, and his mother and I remain very proud of him.

THE WORDS UPON THE WIRE

THE NEW DECADE STARTED MUCH THE SAME AS in recent years, with a flight to Omaha to record guests for River City Folk. I would always try to book some concerts back that way too, to make those couple of weeks more productive and lucrative. That year, I did a concert at an Omaha church and another at a library in Ames, Iowa, where Dylan joined me on bass for the entire show.

When I returned to the Northwest, I started another tradition that still carries on – an annual house concert at Tom Bryson's and Claire Levine's home, where I most often stayed when I was working in Portland during those years. It is hard to put into words the gratitude I feel towards those gracious friends, but no doubt their kindness and counsel through the years to me saved me from making even worse choices than I did – and kept me warm and safe during a period of great turmoil in my life.

There was an exceptional Winterfolk program that year, featuring both Utah Phillips and Rosalie Sorrels, then the annual St. Patrick's festival at Kells. Kells was putting me and Mark in luxury rooms at the downtown Embassy Suites these days, just a block from the event, and we reveled in "the kind of accommodations we would like to become accustomed to."

"I WOULDN'T COUNT ON IT" — CONFESSIONS OF AN UNLIKELY FOLKSINGER

I HAD BIG plans for the springtime before Dylan graduated from high school. I had booked a concert tour for David Rea and myself back in our old stomping grounds of Ontario, Canada, with the caveat that Dylan would join us on bass for the shows. I wanted him to see where his father started out and to have the experience of performing on a real tour.

Unfortunately, Gordon Lightfoot would not be home in Toronto at that time, so we could not connect there with him. However, Gord was to be in Lincoln City, Oregon, doing a show the night before our tour began. So I put David, his wife Barbara, and his business manager, Kathleen, into Maggie the van, and away we went. It was a good concert, and we had a lengthy visit afterwards with Gordon at the restaurant next door to the casino where he had performed. Kathleen took a smiling photograph of David, Gord and me that night, which I treasure.

It was pouring rain as we headed back over the coast range to Portland late that evening. I had just a few hours of sleep on Kathleen's couch, and then I was off to catch the flight. David was taking a different airline that went through Victoria, British Columbia, and would meet us at the Toronto airport.

Dylan flew to St. Louis, where he met our friends Mark and Judy Moebeck during his layover at the airport. I was connecting there, where I would hopefully rendezvous with Dylan and we would fly together to Canada. Everything went just as planned, surprisingly enough. In Toronto we cleared customs and immigration and figured we would have to wait quite a while for David to hook up with us. Amazingly, just as we walked by the Air Canada arrival immigration point, the sliding doors open, and out he comes.

In Toronto we all bunked with my old pal Peter Mathieson and his sweetheart Theresa, who had a comfortable home in the very desirable "Beaches" section of the city. I engaged a rental car for the duration of the week to get to the gigs. Peter and Theresa could not have been more hospitable. Unfortunately, Theresa took it a little too far when she showed David where her prized single malt scotch collection was and invited him to help himself. That precious aged whiskey was not long for this world.

Our first concert was at the Tranzac Club in Toronto, for a longtime organization called "The Flying Cloud Folk Club." I rented Dylan a bass and an amp for the shows, and we had a day or so to rehearse with David before that first gig. The performance was a mixture of my songs, David's songs and some well-known "Canadiana," such as the David Whiffen piece, "More often than not."

That first show was brilliant. Paul Mills, the famous Canadian Broadcasting Corporation producer who had been responsible for much of Stan Roger's success, was there and was very complimentary, as was my dear friend from Elora, Ontario, Earl Chamberlain. Dylan was an avid Stan Rogers fan and was thrilled to meet Paul Mills. Peter and Theresa also attended of course, and other old pals and folkies made it a very respectable crowd. We all played well and received a couple of encore requests.

TOM, GORDON LIGHTFOOT, DAVID REA

"I WOULDN'T COUNT ON IT" — CONFESSIONS OF AN UNLIKELY FOLKSINGER

I was encouraged by this, because I had been somewhat worried by the volume of David's alcohol intake since we arrived in Canada. David was always a heavy drinker, but *most* times seemed to be able to keep it under control when he needed to.

That wasn't particularly true the rest of the week. At a concert in Barrie, he was a great embarrassment. After he tried to pick up the promoter's wife and then played very badly in the first set, I had to pull him aside and tell him that if he ever did that to me in the future I would never perform with him again. That seemed to get his attention, and the following gigs went more smoothly.

We completed the week with a successful show in Ottawa, though we wound up having to bed down on the promoter's floor afterward. It was almost impossible to sleep in the same room with David, with his snuffling, groaning and snoring. Dylan and I woke him up, and we departed before sunup, sneaking out of the place without waking up the resident.

Plans had been made to visit Ronnie Hawkins at his compound in Peterborough, Ontario. Ronnie Hawkins was a Canadian legend, originally from Arkansas, who put together the group that came to be known as The Band. The members, Robbie Robertson, Levon Helm, Garth Hudson, Rick Danko and Richard Manuel were renowned for not only their own songs, but also for their stellar backup of Bob Dylan. Hawkins had a big 60's hit with the song, "Who Do You Love?" He was also a longtime pal of Gordon Lightfoot, and I had met him briefly in the 1970's.

David Rea and Hawkins knew each other quite well, so that was our entree. Dylan was not only excited about meeting him but also about seeing his barn, which Beatle John Lennon had used as a backdrop for one of his album covers.

It was altogether a weird visit. After we arrived at the walled estate, we were escorted from the main house to a boathouse, where we were joined by one of Ronnie Hawkins' security guards. Some very bad jug wine was passed around, as were a few generously large joints of pot. David and I played some songs for Ronnie, who was not in particularly good health.

Hawkins did have some funny stories about Gordon, Ian and Sylvia, and other well-known northern artists. He complained about Lightfoot frequently staying with him and then not picking up his part of the phone bill in the old days, which Gord had evidently run up quite a bit. After that, Ronnie Hawkins began referring to him as "Gordon Tightfoot." Through all of this, Dylan was quiet, just taking it all in, What an experience for a teenager.

After we had been there for an hour or so, Ronnie says to David, "Why don't you stay around? I'll book a bunch of studio time, and you and I will make a series of records of old and new songs. I'll pay your expenses and for your picking, and we'll have a hell of a time and make some good music."

Now, this sounded like a bullshit offer to me if ever there was one. There were no specifics, no starting time, no set fee, no guarantee of when they would be done. Nothing. David was already in his cups, however, and it sounded good to him. So, after asking him three or four times if he was sure this is what he wanted to do, Dylan and I left him behind. All our booked shows were done at that point in the tour, so that was not a problem.

After spending a whole lot of time with David the previous few days, Dylan and I both felt as if we were now on holiday. We drove back to Toronto and spent a couple of more days in that great city before flying back across the border.

David would wind up not making a dime from Ronnie Hawkins' proposition, and while there he quickly went though all the money he had made on our tour. They never actually recorded anything together, though I wager a good deal of whisky disappeared. After a couple of weeks, David had to make a desperate call to his wife, Barbra, to ask her to scrounge up the money for his additional airfare to get back to Washington State. Needless to say, she was less than amused.

"I WOULDN'T COUNT ON IT" — CONFESSIONS OF AN UNLIKELY FOLKSINGER

I FLEW BACK to Nebraska with Dylan and rented a car to do a month of River City Folk tapings, along with concerts in Nebraska; Lexington, Kentucky; Illinois; and St. Louis. I had great fullness in my heart when Michaela welcomed me into what had been our home together for Dylan's high school graduation party. A couple of days later he graduated from Benson High School in Omaha.

Early the following morning I was on a plane to Portland to pick up my van that I had left at Kathleen's house. As soon as I got behind the steering wheel, I pointed the van toward Port Angeles, Washington, where I was to start my responsibilities at the annual Juan De Fuca Festival at 8 AM the next morning. It had been a journey of lots of music, laughter and some frustration, too – capped by the great joy of seeing my son launched on his next adventure.

I HAD BOOKED almost three full weeks of performing at the Grand Lake Lodge that summer and planned to be there from late June right through the 12th of July. Dylan by now had a waiter's job in the restaurant there and was starting to make some good money at it. Cliff and Avery joined me for a portion of those dates, and occasionally Dylan would play bass with me for a night, too.

On July 2, Michaela called the lodge, trying to reach me – there were no phones in the cabins, and most folks did not have cell phones back in those days. Fortunately, my pal Avery was walking by the front desk at just that moment and talked to Michaela.

My father, long ago retired, was a volunteer for Radio Talking Book in Omaha, reading books and newspapers for the blind on a special radio broadcast band. He had been returning books to the organization's office and had boarded the city bus, as he did most days of the week (he had stopped driving years ago). As he was heading back to his seat and before he could sit down, the bus driver abruptly hit the brakes, causing my father to fly through the air and hit his head on the bus's windscreen.

He had been taken to the hospital in extremely critical condition. Avery came and gave me the bad news. Dylan and I decided to leave for Omaha in my van before daybreak the next morning, hoping we could make it to the hospital while my father was still alive.

My mother had died in 1998 after a series of strokes, and my father had adapted much better than I thought he would to her death. He had done some traveling, even coming out to Roseburg, Oregon, to visit a long-lost brother who had been separated from him when he was a child. Despite his fragile health and many medical issues, he walked a couple of miles a day and generally enjoyed his volunteer work and his retirement.

Dylan and I crossed over the 12,000-foot-high Trail Ridge Road as the sun came up, heading for the plains of Nebraska. We drove straight to the hospital in Omaha, and arrived there about 5 PM. The medical staff explained to me that my father was only being kept alive by life support. He had no chance of surviving his injuries. Michaela was there, bless her heart, and her good sense, compassion and empathy was so invaluable at such an emotional time.

Despite the doctor's pronouncement, I could swear my father knew I was there when I squeezed his hand and talked to him. It was almost as if he had been waiting for us before he let go. I don't know if that was true, but that is how it seemed to me.

The life support was disconnected, and the nurse said it could take anywhere from minutes to days until he died. I was determined to stay with him and keep him company, talking to him and hopefully comforting him, whether he knew I was there or not. Michaela offered to take Dylan home with her, but much to

"I WOULDN'T COUNT ON IT" — CONFESSIONS OF AN UNLIKELY FOLKSINGER

his credit, and my pride, he decided to stay with my father and me until the end.

My father mercifully passed away in less than an hour after all the tubes and IV's were removed. Dylan and I both held his hands and cried together.

After a difficult experience with extremely jumbled finances after my mother died, my father had put everything in order in regard to his estate. I had a sister who was just one year younger than me who had been living with him at his house, but she was pretty well detached from life – her story is a sad one.

It was up to me to sort through all the details, including moving everything out of the house and putting it up for sale, finding her an apartment and moving her, and distributing the assets. I had a friend, Mick Shannon, who I had been staying with often when I needed to be in Omaha. He was a great help, referring me to an attorney, helping me sell that house, putting up with my presence in his house, and more.

It did require more trips to Omaha, in between gigs, to facilitate all of this. Through it all, Rebecca never offered to come with me or to help with any of the details. Since I seemed to be on my own anyway, why was I still in a partnership with this woman? I had plenty of time to mull it all over as I traversed the West repeatedly, by Chevy van and airplanes that July and August.

On one of those many trips across the western U.S. that emotional summer, I did another concert in Cody, Wyoming. After the show, I had one of those rare nights when I just couldn't sleep, as I thought about my father's life and my own decisions that needed to be made.

I was on the road well before dawn and headed south toward Chris Kennedy's house in Rock Springs. As I drove down vacant Wyoming Highway 125, there were a few sprinkles just before I got to the picturesque little town of Meteetse, Wyoming. Up in the sky I saw the most dazzling display of colors I have ever seen in all my travels, as the early morning sunlight was refracted by the moisture in the clouds. There were purples, a dozen shades of red, yellows and blues.

It was so very beautiful. I knew right then I was on the path I needed to be on, and that everything would turn out okay. That experience would eventually be the inspiration for the title song of my 14th album, "A Road Worth Driving Down," recorded in 2018.

♪ ♪ ♪ ♪ ♪

DYLAN WENT BACK to Grand Lake to finish off his season there, and I picked him up in late August and drove him back to Nebraska. After giving him a couple of days to pack his supplies for college, we headed Maggie back west to take him to his first year of college at Evergreen State University in Olympia. We stopped along the way, and I performed again at the Willow Tree Festival in Gordon, Nebraska – and Dylan joined me on stage.

It was very gratifying and a great pleasure to be able to transport my son to this new chapter in his life.

Along the way, I had decided it was time for me to turn a page in my life, too. I had resolved I would tell Rebecca I was moving away from her and Eatonville. I already had secured a small apartment in Vancouver, Washington, just over the Columbia River from Portland.

Dylan and I would be in Eatonville for a night. I would take him to school the next day and move him into the dorm and would return later that day and tell Rebecca of my plans. As you might imagine, the conversation did not go particularly well. I had a full van load of my possessions the next morning and headed off to start my new life in Vancouver.

I would jokingly refer to that apartment complex as "the methamphetamine arms," because some quite unsavory types lived and did business there. It fit my price range, however, and truth be told, no one ever bothered me.

"I WOULDN'T COUNT ON IT" — CONFESSIONS OF AN UNLIKELY FOLKSINGER

Before I really settled in, I had to return to the Mt. Rainier area to direct the second annual Lark at the Mountain Festival. I had written a $20,000 grant that was approved by the Pierce County Visitors Bureau for the festival and for a subsequent concert series. The bureau collected a tariff from local businesses and restaurants for such purposes.

That festival was, unfortunately, kind of a disaster. It started well, with David Rea and me doing a packed concert at the picturesque Paradise Lodge at Mt. Rainier. The other mini concerts at Longmire Lodge did okay too, featuring our old friend Elizabeth doing a kids' presentation and Curtis and Loretta from Minneapolis.

Then, the heavens opened with a deluge that was a remnant of a tropical typhoon. The penultimate day was supposed to be on an outside stage on the Sunday, but we had to move it inside to a grade school auditorium.

I had flown David Mallet in from Maine to be the headline act. Probably fewer than 30 people were in the audience for his set.

Despite having the front page of the Tacoma's newspaper entertainment section, it was a dismal turnout. The weather was just too terrible to expect people to drive up the mountain. So, that particular event did not last beyond that ill-fated year, though the other concerts I had included in the grant still took place.

I BEGAN TO make plans for my next album, which was slated to begin recoding in 2001. I was funding it by my father's kind stewardship in his bequest to me, and I would record it at Billy Oskay's Big Red Studio, which had just recently been completed. It was a carefully designed space, with an exquisite sounding Trident analogue mixing board that had come out of the famous Automat Recording Studio in San Francisco. (Ella Fitzgerald and

Stevie Wonder had albums recorded on that board, as well as dozens of other big names.)

Billy also had a splendid grand piano and an incomparable assortment of Neumann microphones – state of the art for the recording industry, then and now. Dave Carter and Tracy Grammer, who by now were the toast of the folk music world, would record their next album at Big Red in December. I would start on my new project immediately after them, in January.

Pal Clete Baker had agreed to come out from Omaha to produce and do the tracking for the album, and now it was up to me to gather some musicians to help fill out the sound. Fuzzy Purcell from Salem was quite willing to help by both performing and consulting on the project, and he suggested a bass player who would eventually come to do dozens of shows with me over many years. Fuzzy also provided pre-production help, recording reference versions of the songs we would be working on at Big Red.

I had planned on having my son, Dylan, play bass on a couple of the cuts, but I knew I needed a more experienced hand to tie down the rhythm and bottom on other songs. Besides, Dylan was pretty busy acclimating to his new life and studies in Olympia, which certainly was closer than Omaha had been, but still was a couple of hours from Portland. It was a lot to expect him to drive back and forth from the university more than once.

Fuzzy introduced me to a bass player who had been a friend of his for years by the name of Donny Wright. Donny had played in various sorts of bands for decades and was also a very gifted, intuitive harmony singer. We had a couple of rehearsals before the recording again, and I realized he was really an exceptional musician.

Coincidentally enough, Dave Carter and Tracy Grammar had recorded much of their first album with him on bass, and he was scheduled to play on the album they were doing at Big Red in December, too. For percussion, Donny suggested Carlton Jackson, who had a sensitive touch on the parts he eventually added to the album.

The stars seemed to be lining up for this venture. On fiddle I engaged Eddie Parente, an expressive player who I had first met in early 80's when he was playing with the famed Irish songstress Triona Ni Domhaill (of Bothy Band and solo renown) at McGurk's in St. Louis. More recently Eddie performed regularly with my old pal Peter Yeates, as well as doing regular concert tours in Russia.

I had always admired the virtuosity and versatility of Orville Johnson from Seattle. He had been a guest on River City Folk, and I was very taken with his prowess on the dobro, one of my favorite instruments. But that guy could play anything: banjo, guitar, mandolin, he was a master of them all. We came to an agreement, and he traveled to Portland to work on the project.

DAVID REA, AT 2001 RECORDING SESSION

David Rea also was dying to play lead guitar on the recording, and Avery flew out from Denver to add some piano for me in the studio and to be part of the endeavor – and also to drink some wine with me.

The aforementioned Elizabeth now lived in Vancouver and

was teaching school there. We had spent time together since we both had become unattached, and we shared some songs, too. She had an unusual, huskily textured contralto voice, and she had an uncanny aptitude for vocal harmony. I invited her to participate in the new venture, too.

My old friend Terry Prohaska agreed to add his hammer dulcimer to a couple of tracks and even offered to write a score for two recorders to add to one of the cuts. Elizabeth would play the second recorder: Terry knew her from the renaissance/old music community.

So, the stage was set, and the players were all anxious to get started. I picked up Clete from the airport, and we began working on the album eventually known as "Vested" on the 7th of January 2001.

Billy Oskay was well known for his engineer chops and also for his tasteful fiddle work with the group Nightnoise, which he founded in the 1980's – and which went on to tour the world. He is an extremely opinionated and personally invested engineer in projects he believes in, and it was difficult at first to get used to his relational style. Eventually, however, we grew to be close friends – and we created some beautiful musical portraits together.

I believe "Vested" is the most sonically pleasing album I ever did, as I mentioned earlier. Part of the credit for that has to be given to the special Studer microphone pre-amps we were able to borrow for the session through Billy's efforts. Those pre-amps, along with Billy's superb microphones and his expertise in placing and recording them, really make the vocal quality on "Vested" something special.

The songs were among the best I have ever written. "Trial by Fire" is a tribute to wildland firefighters, particularly those who worked the deadly fires in Montana and Colorado in 1949 and 1994. It is accented by the dramatic interplay of Fuzzy's lead guitar and Orville's dobro. As on most of the cuts on this album, Clete and Billy wrote the basic instrumental themes that would frame the lyrics.

"I WOULDN'T COUNT ON IT" — CONFESSIONS OF AN UNLIKELY FOLKSINGER

The songs were recorded "live on the floor" again, with myself playing guitar and singing, joined by bass and percussion together on the ensemble pieces. We overdubbed the vocal harmonies, fiddle, dobro and other touches later.

I have always been impatient in the studio, particularly with my own work. It was hard to adjust to a different pace, especially during the mix, which Billy approached in a very different, much more time-intensive way

than I had experienced before. Proof is in the pudding, though. The results were worth every minute and every penny.

Also, Billy charged you for the day, not by the hour. He would work many more than eight hours if you had the energy to keep up with him. I was very lucky to have Clete and Billy both on this effort to make sure I relaxed a little and curbed my inclination to rush things.

Another highlight on this CD is the interplay between dobro and fiddle on "Rose of the Riverwalk." We also added in a Cajun style squeezebox to give it a Tex-Mex feel. "Forever Lost and Found" was augmented by Elizabeth's expressive background vocals. On Gordon Lightfoot's "Shadows," the duet of recorders playing the musical parts Terry Prohaska wrote provide a completely different texture from anything else on the album.

I think the whole CD "Vested" still stands up well, even after almost 20 years. Fuzzy not only played guitar and mandolin on some cuts but also took a vacation from his job and helped with all of the tracking and mixing. Dylan did a fine job on the two songs he added bass to, and he enjoyed his first studio experience. Donny was workmanlike and superb, as I suspected he would be. This was the first project of many for which he would be the linchpin.

Dave Carter and Tracy Grammer passed my finished album along to their label – Signature Sounds, out of Northampton, Massachusetts. That label did give me an modest offer on it, but considering where I was in my life at that time, I resolved to just release it myself.

The night we finished mixing "Vested," Billy Oskay called a friend of his who lived not far away and procured for us all a bottle of 1983 French Margaux wine. Billy had really appreciated the fact that we had lots of wine at the studio and would enjoy it with the many friends who visited toward the end of each evening's sessions, when we were listening back to the day's efforts.

Drinking that Margaux was like having stars dancing on your tongue. It was a fabulous wine, one of the best I have ever tasted – and a fitting punctuation mark to a successful piece of work. I still have the empty bottle.

"Rose of the Riverwalk" from "Vested" continues to be a popular song with audiences and one that I rarely go through a night without performing. It was inspired by a couple of days in San Antonio, after the 1996 Kerrville Folk Festival, and was written in my head as I sat in the sauna of the downtown YMCA in Omaha, reflecting on that romantic Texas multi-cultural crossroads.

Rose of the Riverwalk

Chorus
Won't you be my rose of the Riverwalk, a Texas Fleur-de-lis
bring the margaritas in the moonlight, we'll have a Lone Star Jubilee
hear the big guitar bands a playin', Mariachi melodies
be my rose of the Riverwalk, remember how we used to be

There are lanterns hangin' by the bridges, brightly colored lights of
    red and blue
short skirts swayin' in the evening breeze reminding me of you
young people linger in the doorway, sweatin' as the sun goes down
deep in the heart of old San Antone there is romance to be found

Repeat chorus

There's an old man paintin' the Alamo, paintin' lizards and Kokopelli
    too

with a soft cotton shirt for the hot July, a sombrero to keep him
    cook
underneath a red umbrella, two lovers bid a fond goodbye
there is heat in the humid southern nights, there is passion in their
    eyes

Repeat chorus

There are barges floating down the rivers, diners with a glass of
    wine
a pretty senorita in a crimson dress from another place and time
a fiesta of light and color, flamenco dancin' in the city square
the lovin' sounds of the Spanish tongue sing that I need to bring
    you here

So won't you be my rose of the Riverwalk, a Texas Fleur-de-lis
bring the margaritas in the moonlight, we'll have a Lone Star
    Jubilee
hear the big guitar bands a playin', Mariachi melodies
be my rose of the Riverwalk, remember how we used to be
be my rose of the Riverwalk, bloom once more for me

Tom May copyright 1996 Blue Vignette, ASCAP

DURING THE PROJECT, Elizabeth and I had become lovers. I had permanently (or so I thought) split up with Rebecca over the holidays. I was running off a double dose of euphoria, heavy on the **dope**amine, after the rush of both a successful album completed and a new romantic affair. I didn't have the sense god gave a goat. I was jumping from one hot griddle onto a fresh bonfire.

Still, at that time it seemed all was well. After a trip to the Folk Alliance in Vancouver, B.C. in February and another sold out Winterfolk in Portland, I proposed marriage to Elizabeth. All

I can say in my defense is, it seemed like a good idea at the time. Much to both of our eventual regrets, she accepted.

Elizabeth was not a bad person in any way, shape or form. We simply did not mesh. We were both too used to being the boss, musically and otherwise, and that is not a recipe for a blissful relationship. I was doing my regular round of gigs, including Kells and other local destinations. In the spring I needed to go back to Omaha to record more radio programs and did concerts in Rock Springs; in Red Lodge, Montana; a week in Coffeyville; Minneapolis and other cultural meccas along the way.

The agreement with Nebraska Public Radio to underwrite River City Folk had only lasted a year, so I had figured the jig was up there. Clete Baker had resolved, however, that he still wanted to produce the show if I was on board too. Neither of us would continue to be paid for the production, though. For the first year we were on our own, I used some of the money my father had kindly left me to pay for musicians and for recording time in the Pacific Northwest.

That was not sustainable over the long term, of course. I had decided River City Folk was destined to be dead in the water, when a couple of miracles appeared in the form of Fuzzy Purcell and Dan Rhiger. I had met Dan up at Big Red, when Dan was building his own studio in Portland and Billy was sharing information and tips with him. Fuzzy, of course, I knew well from his previous work with me.

Billy Oskay at his beautiful Big Red Studio also underwrote a few River City Folk programs, but that recording space was his sole livelihood. I could hardly expect him to donate his time, talent and facilities on a regular basis.

Fuzzy had a "project studio" he would set up in his living room and adjoining room, and he competently recorded quite a number of shows for River City Folk there in Salem. It was awkward to intrude on his space, though, and he always had to take off work from his day job to make it happen, or we needed to record on weekends. That was problematic for me, as I was always performing on Fridays and Saturdays, frequently far away from Salem, Oregon.

Dan Rhiger had done a marvelous job of creating an intimate space in a building he had built from the ground up, to exacting specifications. I became acquainted with him and his wife, Rahmana, at folk events they played at, and they had come to hear me at Kells and other places. At that time his studio was being underutilized, and his wife strongly suggested to him that he take over production of River City Folk as a favor to the folk music community – and to keep busy. Little did he know what he was getting himself into.

I still record the program at Dan's Medicine Whistle Studio today, thanks to Dan's generosity of spirit and commitment to the soul of this music. I believe he would agree the arrangement has worked out well for both of us, as well as for the performers we have helped and featured. I have also done all I could to try to turn Dan and Rahmana on to gigs. They are fine multi-talented writers, singers and musicians. The venues who feature them are the lucky ones here.

Dan is one of the nicest, most talented guys I know, and the program would not still be going without him, or without the ongoing efforts of my partner Clete Baker back in Omaha, who still edits, masters and posts every broadcast. Clete, Dan, Fuzzy Purcell and Billy Oskay felt as I do – that this music is important, that it deserves to be heard, and that it's a privilege to record and produce it. I get a lot of the credit, because I am heard on air and it's originally my baby, but it would not exist without those folks.

I MOVED IN with Elizabeth in June of that year, but it was obvious there were conflicts. We saw a counselor that she had been consulting with, who after a few sessions said, "You two can't get married. You have way too many issues you haven't worked out."

So, we did what people our age should have been smart enough not to do: We got married anyway, despite her observations, sure that holy matrimony would solve our problems. Before we followed through on those nuptials, we went to a family reunion of hers in Hawaii, my first trip there, and to Grand Lake, Colorado, where she joined me on stage, along with Chris Kennedy, and with Cliff or Dylan on bass.

"Vested" was released in October of 2001, and it received terrific reviews as well as substantial airplay throughout the U.S. on public radio – my most significant recording success to date.

In November, the Horse Brass Pub in Portland celebrated its 25th anniversary. I put together a slate of performers for my dear friend Don Younger on the Sunday during the festivities and coordinated the music. It was quite the blowout. Don had brewer friends he had known for decades custom make a custom beer for each day of the 10-day celebration.

One of the simple, enduring pleasures of my daily life since I had moved to the Pacific Northwest was to frequently stop in at the Horse Brass in mid-afternoon and catch Don there, as he was generally gone by evening. He and I would sample the latest and greatest beers and converse, argue and deport ourselves in a garrulous manner.

Don Younger was actually the opposite of clannish. Typically his best friend in the pub that day was someone he had just met, who had walked into the

WITH DON YOUNGER AT HORSE BRASS PUB, 1997

"I WOULDN'T COUNT ON IT" — CONFESSIONS OF AN UNLIKELY FOLKSINGER

Horse Brass for the first time. This was one of his more endearing traits, along with his undue fascination with women, although he was a lifelong bachelor. Many a stranger had the opportunity to be schooled and entertained by this unusual looking character, with his shoulder-length long hair, white beard, and a constant lit cigarette in his mouth. If you were lucky enough to meet and chat with Don Younger, you would never forget him.

THE REST OF that year I was working through my regular set of engagements, when I was invited to perform at the 2002 Winter Olympics which took place in and around Salt Lake City, Utah. I had met folks who lived close to Salt Lake in Heber City, Utah, and had done a number of performances they had arranged for me through the years. They put me in touch with the powers that be in the Olympic organizing committee and also arranged some other gigs while I was going to be in the area.

I drove across the western U.S. enveloped in the frozen February landscape, first traveling to Evanston, Wyoming, close to the Utah border. Another couple of long-time fans there booked me to do a concert, inviting all of the Olympians and their host families who were staying in the area, as well as locals. I was scheduled to come on right after an autograph signing event with the Jamaican bobsled team – which was were very hot at that time after a movie that had featured them, titled "Cool Runnings."

The Jamaican bobsled team was running on Caribbean time and started late and went quite long. By the time I performed, I only had a small crowd to sing for, but that was okay. The sponsors were quite kind to me and enthusiastic about my show. Fortunately, my pay that night was not dependant on a door charge!

After Evanston, I doubled back west on Interstate 80, then turned south on U.S. 40 to Park City and Heber City.

The Words Upon the Wire

There was a real feeling of excitement in the air, as athletes from all over the world descended on Salt Lake and all of the satellite locations.

I played my "New Songs of the Old West" program as part of the Heber City Olympic venue opening. You can imagine what the security was like after the shock of 9/11, just a few months before. Getting me and my guitar inside, even with all the passes and documentation I had, was an incredible pain in the ass – and I had to arrive two hours before I was due to play.

Ordinarily, this would not be a problem. I have always preferred being early for gigs, particularly at unfamiliar venues or festivals. That morning, however, it was about 20 degrees below zero. The sky was blue and the weather was perfect – it was just colder outside than a Republican's heart after a winning election.

I mingled with other performers and staff in the heated tent they had set up, but it was still damn cold. Oh, and there were security guys and soldiers with guns everywhere.

When I finally did get to do my bit, it was still very, very chilly. I was worried about my guitar staying in tune in that temperature, but it actually did pretty well. I had brought my old, beat up Martin D-28, which had seen decades of tough use and abuse. Mounted heaters on the stage blew hot air underneath the plexiglass shields right in front of you that extended above your knees. The stage was also covered. The result was that my front was tolerably warm – but my backside was still below zero. I now had some idea what a half-cooked frozen chicken feels like.

Still, it was a rush to be there. Thousands of people milled about the big, snowy, meadow in front of the stage, and many of them took part when I asked them to help me out on David Rea's jocular song, "Hands Up," where I ask folks to put their hands in the air and shout back those two words to me, during the chorus. I could see the cross-country skiers and biathlon athletes doing their thing in the distance. It was an unforgettable, unique engagement, and I knew I was fortunate to be invited.

"I WOULDN'T COUNT ON IT" — CONFESSIONS OF AN UNLIKELY FOLKSINGER

The rest of my time in that area I performed at an upscale chalet/lodge called the "Blue Boar Inn." I did three or four nights there for a generous sum of money and had such a good time meeting folks from all over the world. Back across the snowy western U.S. I traveled after that, home to Vancouver, Washington, and "marital bliss."

ON THE ROAD IN COLORADO, 2001

I REALLY DON'T mean to sound too negative about Elizabeth. We both did the best we could, but it was like blending oil and water and expecting fine Bordeaux to be the outcome. One distinct benefit of our time together was that I met some wonderful folks though her, many of whom are still close friends.

The Words Upon the Wire

In particular, Wayne and Karen Hoffman from north Clark County, Washington, would turn out to be life companions and pals. They were in the audience one night when I shared a presentation with Dave Carter and Tracy Grammer at a bar in North Portland. It was the first time Wayne and Karen heard them, and they became devotees of their music.

In years to come, it would always seem that for significant turns of my fate, including Wayne being the bartender at my wedding to Elizabeth, Wayne and Karen would wind up being there as supporters and confidants.

Wayne is a fine guitarist and singer, though he sensibly made his living in other ways. When he found himself with more time later in life, he established and continues events that make an impact through what he gives to the music and to the community. For almost 20 years, Wayne has run a series of open mic nights that welcome everyone. Karen often cooks for the gatherings that turn up at their home afterwards – and Karen is one hell of a good cook.

Wayne also established and ran a folk festival in north Clark County, Washington, for a few years, whose proceeds went the American Cancer Society. He also has a performing group and likewise donates all monies paid to them to that same organization.

He is a model of the difference one person can make in a community, and I am proud to call both Wayne and Karen two of my closest friends. As the old expression goes, each of them "has a heart made of wool that is 10 yards wide," It was good to have such supportive folks around me, because things were really not going well in my marriage.

I do remember one instance where Elizabeth asked me, "How long are you going to do this for a living? I want us to spend more time with my family." Considering I had already been doing music as a profession 30 years by that point, I assumed she had realized I was not about to become say, a house painter or carpet installer. This was not a good omen for the longevity of the union!

"I WOULDN'T COUNT ON IT" — CONFESSIONS OF AN UNLIKELY FOLKSINGER

As always, I needed to be back in Omaha in the spring, even though Dylan was no longer there, since he was now attending college in Olympia, Washington. His absence made my required time in Nebraska even more depressing than it had been in recent years.

I began to lodge with my producer, Clete, and his wife, Nina, when I was in the area – which was a welcome blessing. They knew how to cheer me up and loved wine as much as I do, and they were, and are, good company. Making my way home from Nebraska that year in a roundabout way, I would perform in St. Louis, Carbondale and Chicago, Illinois and Evansville, Minnesota.

Evansville, Minnesota, is in the western part of that lovely state. The show was a house concert sponsored by a talented duo who called themselves The Granary Girls. I was put up in what had been a corn crib (talk about rustic), but I enjoyed very much the ambience and quiet of that place. I recall being struck by seeing and hearing so many different species of birds that I was unfamiliar with – it seemed they were everywhere. Their exquisite birdsong was a melodious accent to a difficult year.

By this time, when I would do a larger show, I would put together a band of whoever was available who was familiar with my songs. I was booked for the Willamette Valley Folk Festival in Eugene, and the other musicians in my band onstage were Elizabeth, Fuzzy and Dylan. When we arrived at the festival, there was a large crowd. We followed a very popular female folk harmony group, Misty River, who were all friends of mine. They got a warm reception, and I looked forward to playing my tunes for that enthusiastic, knowledgeable audience.

Then it was our turn. When we started our set, there were hundreds of folks there. Halfway into the second song, the heavens opened in a deluge of rain, reminiscent of the stories about Noah's flood. The stage and PA were covered, but for the rest of the set we performed for only about a dozen wet, disheveled people huddling dejectedly under a large Douglas Fir tree. That seemed to be how things were panning out for me most of that year.

The Words Upon the Wire

Elizabeth traveled with me that summer, doing concerts with me in Grand Lake, Colorado, and in Wyoming and Utah. In Green River, I got a call from the Portland newspaper informing me that my friend, the gifted songwriter Dave Carter, had unexpectedly died. The reporter asked me for a quote for the story he was writing.

This was very sad news for anyone who cared about acoustic music. Dave and Tracy had become one of the most heralded and well-known acts in folk music across the U.S., as well as being lovely people and good friends of mine. I was asked to be the moderator at Dave's memorial service, which would take place at Cathedral Park in Portland a few days after we returned from the trip.

It was an emotional afternoon. Joan Baez had recorded Dave's song, "The Mountain," and sang it at the memorial. It was so generous of her to divert her tour bus to arrive in Portland that Sunday. I made sure, per Tracy's wishes, that everyone who had been close to them and had come from far away, like Joan, had a chance to say a few words or sing a song. Dave and Tracy had sung at Winterfolk for me, and we had shared many stages. They are truly among the most talented folk artists I had ever known, and Dave's music still stands the test of time.

SOON AFTER THE memorial, I flew out to do the Tumbleweed Festival again in Garden City, Kansas. When I returned to Vancouver after that weekend, Elizabeth told me she thought things just were not working out, and I needed to move. She would start divorce proceedings.

There was a part of me that was quite upset, but also a part of me was greatly relieved. Elizabeth was right, of course: Marriage to me had been a bad idea from the start, and the sooner we both moved along with the rest of our lives, the better. I checked in with my former abode, "the methamphetamine arms," and they had a two-bedroom apartment available. So, I moved back in there with help from my son and Wayne Hoffman.

As soon as Rebecca found out I was getting divorced, she was down visiting me, calling me, and trying to get back into my good graces. We would see each other periodically over that next year. She wanted to move to Vancouver, buy a house, and have us move back in together, with the idea that we would eventually get married.

I was very non-committal about this plan of action after my recent experience, but as a testimony to my idiocy,

I did continue to see her. I also dated other women, but Rebecca worked on getting her hooks back in me as deep as possible while she had the chance.

In September of 2002, I performed at and helped emcee the Sisters Folk Festival in quaint little Sisters, Oregon. This was a grand affair that really lifted my spirits.

Sisters is nestled beneath snow-topped Cascade peaks, on the eastern side of the mountains. It is an incredibly beautiful setting – as well as being inordinately prosperous and perhaps a little too much in the false-front western town mold, kind of like Sedona. The festival has deep community support – it sells out every year. I was thankful for the chance to connect with so many musical folks from my part of the world. I would appear at Sisters Folk Festival each year for the next three years.

I also consoled myself about my change in life by going back to Alaska solo in October, performing in Juneau, Skagway, and Haines. By this time my friend Sioux Plummer, now Douglas, had moved to Juneau and hosted a really lovely concert for me at the Northern Lights Church there. There is nothing quite like the beauty and bigness of Alaska to remind you of how small you and your troubles really are.

Donny Wright, the bass player from the album "Vested," had begun to join me in my Thursday night gigs at Kells, which fell once a month at the end of a five-day stretch there. He had also joined myself and Elizabeth a couple of times on stage, and I was becoming increasingly fond of not only his welcome musical additions to the songs, but also his good humor and friendship.

The rest of the year was filled with my usual rounds at the Horse Brass, Kells, Pacific City, and other regional engagements. The work of recording River City Folk had almost entirely shifted to the Pacific Northwest, though Clete back in Omaha was still my partner in the venture. I would continue to travel back there once a year to work with him.

After Nebraska Public Radio had declined to continue funding River City Folk, Steve Robinson had moved to a new job as director of the WFMT Radio Network in Chicago. WFMT distributed nationally a number of different broadcasts, most of them classical in nature.

Steve had always been a believer in River City Folk, and through his advocacy our program wound up being distributed on his network. Though it didn't mean any funding for our show, quite a number of new affiliates did begin to broadcast it, just by the nature of it being carried on the WFMT satellite. The network also had an active promotional department, and that helped with getting out the word on the program.

Steve Robinson also facilitated a major coup for River City Folk – getting it carried on the new XM satellite radio network. XM was a pay-network that had dozens of channels and had one channel (The Village, Channel 15) totally dedicated to folk music. River City Folk aired on XM for years, along with Bob Dylan's program and Rich Warren's Midnight Special from Chicago. That lasted until The Village was relegated to member/computer-only reception, with no availability in cars or on other receivers. For a few years previous to that, however, it could be heard on Direct TV and other reception platforms XM provided.

XM eventually merged with its competitor, Sirius. However, that combined entity, consisting of more than 200 channels, does not have one dedicated folk music channel – though it does have numerous NASCAR channels! There are a lot of explanations for this, but my theory is that as we continue to become a post-literate country and fewer people read books, newspapers or can follow a story, the more nuanced forms of music like folk, classical and jazz have suffered accordingly.

Except for perhaps a brief time during the Folk Revival of the early 60's, when there was real money to be made in the genre (which unfortunately also brings in extremely non-altruistic opportunists), folk music is created for its own sake. It focuses on human issues, work, politics, history and all kinds of other subjects most Americans can't be bothered with. A superb book written in 1985, called "Amusing Ourselves to Death," by Neil Postman, presaged the destination modern tastes have devolved to.

MY 50TH BIRTHDAY in early 2003 was not quite as rambunctious as the 40th had been, but it still was a lot of fun.

A dear friend in Portland, Kim Cook, put it on for me at her comfortable home. A lot of fine wine was consumed and good music shared.

That year Winterfolk was on its now-usual date, the first Saturday night in February at the Aladdin Theatre. As it was the 15th annual gathering of this important benefit for Sisters of the Road Café, we recorded another CD documenting the event, which Clete Baker graciously came out to Oregon from Omaha to record. It is really an accurate record of that night, and it begins with Chris Kennedy singing a humorous song that was only too appropriate at that time, called "Big Dick Cheney Man." It is a classic, and Chris brought down the house.

After Dave Carter's untimely death, Donny Wright had begun working with Tracy Grammer, who was trying hard to keep the

The Words Upon the Wire

momentum going that her and Dave had established. Winterfolk 15 was the first time Tracy and Donny performed in public, and they did a fine set of some of Dave's best loved songs. It was particularly moving since Dave and Tracy had performed together at Winterfolk just the year before.

Old friends Kate Power and Steve Einhorn also did a memorable selection of tunes, including a new song Kate had written, entitled "Travis John." It is a sensitive, thoughtful memorial to a young man they had known well, killed during the second Iraq war that was raging at that time. The contemporary anti-war song created an incredibly moving moment in the hall when they performed it. It would also be one of the highlights of the CD, and it went on to win an award from the Kerrville Folk Festival as the hardest-hitting topical song of the year.

With Utah Phillip's always-riveting presentation of songs and stories, and myself doing a couple of pieces off "Vested" with my son Dylan and Fuzzy Purcell, it worked out to be a really fine concert recording. Andrew Calhoun from Illinois performed evocative songs from his new album, "Tiger Tattoo," and the very popular female group "Misty River" electrified the Winterfolk audience with their tight harmonies and mix of traditional and original music.

Andrew Calhoun's record company in Chicago, Waterbug, released the project nationally. Thanks to the efforts of so many, lots of money was raised for Sisters of the Road Café, and a lasting record of the event was heard on radio and in folks' CD players around the U.S.

AT HORSE BRASS PUB, 2001

"I WOULDN'T COUNT ON IT" — CONFESSIONS OF AN UNLIKELY FOLKSINGER

IN THE SPRINGTIME, I headed Maggie back east for another round of concerts and radio tapings in Omaha.

It seemed I was dodging tornados frequently that season, but I did get to quite a number of places I had not performed before: Boise and McCall, Idaho; Little Falls, Minnesota; and Jefferson City, Cape Girardeau, and other southern Missouri locations. On the way back home, I did shows in Laramie and Rock Springs, Wyoming, and discussed with my pal Chris Kennedy what I should do about my whole situation with Rebecca back home.

He and my old friend Avery Grimes had both cautioned me about going down that path again, but I figured when she actually found a house she wanted to buy, I would worry about it then.

Unfortunately for me, that summer, while I was back in Colorado performing at Grand Lake, Rebecca located a house in Vancouver she decided to purchase. It was like being in a poker game and called to show your cards. I had to decide what to do.

Much to my eventual chagrin, I moved in with her again that August. It wasn't a money-saving move – it would actually cost me far more a month than I was paying for my apartment. Despite virtually everyone who knew me well counseling me against it, I decided to give our relationship another try. What a chump.

Late that August there was an embryonic concert series that I was recruited to do for each of the next three years, located at Mt. Hood's Timberline Lodge. Donny and Fuzzy would join me for three afternoons of songs each Labor Day weekend, in exchange for a decent fee and lodgings. Friends came up to party with us, and we had a delightful time.

Timberline Lodge was built during the Great Depression of the 1930's and dedicated by Franklin Roosevelt. It had employed struggling Northwest artists at that time to decorate and construct its monumental facade and interior, and it remains one of the nation's treasures.

Back in Vancouver, it was a beautiful home that Rebecca had purchased, and at first things went well. By Thanksgiving, however, there were extremely troubling signs that I had put myself right back in the uncomfortable situation I had been in before with her – except this time it was costing me a lot more money. Hearts and flowers were not carrying the day.

EARLY IN 2004, I joined old friend Terry Prohaska at a venue called The Alberta Street Public House, run by accordion-player deluxe Mike Beglen, former owner of The East Ave. Tavern. This would begin a tradition of our January reunion gigs that would occur for the next few years. Terry always makes me laugh. He is a fine, multi-talented musician and singer and a stimulating drinking buddy, but he also has an irreverent sense of humor about music, women and life in general that he and I shared.

A couple of years earlier I had re-met the banjo player-author Dick Weissman at a festival in Richland, Washington. Dick has a colorful history. He had been one third of the group The Journeymen during the Folk Revival of the early 1960's. The other members were John Phillips, founder and primary songwriter of The Mamas and Papas, and Scott McKenzie, who had the monster single in the 60's, "If you're going to San Francisco." Dick had gone on to be a sought-after record producer, solo artist and also an author of numerous books about the music business for publishers such as Mel Bay and Routledge.

Dick and I hit it off and would frequently meet for coffee and observations and complaints about the direction our beloved music was heading in. I joined him to present a songwriting workshop in Astoria, Oregon, later that winter, and we would work on other musical collaborations as well.

In February, Creighton University in Omaha flew me back to do a concert for its 150th Anniversary. Creighton University was founded by two brothers, immigrants from Ireland, who made

"I WOULDN'T COUNT ON IT" — CONFESSIONS OF AN UNLIKELY FOLKSINGER

their fortunes by laying the first telegraph cable to California. It was an incredible risk at the time, but it eventually garnered tremendous wealth and influence for them.

That telegraph line, completed in 1861, put the Pony Express out of business – and insured that both California and Nevada would remain in the Union during the Civil War. Since a significant percentage of the Union effort was funded by those silver and gold deposits in Nevada, this was not an unimportant event.

I thought about my father coming along 90 years later, without family or prospects, and how the profession of telegraph operator had rescued him from the grinding poverty of the great depression of the 1930's – a kind of desperation we modern Americans really can't conceive of.

I combined those two stories into a song titled "The Words Upon the Wire," in tribute to the first time in human history a message could travel faster than a man could walk or than a conveyance like a boat could carry the words along.

> **The Words Upon the Wire**
>
> My father was abandoned, cast out upon a sea of grass
> he had to learn to find a way to feed himself and forget the past
> he learned to play the Morse code key like a fiddler's farewell tune
> he met the gamblers, and the railroad bums, in the smoky office
> > rooms
>
> Now the Creighton brothers came from Ireland, not a penny to their
> > name
> converts to their adopted land, where a man could stake his claim
> a century before my father, they felt the winds of change
> took a chance upon a crazy scheme, and the world would never be
> > the same
>
> Chorus
>
> My father worked the Morse code key from Georgia to Wyoming

The Words Upon the Wire

in small towns finally tied, to a country ever growing
from railroad stations, ships at sea, the sentences went like fire
there is nothing changed the world so much as the words upon the wire
the words upon the wire

He met a bride from Nebraska, she came from a humble place
born in a sod house, raised on the open spaces
together they would forge their life in the days of the model T
a telegraph operator, he traveled endlessly

Now the telegraph tied the country together, along with the Civil War
telegraph poles like sentinels marching in line, from shore to shore
all the way to California, Creighton strung the first long lines
from Omaha, to Frisco, and the Nevada silver mines

Repeat chorus

In the days of Lewis and Clark, nothing moved faster than a horse
or the speed of a river current, as a boat struggled to change its course
it is hard for us to remember, and ever harder to understand
the difference that those men did make, to the way things had ALWAYS been

Now the vision the Creighton brothers had, is still alive today
the messages that my father sent, still have things to say
that knowledge along with wisdom, makes a difference still somehow
that it still can make the distance, between us then and now

Repeat chorus

Tom May copyright 2004 Blue Vignette ASCAP
from the album "Blue Roads, Red Wine"

As far as I have been able to research, this is the only song in our times that has ever been written specifically about the telegraph and Morse code, which is surprising, given that it is the basis all of our future technological advances were built upon. It is a tribute to my father and his struggles and life, and I wish he would have had a chance to hear it.

♪ ♪ ♪ ♪ ♪

AS I MOVED on into 2004, I had thankfully all the work I could handle. With the invaluable help of Fuzzy, we recorded a series of Live at Artichoke Music radio programs, in front of an audience. My guests include Claudia Schmidt from Michigan, the legendary Celtic fiddle player Kevin Burke, and the outstanding ensemble from Vancouver, British Columbia, Tillers Folly. It was a pretty labor-intensive operation that required us setting up our own PA and Fuzzy bringing in lots of gear to record the show, but we captured some terrific performances for the broadcast.

There were new gigs and festivals to do too, including a concert at Eastern Oregon University in LaGrande and a Celtic Festival at Ocean Shores, Washington, as well as the usual rounds of regular shows.

I don't ever mean to appear too negative about the prospects for young folks doing this profession today. I know some fine talents who are diligently trying to make a go of it. There are just so many obstacles and hurdles now that didn't exist when I began to ply this trade, not the least of which is the pitiful pay for the aspiring novice performer.

In addition to the general dearth of venues today and lack of decent paid performing opportunities of all kinds, (Dick Weissman would tell of a coffeehouse in Portland that made you sign a contract – confirming you would be paid zilch) a significant change in recent years would be the abruptly diminishing sales of product.

In the mid-2000's, everyone's CD sales begin to slack off

dramatically, as folks preferred to buy just one song online for their iPods or took the course of just acquiring the music they liked from the internet, at no charge. This was really a blow for those of us making a living in alternative forms of music. You would sell some cuts on CD Baby or other digital outlets, but it would never make up for the sales you could regularly count on at a concert or gig. Most full-time performers I know like myself confirm the drop in product sales was around 75 percent at that time, and it has never recovered.

Just to give you some idea, previously, even at Kells on a Sunday through Thursday night, I would sell upwards of $200 dollars a week of CDs. At a concert that was well attended I frequently could move $300 to $800 worth of product. Losing that income was a blow. In some forms of rap and pop music it has worked out okay for bands (so I hear), but in folk, jazz and other more esoteric genres it has been a disaster.

Thank goodness, there will always be folks who don't mind sleeping in their cars or living on next to nothing while they are out gigging, and the world is richer because of them. But as far as these kinds of music being a bona-fide, long term way of supporting yourself, as has been the case for me, I am extremely pessimistic.

BLUE ROADS, RED WINE (AND A ROSE SCENTED WOMAN)

At the last minute, in late May of 2004, I was booked at the Spiral Rhythms Festival, which took place upon the high wilderness benchlands above the Columbia River, a couple hours from Vancouver, Washington. The festival was put on by Ian Drake, who had been involved in many productions of acoustic music.

Ian has a 1960's ethos and truly believed that music and friendship made a difference. He is another one of those unsung heroes who has changed the world for the better through his volunteer efforts to build community and dedication to making the arts accessible to all.

By this time, I was really getting discouraged about how my relationship with Rebecca was going. At least I had not married her, which made contemplating yet another relationship split a little easier. She had rarely attended or gone with me to any gigs since we had moved back in together (which was ironic, I thought), and she was not interested in going with me to this festival, either.

Which by this time was fine with me. I figured it would be a hippie gathering of fun, counter-culture types, and I was right.

When I got there, Ian had arranged for one of his staff to have good red wine there for me to enjoy while I was at the festival. She brought me a bottle of Hedge's Cabarnet/Merlot blend, and we began to chat.

Her name was Debbie Dutton. She was a nurse at a Vancouver hospital, and we had a lot of similar interests.

We talked and talked, before and after my presentation. That set of music was the only time I have played songs through a PA powered by a car battery!

I stayed much later than I should have, and I slowly made my way back down the winding roads to the Columbia River. I did not realize it then, but my last minute acceptance of the invite to perform at that little festival would alter the course of my life yet again.

I HAD PERFORMED a couple of weekend band shows at Kells with a makeshift lineup, but the owner asked me to put together a regular group to fill in more of those Friday and Saturday dates. In those day, on the weekends, Kells was quite a scene: Young people would stand in line to pay the cover charge and get into what was one of the most happening places in town.

The hours for the bands on the weekends were 9:30 PM to 1:30 AM, harkening back to the hours I played when I started out in this game back in Ontario. The money was attractive, however. Kells always paid exceptionally well, and the weekends, along with the St. Patrick's Day festival, were the most lucrative dates to play. You did, however, earn every penny of it.

Donny was on board with me for those weekends, but I figured we needed a fiddle player too, so that I would have a break from singing every song by filling in with some instrumental Irish tunes. Eddie Parente did a couple of nights with us, but he was

"I WOULDN'T COUNT ON IT" — CONFESSIONS OF AN UNLIKELY FOLKSINGER

very committed to other bands. Donny suggested a fiddle player he had worked with before by the name of Peggie Moje.

Peggie's primary background was in bluegrass, but it turned out she had always wanted to get involved with Irish music. She was a competent singer, too, which meant we could work out some three-part harmonies on the songs.

So, after just a couple of rehearsals we began doing weekends at Kells, mostly smoothing out the rough edges on stage as we went along. The audience by and large didn't know the difference, anyway.

But a funny thing happened during those nights on that cramped, high platform. I had always worked at getting the crowd involved when I was at Kells, but on those packed weekend nights I really improved at the art of inciting the audience to help us out by clapping, singing, shouting – and just generally doing what I told them to do. The trio sounded so damn good together and had such a forceful presence that it really got patrons of all ages up tapping their feet and onto the small dance floor.

Turns out you can teach an old dog new tricks.

The young affluent girls, dressed in their scanty finery to attract the cool dudes, would prance around the dance floor, and some nights it seemed as if we could do no wrong on stage. The spirited ovation for us would resound throughout the Celtic-decorated walls. Conversely, sometimes for no apparent reason, the crowd would be totally uninvolved and passive, but this seldom happened. Donny had a rock-n-roll sensibility, and he pushed me toward more upbeat versions of those classic ballads. I had to chuckle to myself on stage, as I watched randy young folks boogying to 400-year-old songs.

Performing my own heartfelt, emotional, historical songs in a concert was one thing: This was quite another.

Though I had performed at Kells for more than 10 years at this point, those weekday nights were much more relaxed, and I did pretty much as I pleased. The Fridays and Saturdays were more like a rock concert, with people who couldn't find seats

Blue Roads, Red Wine (and a rose scented woman)

DONNY WRIGHT, TOM, PEGGIE MOJE, FUZZY PURCELL PORTLAND OREGON 2005

standing throughout the joint, and the crowd on many weekend nights being over 350 at any given time. Kells would have four bartenders and who knows how many waiters and waitresses, pouring and serving trays of drinks and shots as quickly as the taps would run.

I did not use a set list there, but rather just decided what was next, and gave my spoken intro for the song – generally a short little history or story. Donny and Peggie recognized from that intro what was coming, and away we went.

When we did our bombastic version of "Follow me up to Carlow," a traditional song written about the last great victory of the Irish clans in the sixteenth century, the kids would roar after we hit the big finish. At some of those times, I got a rush that gave me some idea of how the Rolling Stones felt after shouting out one of their big hits. Smaller audience perhaps, but same kind of rush – totally unlike a folk music concert crowd, but invigorating, nonetheless.

Shouting was indeed the operative word on many of those nights, with the ambient noise in the pub and the volume we played at, there wasn't a lot of room for nuance. Typically during the day between the Friday night and Saturday night performances, I was so hoarse I didn't know how I would do the show that evening. But after throat coat tea and not speaking all day, I was always able to somehow croak my way through the performance. The adrenaline rush from the audience was also a wonderful healing tool.

"It's never too late to buy the bass player a round of whiskey," was Donny's theme through those nights, and though I generally did not indulge in a glass of wine until the break before the last set (if I did, I just lost too much energy), we did indeed all have a good time most of our nights there. I never ceased to be amazed that old folks like us, singing even older ballads, could fire up those vital young souls as we did.

Nirvana, eat your hearts out.

♪ ♪ ♪ ♪ ♪ ♪

THAT JUNE WE celebrated the joyous occasion of Dylan graduating from university at Evergreen State. Michaela and her husband, Harold, came out for the ceremony (she was remarried to a really kind, caring man back in Omaha), and I of course put that weekend aside to celebrate my son's landmark achievement.

Rebecca did grudgingly come to his commencement, though she punished me for her attendance by her resentment about being expected to do so. Her negativity and ill humor really colored what should have been a celebratory day for all of us. I considered her behavior that day unforgivable. I stayed in Olympia by myself that night while she returned home and contemplated the relationship pickle I had gotten myself into – again.

Debbie, who I had met at the Spiral Rhythms festival, began to attend some of my shows whenever she was able to do so. I eventually told her I was living with Rebecca, as there was no way Debbie could have known that. (I had omitted that salient bit of information when we first interacted, and Rebecca was at a point where she no longer came to any of my performances.)

After a Pacific City weekend of gigs and five nights at Kells, I was off for my annual expedition to Colorado and Wyoming locations. I had a chance to discuss everything that was going on with Chris and Sue in Rock Springs, who always provided a non-judgmental, wise sounding board for me.

I gave serious consideration during that trip to packing it all in with Rebecca and exploring what a relationship might be like with Debbie. By the time I returned to Washington, however, Debbie had gotten involved with someone else. It seemed the goddesses were telling me to really play out this string until the bitter end this time around.

Knowing by now it was foolish to defy goddesses, I decided to renew my efforts to try to make things work with Rebecca – at least for awhile longer.

I WAS AS busy as I have ever been in my musical life, doing more than 200 dates that year. Timberline Lodge Festival, Sisters Folk Festival, Galway Bay Festival, and all those dates at Kells – and that was just September.

In early November, I was set to do a concert as part of the Stormy Weather Festival at the Coaster Theater in idyllic Cannon Beach, Oregon. As this was a performance of my own songs, rather than Celtic music, the ensemble would consist of Donny and

Fuzzy. While we were rehearsing for this show, I played the guys some lyrics and a melody I had been messing around with. Donny in particular made some helpful suggestions, and throughout that month I would put the finishing touches on a song that would become a theme of sorts for me: "Blue Roads, Red Wine."

> **Blue Roads, Red Wine**
>
> Blue roads, red wine, and a rose scented woman,
> that's all this old fool needs
> just a blue road, red wine, on a cold Wyoming morning,
> and a few good books to read
>
> In the shadow of Mt. Rainier, a voice whispers to me soft and clear
> of the promise of a young man, whose miles have gone too fast
> as that mountain fades from view, I wonder what became of you
> when my only heart's desire, took me home to you at last...
>
> Blue roads, red wine, and a rose scented woman,
> that's all this old fool needs
> just a blue road, red wine, on a cold Dakota morning,
> and a few good books to read
>
> Through the eyes of my only son, I remember 21
> two lane roads so carefree, and my heart belonged to none
> never mind the busted cars, just my thumb will get me far
> past abandoned routes and railroads, where the wild deer still run
>
> Blue roads, red wine, and a rose scented woman,
> that's all this old fool needs
> just a blue road, red wine, on a cold Nebraska morning,
> and a few good books to read
>
> Now those years have disappeared like my taste for lager beer
> I've borrowed to the limit, to live the life I've had
> from the bedrooms to the bars, tasting life from a mason jar

Blue Roads, Red Wine (and a rose scented woman)

> turning back towards old Montana, when the weather gets too bad
>
> Blue roads, red wine, and a rose scented woman,
> that's all this old fool needs
> just a blue road, red wine, on a cold Alaska morning,
> and a few good books to read
>
> Blue roads, red wine, and a rose scented woman,
> that's all this old fool needs
> just a blue road, red wine, on a cold Wyoming morning,
> and a few good books to read

Tom May copyright 2005 Blue Vignette, ASCAP
from the album "Blue Roads, Red Wine"

♪ ♪ ♪ ♪ ♪

IN MY PERSONAL life, the quarreling with Rebecca became steadily worse. It was becoming obvious I was going to have to make different living arrangements, no matter how difficult that was going to be for me. I stayed through the holidays into early March, and then I told her it was time I moved on. It was not news that was received well, despite all of the conflict. At least I never married her. She was a great passion of my life, but some things are just not meant to be, for whatever reason.

In this moment, I wish I could have had more compassion for her pain and her illness, but I lived with her for six years, changed my life to be with her – and did my best to make it work. In the end, I was reminded as I said earlier, that you can't take away anyone's pain – no matter how much you love them or they love you.

It was also time to say goodbye to Maggie, my beloved Chevy van. She was getting pretty tired, with over 400,000 miles on the odometer. What a trooper she was. I hated to see her go far more than most of the women I had split up with. She was replaced with a 1999 Chrysler Town and Country.

"I WOULDN'T COUNT ON IT" — CONFESSIONS OF AN UNLIKELY FOLKSINGER

TOM AND DONNY AT ARTICHOKE IN PORTLAND, (SCOTT DOCHERTY)

Winterfolk that year featured the guitar virtuosity of Beppe Gambetta and Dan Crary, along with the always thoughtful, inspiring and funny words and songs from Utah Phillips. I had some new songs too, and it was a pleasure to play them there with Donny and Fuzzy joining me.

Other memorable concerts for me that month were a show at the Civic Center in the Dalles, Oregon, and a performance with Donny before an astounding sized audience of over 400 in little Madras, Oregon, – Donny's home town.

I also began to see Debbie Dutton again on a regular basis. The other relationship she had been in the previous summer had not worked out. There was something about Debbie that was just so attractive and welcoming. We would talk for hours, and we quickly fell very deeply in love.

I suppose I should have been more cautious, having just gone through another wrenching ending, but life is for the living. When the seemingly right person comes along, I have never been afraid to take a risk – though obviously there are a few instances when I should have looked a little closer before I leaped!

Debbie and I have rarely been apart a day since that tumultuous springtime of both endings and beginnings.

AFTER CAMPING OUT on kindly friends' couches and in their spare bedrooms and putting my meager goods in storage, I found a nice apartment – definitely a step up from the "methamphetamine arms." I would move in after my spring tour back east.

I started out with a show for Chris Kennedy at Western Wyoming Community College in Rock Springs. After an evening concert, I did a songwriting workshop the following afternoon, then he waved me "adios" as I took off down Interstate 80 in that Chrysler mini-van. Breezing past Cheyenne at 75 mph, I heard a loud clunk – never a good sound. The van rolled powerlessly to a stop on the side of the road.

The tow truck hauled me the few miles back to Cheyenne – and of course it was a weekend, the worst time for a breakdown – where I found out I had blown the transmission. I had a bunch of lucrative concerts on this trip that I was loath to cancel, so I left that damn mini-van behind to get a very expensive repair, rented a car and took off for central Nebraska, my next stop.

After a concert on the Thursday in Auburn, Nebraska, I headed all the way back to Cheyenne to pick up the repaired Chrysler – to the tune of over $3,000 – then back to Omaha, Lincoln, Chicago, Milwaukee and a few other whistlestops, finally returning west taking the northern route across I-90.

It was the worst automotive disaster I ever had in all the years of doing this profession, and I had to borrow money to make the repairs on that accursed Chrysler. Chris Kennedy would tease me for years about our carefree parting that day, as I blithely drove off towards disaster. As with everything else in this life, however, it could have been worse. I always had the AAA motor club extended coverage that would tow me a hundred miles free – but in some remote parts of the west, even that would not have been enough.

Cheyenne is a pretty large regional center too, so they were able to get the parts for that piece of junk quickly. Had I been in Meteetse, Wyoming, or at Frenchman, Nevada, it would have been a far different story, and I wouldn't have so easily procured a rental car to get me by.

As it was, I didn't miss a concert. I have always tried to be as professional as I could about this occupation, and the very worst thing you can do is cancel a performance. Occasionally I have missed a bar gig because of a flu or bad head cold, but very seldom. And never have I cancelled an important show, no matter how lousy I felt (or sounded). A wise man once said 90 percent of life is just showing up. That is certainly true in the entertainment field. Though you may think you sound awful when you have a cold or flu, most of the audience will never even know, providing you show up, don't whine too much about it, smile and do your best.

That somewhat snake-bitten journey in the spring of 2005 would be the last performing tour I would ever do solo, as a lonely folksinger on the way to god-knows-where. Debbie loved to travel and see new places, and at least in the beginning she couldn't get enough of the troubadour's life. (Nowadays she prefers it when we go places where I'm not playing music, though she kindly still accompanies me to far-flung shows on the odd occasion when I book them.)

I never imagined I would so much enjoy the company of a woman on my travels. When I had tried it in the past, it hadn't worked out particularly well, but Debbie and I got along so famously, even during tiring and stressful times. Because she is a nurse, she is able to structure her schedule to tour with me, and I never again booked a performance journey where she was not able to join me.

It is odd how our attitudes adjust as we grow older. In my youth I was fiercely independent and didn't want anyone riding along with me on my long tours. If I wanted to wake up at 5 AM and take off, I didn't want to consult with someone else. If I chose to sleep in the van a few miles down the road, rather than bunk down on a cat-hair covered couch, I didn't want to take a vote.

I found, however, Debbie to be a wonderful companion who enhanced, rather than detracted, from the traveling lifestyle. It was I who had changed as I got older, encouraged by the joy of being with Debbie, to laugh with and to love as the miles went by.

That first year together, she joined me at the Juan De Fuca Festival in Port Angeles, in Ocean Shores and Seattle, Washington, in Grand Lake and many other picturesque destinations that I delighted in sharing with her. Likewise, she introduced me to some of her favorite spots on the Olympic Peninsula in Washington, as well as the pleasures of Victoria, British Columbia. Life was good.

TOM AND DEBBIE, BALLYVAUGHN, COUNTY CLARE, IRELAND, 2006

THAT AUTUMN, I played one of the most unusual concerts ever, at Richmond, a ghost town hidden in the remote rocky outcroppings of central Oregon. Donny and his wife, Connie, joined Debbie and me. We all had one hell of a time finding it. It was put on by a promoter who had sponsored shows there for Ramblin' Jack Elliot and other well-known celebrities in the folk world.

It was October 1, and the rain was softly falling. Debbie and I passed the old barn where the concert was to take place at least three times before we noticed some red folding chairs leaning up against the weathered structure. It was down in a grassy, soggy meadow, with no signs or indication that it was the place. Donny got there a few minutes after us, and he only found the spot by catching a glimpse of my van sitting there.

"I WOULDN'T COUNT ON IT" — CONFESSIONS OF AN UNLIKELY FOLKSINGER

We set up my PA and readied for the evening. The big question all of us had was, "Who in the world is going to come to this event?" The closest town of any size, Bend, was more than 60 miles away. On that little side road, there had been no signs of life at all – just abandoned outbuildings.

The barn was cool, though. It was over 100 years old, and extremely rustic. There was an old pot-belly wood stove warming the space, and it was large and cozy.

Our opening act droned on for almost an hour to around a dozen people. By the time Donny and I performed, however, the place filled right up: There were between 40 and 60 people there, I'd estimate. To this day, I have absolutely no idea where they all came from. Two bats flew in concentric circles above us while we played, which was kind of an eerie feeling – but the show was unqualifiedly a great success. You just never know.

DEBBIE AND I were so happy together, and other things unexpectedly fell into place, too.

Dick Weissman and I had made a habit of getting together for coffee every couple of weeks or so, recounting old war stories from the folk music trenches. We would also gossip about folks we knew and other aspects of the business, such as songwriting and the recording industry.

He was engaged to write a series of books for the well-respected publisher Routledge, located on Madison Ave. in New York City. Dick phoned me and asked me if I would be interested in writing the songwriting/performing book of the series, based on my experiences making a living in this trade over the previous 35 years.

The longest piece I had ever written was my high school term paper, and I don't suppose it was very good.

Still, I figured how hard could it be? I would certainly be

"writing about something I knew," one of the first suggestions any author gets.

I first put together a basic outline of the proposed book and submitted a writing sample from one of the possible chapters. My idea was to have this book be more accessible than many of the similar books that flood the market: Real "how to" suggestions on booking shows, equipment, wage scales, pitfalls to avoid, etc. I also thought I would use some of my contacts from over the years as interview subjects, giving their insights into this very competitive profession.

To my surprise, Routledge accepted our proposal. I would write 80 percent of the book, and Dick would fill my knowledge gaps with specific current info about royalties, placing music in film and television, and a few other more arcane aspects of the business.

We would be paid a fair amount to write the book, half of the fee as an advance, the other half to be paid upon completion. The contract was for a 75,000-word project, with a two year deadline. I was very pleased, if somewhat nervous, about taking on such an ambitious undertaking in a field new to me. Like the radio and television program though, I figured the way to get beyond my trepidations was just to dive right in.

The very first step was to get an entertainment business celebrity to consent to an interview that would be used in the book. Having a marquee name like that on the jacket of the tome would help it sell. Since the person in that category I knew best was Gordon Lightfoot, I decided he would be my first choice to approach.

Gord does not really like excessive publicity, particularly television, and has been misquoted and misunderstood an inordinate number of times in his career. Still, I had kept in contact with him over the years and considered his current business manager, Barry Harvey, a friend. So, I figured I had at least a 50-50 shot to garner Lightfoot's help on the book.

I began with a formal written request to Barry, which is the proper way to go about such things. I explained the concept of the book and laid out the kind of interview I hoped to do with Gord. I didn't receive a response for a few weeks, so I was beginning to get concerned. But then Barry phoned me and set up a time for Lightfoot's first interview with me.

He gave me an illuminating series of interviews on his career, and I had very carefully scripted the questions I would ask. As much as I thought I knew about Lightfoot's career and life, I found out much more that I believed would be of interest to readers.

I taped the interviews and then transcribed them and sent them to Gordon for approval. I didn't want anything he was uncomfortable with to be in the book, and indeed, there were numerous statements he made on tape he would strike as being pronouncements he did not want to be out there in public. We would go on to do many conversational sessions, and they became some of the primary foundations of the book.

I hope I corrected in the book some misconceptions about Lightfoot's career that had been printed on album sleeves and in newspaper articles many times through the years. One of the facts I really was surprised by was that it was Peter Yarrow, of Peter, Paul and Mary, who really gave him his big break.

Ian and Sylvia, the Canadian folk celebrities of the 1960's, had learned Gord's song "For Lovin Me," and played it for Peter Yarrow. Peter then recorded it, and it became a minor hit for Peter, Paul and Mary. That prompted Albert Grossman, who managed and was instrumental to the success of Peter, Paul and Mary; Dylan; Odetta; and others, to sign Lightfoot to a contract. I had always read and heard that story told very differently.

Gordon's humility and awareness of his good fortune, which had blossomed in his older age, was very apparent in his words. One of his statements that I was particularly taken by was, "I have had far more failures in my life in the music business than I ever had successes."

I would also interview Eliza Gilkyson, a Texas songwriter who had – and still has – a thriving independent career; Harry Manx,

Blue Roads, Red Wine (and a rose scented woman)

a riveting Canadian performer who incorporates the unusual Indian instrument, the mohan veena, into his presentation; and Terry Currier, proprietor of Music Millennium in Portland, one of the most successful independent CD/record stores/distributorships in the U.S.

I incorporated segments of all of these interviews throughout the book in appropriate chapters. Dick Weissman did his usual masterful job of explaining in readable language how the complex copyrighting/royalties system works, and also how to place music in films and television. Chris Kennedy wrote an introduction that was friendly, humorous and welcoming.

After a lot of editing and many rewrites over about an 18-month period, the completed book was ready to go to the publishers. I thought the title should be something that had a little more juice to it than just, "Promoting Your Music," which was the working name. I contacted Pat Garvey, the writer of the classic song, "Lovin' of the Game," and asked permission to use his title as part of the book name. It is a spirited tune about the reward of pursuing your passion for a living. He consented, and "Promoting Your Music, The Lovin of the Game," became available at stores around the country in June 2007.

Though it has never sold large numbers, (shortly before it was released, Routledge was bought out by the conglomerate Taylor and Francis, which severely impacted the amount of publicity that would be done for the book), "Promoting Your Music, The Lovin' of the Game" got terrific reviews from critics and readers alike.

Most important to me personally, it caused me to look over my career in an objective, detached fashion. I came to the conclusion that yes, this profession has been and is important and worthwhile. It is just is a very hard road to hoe. I believe that is true now even more than it was in 2007.

Also, I had the great experience and challenge of writing a narrative that made sense as a whole. Just the physical and mental task of making yourself sit down to put words to paper for hours

"I WOULDN'T COUNT ON IT" — CONFESSIONS OF AN UNLIKELY FOLKSINGER

AT KMUN RADIO ASTORIA, OR, 2018

each day was a fulfilling and challenging task. I will always be grateful to Dick Weissman for giving me the opportunity to do so.

♪ ♪ ♪ ♪ ♪

THE OTHER SIGNIFICANT project Donny, our fiddle player, Peggie, and I undertook in late 2005 was a CD that represented the music we performed at Kells Pub. Titled "Just Another Night at Kells," it was a compilation of Irish and Scottish ballads and tunes we would play on the typical weekend at that establishment. Most were traditional, with the exception the album title song I composed (which crowds went crazy for there, as we got them to clap along at the end of a set) and "Lover's Heart," by the gifted Scottish writer Andy M. Stewart.

We recorded the project at Dan Rhiger's Medicine Whistle Studio, where I was also taping almost all the River City Folk programs by this point. Dan is such a delight to work with, and he really did a terrific job on the album. My favorite piece from that session is "Lover's Heart." Donny plays a soulful fretless bass part, and he and Dan's wife, Rahmana, add evocative harmonies to the chorus. Fuzzy plays a pensive octave mandolin part, and I grew to like the recording of that song so much I would use it again on a future album.

Though "Just Another Night at Kells" is not the most perfect, meticulously assembled CD I have ever done (I didn't want to spend a large sum on the production and whipped through the recording pretty quickly), it sure did sell a lot of copies to the audiences in the pub, particularly at that St. Patrick's Festival in 2006. That was before CD sales in general really began to slide.

DEBBIE AND I made plans to travel to Ireland in May of 2006. I would do some concerts while we were there, but primarily I would share with her that country that I find so endearing – the repository of learning and knowledge during the dark ages in Europe and the cradle of so much of the musical tradition I have spent my life pursuing.

We landed in the west of Ireland, at Shannon. The second night there we wound up in the postcard-perfect little town of Ballyvaughn, in County Clare, at the edge of the Burren, with its stunning rock formations and flowers. After dropping our bags at a bed and breakfast, we adjourned to the Hyland's Hotel in the village, where years earlier the owner had invited me to perform for the summer. I always wished I had taken him up on that.

Before we left the Pacific Northwest, I had purchased a ring for Debbie, and I asked her to marry me while we were sipping Guinness at Hyland's. We both had been through the marriage mill more than once, but this just seemed so right. I was very joyful when she said yes.

The rest of that excursion was a charmed journey. Probably the most successful concert was in Dublin, in the old part of town, at a place called The Boar's Head on Caple Street. Martin Sneyd, a fine musician, has been a good friend for decades, ever since I met him in Omaha in the early 80's. He had helped me many times book concerts in Ireland, pushed my recordings on Irish radio, and has always been so very hospitable. He promoted the show that night, and the place was packed.

Even the glow of a successful performance, however, did not rival the sense of well being and romance that permeated that entire journey with Debbie. After some desperately ill-advised detours, I had finally found a woman who seemed to understood what I was all about and loved me unqualifiedly – as I in turn loved her.

After our return home, the television program Oregon Art Beat on Oregon's public broadcasting station did a flattering profile of me and Winterfolk that was seen around the region. I was so very busy and so very happy, too. Debbie and I got married in the garden of her lovely home on July 2, surrounded by family and friends, and we celebrated with an abundant quantity of excellent red wine and champagne.

Later that July, it was the end of an era when Chris Kennedy, Cliff Jones, Avery Grimes and I did our last performance at the Grand Lake Lodge. The old place had just become too expensive to run (it was only open through the summer months, because of the cold and snow), and the James family had decided to sell the property.

It was a bittersweet weekend, though it was great fun to have everyone there doing one last show on that stage. I was also very happy that Debbie had at least gotten to spend a couple of summers with me in the rustic comforts of employee cabin #42. I still dream some nights I am sitting on one of the expansive porch swings at the main lodge, looking out over the swimming pool, the village of Grand Lake and the pristine lake itself, surrounded on all sides by peaks of Rocky Mountain National Park.

Eventually the lodge would be sold, and the employee cabins would be torn down. I haven't been back there since that last performance, but I am so grateful for all those years of gigs, enveloped in the incomparable beauty of that part of Colorado, surrounded by friends and family.

THE REMAINDER OF that busy year was filled with gratifying concert dates, including a Portland Parks concert with Donny and Fuzzy, a prestigious show for the trio at Skamania Lodge, close to Stevenson, Washington, and various other festivals, dozens of dates at Kells, and a trip to Vancouver, British Columbia, with Debbie to see and visit with Gordon Lightfoot.

The anniversaries were piling up too quickly now. November was the Horse Brass 30th anniversary, and I would once again book, perform at and arrange the Sunday celebration for Don Younger, along with Donny's PA help. As always, it was the occasion for much merrymaking, consumption of superb craft beer, and musical reunions with old pals.

As the year flipped to 2007, Debbie would join me in Omaha while I recorded a new crop at programs at Clete's Studio B in Nebraska. While I was there, I got a call that marked the end of another era: Bruce "Utah"Phillips phoned me to say he was too ill to perform at this year's Winterfolk XIX, coming up in just a few weeks. I wished him well, thanked him profusely for all he had done for the event and for Sisters of the Road, and we both agreed there was no way he would miss the next year's event; the 20th Anniversary of Winterfolk.

Alas, it was not to be. Utah Phillips never regained his health,

"I WOULDN'T COUNT ON IT" — CONFESSIONS OF AN UNLIKELY FOLKSINGER

and this poor old country lost one of its most gifted raconteurs and artists when he died in May of 2008.

♪ ♪ ♪ ♪ ♪

ALONG WITH THE usual gigs, this year proved to be a creative time, as well as a peaceful, settled period with my wife, Debbie. I wanted to take her to Montana and introduce her to some of my favorite venues and folks back there, so I booked a tour that included Butte, Bozeman, Billings and Red Lodge. We had a grand time there, and the crowds were good. I was reminded how much I loved the Big Sky country and the wide-open ranchlands bordered by the various mountain ranges.

Unfortunately, to my mind, there were lots of changes even in that landscape. Eastern Montana remained as sparsely populated and rural as ever, but the scenic areas of the western part of the state were filling in with urban sprawl and fancy subdivisions. In particular, the main street of Bozeman was unrecognizable. It was no longer a rustic, ranching mountain community: It had become a smaller version of Jackson, Wyoming, with chichi shops, brewpubs and young folks in expensive outdoor togs.

I know it is unrealistic to expect such a scenic location to remain the same, and the development undoubtedly created more, although minimum wage, jobs. I missed the days, however, when the Mint Bar on Main Street was filled with cowboys and ranchers, rather than with over-privileged young folks with no calluses on their hands, spandex trousers and haughty attitudes.

There were more festivals and regular gigs to perform at when we returned home and a couple of landmark performances I am especially thankful now I took the time and effort to make happen.

Terry Currier, the owner of Portland's iconic Music Millennium store, had encouraged me and David Rea to do some concerts honoring our old pal and mentor, Gordon Lightfoot.

Gord had weathered a serious illness that nearly killed him, but he was back working on the road again. Terry thought it was time that two of the guys who knew him well did a tribute concert incorporating those memorable songs.

After carefully selecting Lightfoot's compositions that we would highlight, we rehearsed for a month or two. Donny joined us on bass, and we did the first show at a concert club in Portland.

The second and final one of those shows we did was the most successful, taking place at the newly renovated outdoor amphitheater at Mt. Hood's Timberline Lodge. We had a very responsive, enthusiastic crowd there, as we ran though such Lightfoot favorites as "Rich Man's Spiritual," "Ribbon of Darkness," "Early Morning Rain," "For Lovin' Me," and some of his 70's hits, as well.

It was always a thrill for me to hear the signature licks that David had played on Gord's first album sounding behind me while we picked and sang those classics.

♪ ♪ ♪ ♪ ♪ ♪

GREEN RIVER, WYOMING, had been another regular stop for me through the years. The Parks and Recreation director, Roger Moellendorf was supportive of my music and had come to love Chris Kennedy's music, too. We performed for him numerous times, both individually and as a duo.

One venue he would use for the shows was Expedition Island, the launching point for John Wesley Powell's famous trip of exploration in the late 1860's, down the Green River and on to the Colorado River and the Grand Canyon. It was a journey akin to taking a spaceship to the moon back in those times.

What a character Powell was: A civil war veteran who had lost an arm, he sure didn't let it slow him down. He and his little band floated down those wild rivers in a backwards-facing rowboat that had to be lifted constantly by ropes and muscle power to get it beyond the precipitous rapids. They were the first white men to explore and map that wilderness. I couldn't imagine making that trip, even with both arms and a motorboat.

Roger Moellendorf was a history buff, well read, and like me, originally from Nebraska. Chris and I bemoaned his departure from Green River to take a job as head of the Parks and Recreation Department in Carson City, Nevada (knowing that those particular gigs Roger booked in Wyoming would most likely not happen anymore).

After Roger had worked in Nevada for a couple of years, however, he and I began to correspond about making some sort of presentations happen down that way. He would eventually put together a series of concerts and workshops that Chris and I have done in Nevada many times over the past few years, the first performances being in that summer of 2007.

Debbie and I rendezvoused with Chris there, and it turned out to be a lovely weekend of shows. Roger and his wife, Donny, were consummate hosts, and any excuse to do a few shows with Chris was a good one in my book.

Nevada can be kind of warm and sunny during the high summer, and with my pasty white northern European complexion – and the bald spot on top of my head – I seriously needed to wear a hat so I wouldn't get badly burned. I had forgotten to bring one with me, so I purchased a big straw cowboy hat to wear for the outdoor gigs and some of the tourist trekking I knew we would do.

With Chris's unerring comedic sense, the first time he saw me in it, he pronounced in his best Walter Brennan imitation voice as he looked askance at me, "You ain't going to shoot him, are you sheriff?" That cracked Debbie and me up, and we both laughed about it through the rest of the trip. You just had to love a guy who could keep you in stitches like that.

During the long drive home through California and Oregon, I began to work seriously on a song idea I had been contemplating

Blue Roads, Red Wine (and a rose scented woman)

for years. One of the great landmarks of the Pacific Northwest, written about extensively by Lewis and Clark and others, was the great falls of the Columbia River – Celilo Falls. Native Americans had lived and fished there for over 10,000 years, and the millions of salmon that migrated yearly over those basalt precipices represented one of the more dramatic nature spectacles in the world.

In 1957, a massive barrier called The Dalles Dam was built, flooding the falls. (It was named after the closest town to it, The Dalles in Oregon; named after the French word for river rapids.) Primarily built as a cheap source of energy to power the region and a huge aluminum plant that was constructed nearby, the fear-mongering during the cold war and promise of good jobs overcame the outrage and objections of the native peoples who had lived by it and harvested the fish for millennia.

To the Warm Springs, Yakima and Deschutes tribes who resided near it, Celilo Falls was more than a source of food: It was the very center of their beliefs in god and the world around them. There was not even a pretense of a treaty that gave away Celilo Falls – it was simply confiscated.

That spring of 2007 had been the 50th anniversary of the construction of that monstrosity. I had always been interested – and appalled – by the story of the Dalles Dam and resolved to write a song about it.

One day I was fooling around down in Salem, Oregon, drinking some good red wine with my compadre Fuzzy, and we talked a little about my idea. It turns out he had been working on some song lyrics about the same subject. We noodled a bit on our guitars and came up with a rough idea of melodically how the verses should sound.

I brought those ideas and the lyrics Fuzzy had already written home with me and proceeded to write another 20 verses or so. Way too many words, but I was full of passion and ideas about this song. I would worry about editing them all down later. Still, it needed a chorus to tie it all together.

"I WOULDN'T COUNT ON IT" — CONFESSIONS OF AN UNLIKELY FOLKSINGER

It was then I recalled one of my favorite books, written back in the 1980's: "Winterkill," by Portland author Craig Leslie. It is an emotional story about a father and son from the Warm Springs tribe and the impact that the damming of Celilo Falls had on their family structures, traditions and personal relationships. A light went on in my head when I remembered a few words the father had said to his young son in the book, speaking about the vanished landmark: "Celilo Falls is only sleeping."

There it was, the first line of the chorus. The chorus would also feature a dramatic melodic shift of keys, from B minor in the verses to A major in the choruses. "Celilo Falls" remains one of the songs I am proudest of, portraying injustice, greed and eventual environmental tragedy (which I regretfully imagine to be the end result) for all of us.

> **Celilo Falls**
>
> There's an echo in the wind of falling waters
> You can hear it if you listen close, from 50 years ago
> long before the white man, long before his roads
> ponderosa pine and alder guard the river down below.
>
> It narrows falling swiftly towards the sea
> at the only point where water breached the rugged Cascade range
> nature's wonder to behold, the falls were liquid gold
> as salmon journeyed home, the air was sweet with sage.
>
> Chorus
>
> Celilo Falls is only sleeping
> tucked beneath a blanket of Columbia River blue
> someday the steel and manmade concrete walls will crumble
> and the mighty roar of Celilo Falls will once again break through.
>
> The old man stares down at the water
> rolling slowly towards the massive concrete dam

Blue Roads, Red Wine (and a rose scented woman)

he remembers standing on the scaffolding
waiting patiently with a dip net in his hand

The young folks they left long ago
for jobs in the city, and the Pendleton rodeo
riding hard to escape the generations call
and the silvery violence that was Celilo Falls

Repeat chorus

By canoe and by foot they traveled there
long before Lewis and Clark ever saw that sea
celebrations in story, dance, and song
where the sacred salmon dried beneath the weeping willow tree

From the Prairies came hides and buffalo
from the seacoast came shells, to decorate their clothes
turquoise and obsidian from the south came forth
a rendezvous of bounty at this crossroads in the north

Repeat chorus

No treaty was ever signed by the elders
in 1957 they were told what the whites would pay
they would take this hallowed land, and build a massive dam
now the salmon run is just a fraction of what it was yesterday

When the gates were closed six hours of rising water
put traditions of 10,000 years to a bitter end
but as with all man's creations, there will come a day
when nature takes her vengeance, and the falls will rise again

Repeat chorus

Tom May and Fuzzy Purcell copyright 2007/ Blue Vignette, ASCAP
From the album "Blue Roads, Red Wine" Waterbug Records

"I WOULDN'T COUNT ON IT" — CONFESSIONS OF AN UNLIKELY FOLKSINGER

It was all sadly true. A cash settlement was forced upon the affected Native American tribes, but they never agreed to it. Even then, not a dime of it was paid for over 20 years. Native American fishing rights, guaranteed under the terms of the building of the dam, were – and still are – repeatedly and shamefully violated.

The salmon population of the Columbia River, one of the greatest fisheries in the world, is now between 5 and 10 percent of what it was before the building of the dams. The largest dam, the Grand Coulee, near the Canadian border, was built without any fish ladders at all, effectively cutting off hundreds of miles of spawning grounds for one of the most bountiful food sources the world has ever known.

The miracle of the yearly returning salmon, the life cycle of which is still dimly understood, continues, but it is ever diminishing. When the salmon fails to run any more, and is extinct, I fear we humans will be on our way out, as well.

WITH A CROP of new songs in hand, I decided to begin working on another album in the autumn of that year at Billy Oskay's Big Red Studio. I really wanted this to be a signature statement for me, as I was aware of timequickly ticking by.

I knew from the very beginning the title of this one would be "Blue Roads, Red Wine," as that song had always gotten a strong response from audiences, and I considered it to be a fair, joyous representation of my life as a musician.

Donny and Fuzzy would again be the foundations I would build the album's arrangements on. Knowing Billy Oskay much better this time around, I would be more trusting and open to his production ideas, too. He had certainly proven himself to be a master during the recording of "Vested."

In addition to my own songs, I would include some pieces by

Blue Roads, Red Wine (and a rose scented woman)

friends, including Chris Kennedy's "Watching the Rivers Flow," Bruce Coughlin's "Somewhere Down the Line," and David Mallett's "Hope for One and All." These were all songs that I felt deserved to be recorded and sung again. (Bruce's "Somewhere Down the Line" had actually never been recorded at all. He had written it with me in mind, bless his heart.)

I again laid in a large supply of red wine at Billy's studio for the recording process to come, and we began work in September. This time around I had Nolan Murray, the virtuosic fiddle/mandolin player from the group Tillers Folly, helping me out, along with Hanz Araki on flute. Donny added not only his impeccable bass work but also his marvelous sense of vocal harmony on many of the songs. Dylan played on Chris's "Watching the Rivers Flow," a song about the irreplaceable resource that is fresh water, which was only appropriate, since he had been hearing that piece since he was a young lad in Omaha.

We worked on that album slowly but surely, and we finally wrapped up the recording and mixing process around Christmas. Andrew Calhoun's highly respected record label in Illinois, Waterbug, agreed to put their imprint on it, and the release date was set for mid-February 2008.

Before that event, Winterfolk XX was to occur. I had been working for a couple of years to enlist Peter Yarrow, of the phenomenally successful group Peter, Paul and Mary, to appear at that milestone event. It all came together after dozens of phone calls, and I had a great sense of accomplishment when Peter Yarrow walked down the aisle of the Aladdin Theatre for sound check that afternoon.

Others among my great friends and musical companions would grace the stage that night; Terry Prohaska and the Rite of Spring; Grammy award winning guitarist Doug Smith; the angelic harmonies of the all-femalefolkie group Misty River; and of course Donny and Fuzzy.

Later that month "Blue Roads, Red Wine" was released on

Waterbug Records and was played extensively on folk radio throughout the U.S. Rich Warren, the producer of the seminal broadcast Midnight Special, named it one of the best folk recordings of the year. All the songs on that CD remain staples of my live performances.

TOM, TERRY PROHASKA, PETER YARROW, WINTERFOLK 20 (SCOTT DOCHERTY)

THANKS

Since 2008, I have reached the time in my life when there are a whole lot more endings than there are new beginnings. One aspect of my life that has been unchanging in recent times, and is a daily joy to me, is my relationship with my wife, Debbie. We have gone through our ups and downs as married couples do, but the years with her at my side have been an unmitigated blessing. There is no way I can thank her adequately for her presence in my life.

I long ago gave up the extensive concert tours and hopes of becoming "the flavor of the month" in the tiny little subculture of the acoustic music world. I do continue to do numerous concerts, festivals and other sorts of gigs every year, and this summer, River City Folk will celebrate its 34th anniversary. Clete Baker in Omaha is still my partner and co-producer, and the talents and work of him and Dan Rhiger in Portland make the radio broadcast possible.

Winterfolk is in its 32nd year and has raised more than a quarter of a million dollars for Sisters of the Road Café, which equates to at least 250,000 meals to give the body and spirit of people going through tough circumstances a little nourishment and hope to keep going.

In 2019 the beneficiary of the event was changed to JOIN in Portland, an organization that aggressively finds housing for the homeless throughout the Portland metro area. It also has a day shelter that provides a stable address that folks can use for job applications and to receive mail. JOIN works with landlords and other entities to try to level the playing field a bit and put a roof over people's heads, something in the richest country on the earth you would think everyone would be entitled to.

My pal Tom Bryson moved to Germany in 2008, following the spiritual questing path that has defined his life the past many years. Though he and Claire Levine are no longer together, both remain incomparable friends and frequent correspondents. I see Claire often, and she still sponsors a house concert for me yearly.

Tom travels the world, giving workshops on a deep, powerful concept called "Constellations." I respect so much his willingness to follow "the road less taken," while reaching out a hand to those who can benefit from his study and mindfulness. He and his wife, Ursula, spend months of each year in Africa, banding and measuring the number and size of the amazing diversity of birds in Namibia, Zambia and Botswana. What stories he has been able to tell since he left Puddletown!

In 2009 I helped produce another album for Chris Kennedy, this time at Dan Rhiger's Medicine Whistle Studio, with Donny, Fuzzy and Dylan helping out. "Postcards from Main Street" has another batch of Chris's excellent, mostly western-oriented songs.

DAN RHIGER MEDICINE WHISTLE STUDIO, PORTLAND, OR

Probably my favorite is "Lincoln Highway," about the first transcontinental road across the country, built in the early years of the twentieth century.

It is also one of the songs he and I perform together when we get a chance to play guitar and sing as a duo, which we do as often as is feasible. That isn't not often enough, now, with myself in Washington State and Chris living in Michigan. For more than a decade we did an annual concert in the park in Rock Springs and other shows when the opportunity arose.

Having talked about the idea for many years, in 2013 Chris and I decided we would do a project at Dan's Medicine Whistle Studio, an album we titled, "Before the Time Slips Away." It is a CD of some songs of his, some songs of mine, and songs by favorites of ours (Gordon Lightfoot, Ian Tyson, etc.). It was great fun to produce. We basically set up two microphones for our voices, two for our guitars, had either Donny or Dylan join us on bass on the track, and let 'er rip. It is the very definition of live and authentic: We recorded all 14 tracks in one day.

As happens to all of us when we get older, there have been some very sad departures of dear friends from my script in recent years. Don Younger, drinking buddy, owner and founder of the Horse Brass Pub, world famous curmudgeon, and great patron of mine, passed away in January of 2011. I miss him every time I have a beer at the Brass, and think of him often.

For his wake, Joellen Piluso, who he left the pub to, hosted a massive tribute to him at the Horse Brass. You had to have an invite to actually get into the pub, it was so crowded, but there was a tent in the parking lot where almost 1,000 additional folks toasted him on that February Sunday afternoon. Don was so esteemed by the hospitality business in Portland that they donated beer, whisky and food for everyone who attended his wake – at no charge. The event reportedly cleaned out the area distributor's stock of Macallan 12 Scotch whiskey for weeks.

I was privileged to be asked to moderate the afternoon in the pub, and I made sure everyone had a chance to speak or sing on microphone who wanted to remember that charming, eccentric, unique soul that was Don Younger. Since it was a private party, smoking was allowed. (In Oregon, smoking in public places had become illegal in 2006 – one of the issues that infuriated Don the most. He would have been pleased to see the Horse Brass again enveloped in a blue haze, in his memory.)

After being ill for a few months, my pal David Rea died one day short of his 65th birthday, in October of 2011.

I helped his partner, Kathleen, put together a musical tribute to him at the Alberta Rose Theatre in Portland that following January. Donny and Dylan joined me at the concert on David's songs, "Hands Up," "Just a Sign," and "The Brass Ring."

**WITH DAVID REA AT ARTICHOKE MUSIC
PORTLAND, OR, 2011 (SCOTT DOCHERTY)**

Lots of other admirers and friends played a song and told a story or two about one of the really colorful talents of our time, who had been right in the middle of the folk revival of the 1960's, and who had never stopped writing, singing, and telling his unlikely stories – some of which were actually true!

We lost Fuzzy Purcell in early 2019, at age 72. He was a lifelong bachelor, kind of an enigmatic character in his habits and ways. But he was unfailingly kind and generous with his time, musical talent and friendship. He also helped keep River City Folk alive in the early 2000's, recording shows at his home studio in Salem.

I stopped performing at Kells in 2012. When most of the patrons aren't even as old as the age of the newest song you play that night, it might be time to call it quits. I am grateful for the hundreds of nights I performed there, and I learned a lot in that venue about how to get audiences involved and excited – and how short and low cut young women wear their partying dresses these days. I do miss that aspect of the gig, but most of all I miss playing and singing those ballads and tunes with Donny and Peggie in front of those raucous crowds.

In 2014 I released that CD of River City Folk duets, that I mentioned earlier, featuring songs I performed with some of my guests through the years. Performers include Italian guitar phenomenon Beppe Gambetta, the gentle poet Bill Morrissey, the peripatetic Bill Staines, Michael Johnson, Steve Gillette and more. I was delighted to discover a digital audio tape I had mixed of those performances that was still in excellent shape, and with Dan Rhiger's help I put it into the structure to release as an album.

There are lots of different styles on that project. It's a fair representation of what the program has always been about: Music that makes a difference. Most of the cuts were originally recorded back in Omaha in the 1990's.

I thought after all of those albums and recording sessions I was just about complete with all that, when I had a resurgence of ideas and songs surface in 2016. "A Road Worth Driving Down" is a collection of 11 self-penned songs which I believe to be some of the best work I have ever done.

Recorded at Dan Rhiger's Medicine Whistle Studio in piecemeal fashion throughout 2017, it features the wonderful accompaniment of guitarist Doug Smith on lead guitar, gifted dobro-banjo player Matt Snook, Donny's always-solid bass work and incomparable ear for harmonies and arrangements, along with fine mandolin work by Tim Connell, Billy Oskay's evocative fiddle, and other contributions by Dan and his wife, Rahmana.

"A Road Worth Driving Down" has and continues to receive a good bit of airplay on non-commercial stations in the U.S. that program this heartfelt music. For me, the highlights are the title song, written about that early morning departure from

"I WOULDN'T COUNT ON IT" — CONFESSIONS OF AN UNLIKELY FOLKSINGER

DOUG SMITH

Cody Wyoming in my Chevy Van, Maggie, in 2000; "Dear Companions," dedicated to the many kind souls without whom I never would have had to opportunity to do this; and "September 1862," about the Civil War battle of Antietam – comparing it to our own chaotic political times.

I had always wanted to write a song set in the Civil War, and I am proud of this effort.

September 1862
a memorial to the battle of Antietam

Johnny, my Johnny, now what's that sound I hear?
see the rows of the ragged men marching northward with no fear
only 50 miles from Washington, see the glint of their polished steel
I hope that they don't spot us, before we finish our breakfast meal

It's warm here close to Sharpsburg, but summer's almost done
perhaps we will be spared, if this battle can be won
we crushed them again at Bull Run, and Shenandoah in the east
if we rout them this far north, perhaps they just might sue for peace

chorus
So c'mon boys, build up that fire, the nights are chilly now

Thanks

forget your homes and your sweethearts far away
break the coffee beans with the rifle butts, add some turnips to the stew
we're camped beside Antietam Creek, it's September 1862

Burnside moves so slowly-McClellan's even worse
even knowing Robert Lee's plans, these generals are a curse
to the brave men dressed in blue, who outnumber the rebels 2 to 1
who will die in bloody lanes, before this battlefield is won

McClellan lacks resolve, but Lee has resolve to spare
so much so that he leaves but one way, for us to escape and get out of there
the two great armies blunder, 'til they meet on that gruesome day
if the rebels can somehow triumph, France and Britain might join the fray

repeat chorus

Stonewall Jackson takes Harpers Ferry, then joins Longstreet in the field
gallant men fall to minie balls and calvary swords of tempered steel
the carnage of the shrapnel, from the cannons relentless fire
makes countless women widows, dressed in funeral attire

advantage gained and lost, until the bridges finally fall
to the overwhelming force of the Union, until no ground is gained at all
The order for retreat is heard, in Lee's reluctant voice
atop his grey mare "Traveler" he can see he has no choice

repeat chorus

No day in our short history, has cost so many brave men's lives
given grudgingly on both sides, so that the nation could survive
so that Lincoln could proclaim, the sin of slavery was at an end

> with a prayer to our better angels, that we could unite again
>
> Now 150 years have passed and the country is restless still
> hear the echoes of Jim Crow, feel the ghost of Emmett Till
> across the land folks are voting again, out of ignorance and fear
> against that battle cry of freedom, they no longer seem to
> > hear.........
>
> chorus

Tom May copyright 2016 Blue Vignette, ASCAP

Finally on the album, "Wherever I Go" is for my wife Debbie – kind of an apology for not always being the kind of man I have aspired to be for her.

Richard Columbo and his partner, Jim Morris, kept Artichoke Music on Hawthorne Ave. in Portland alive – by sheer determination, hard work and talent. It has one of the finest little concert halls in the country, where I performed often and also recorded numerous live radio River City Folk broadcasts in front of enthusiastic audiences.

They have moved on and are now doing an independent series of concerts and workshops in Northeast Portland. Artichoke improbably survived, becoming a non-profit and moving to its current Powell Blvd. location in Portland. It is still a wonderful venue for acoustic music concerts and instruction. There are not many institutions in the United States like Artichoke left: The Old Town School of Folk Music in Chicago and Swallowhill in Denver would be two remaining stalwarts. We are very fortunate that under the direction of Bob Howard, Alexa MacDonald and the rest of the board and volunteers, Artichoke Music perseveres and prospers.

Helping to keep Artichoke Music alive was the web design and promotional work of Scott Docherty. (redhare.com). Scott Docherty has been an important collaborator - and a dear friend – in so many of my creative endeavors of recent years. He is one of the most talented graphic designers I have ever known, as well as being a fine musician, and he ran a self-sacrificing folk venue (is there any other kind?) in Astoria, Oregon, for a few years.

He designed my website, (www.tommayfolk.com), Winterfolk posters and promotional materials, and a number of the album covers for other artists as well as myself. He and his wife, Mary, believed in the Winterfolk mission so passionately they started a similar even, titled RiverFolk, to benefit the homeless in Astoria.

Another patron for just about every creative and charitable project I have directed in recent years is Bill Howe and his wife Joy Botinelli. When River City Folk needed funding to proceed, when a Winterfolk headliner requires expenses, when Wayne Hoffman's North County Folk Festival needed insurance money so it could happen, Bill has always been there with words of encouragement, backed with a check to make those kind of dreams a reality. He believes in funding the arts of music and theatre on a grassroots level and has made a concrete difference with his generosity to a wide variety of arts presentations.

My son, Dylan May, has gone on to front his own funk n' soul band, as well as obtaining his

WINTERFOLK 25

"I WOULDN'T COUNT ON IT" — CONFESSIONS OF AN UNLIKELY FOLKSINGER

master's degree in education and making a positive impact by teaching kids. He released his own hard-hitting, excellent CD, "Empty Fields," in spring 2018. He performs frequently in the area with that powerful ensemble as well as playing solo.

In these days of severe cutbacks to musical programs in the schools, he also brings his bass into the classroom and incorporates songs, singing and the joy of melodic discovery into the basic curriculum. His students are fortunate to have him as their teacher, as I am to have him for a son. I could not be more proud of him – the musician, and most importantly the person, he has become.

"In the late twentieth century, to be a traveling singer/songwriter is the last great romantic endeavor."

This is a direct quote from an old friend in Nashville, Tennessee. He was a little too exclusive, I think – there are a number of other quixotic pursuits in the arts that also fit that bill. That being said, I agree with the essence of those words, and I consider myself among the luckiest of men to have lived my life doing this music I truly believe in.

As far as the result of all of these decades of striving in this alternative vocation, I think the results are somewhere between David Rea's quote, "Ain't nuthin' gonna be okay nohow" – and this book's title, "I wouldn't count on it."

I have made lots of mistakes and done more than my share of things I regret, but I will never look back with anything but gratitude towards the faithful friends, fascinating destinations, blue roads, good bottles of wine and the more subtle yet extravagant rewards of this profession.

> "Memory is like riding a trail at night with a lighted torch. The torch casts its light only so far, and beyond that is darkness"
>
> -Ancient Lakota saying, borrowed from the book, "The Heart of Everything that Is" (Bob Drury-Tom Clavin Simon-Schuster 2013)

I have tried to snatch a bit of light from that darkness in the memories retold in this book.

In 1980, at the Reilly cabin in Colorado, I wrote a song that has become a kind of benediction at the close of my shows over the past decades. I will leave you with this expression of gratefulness. See you down the road, with any kind of luck at all...

Thanks

To all of those who've talked to me, and shared a laugh or two
to the gentleman in Edmonton who showed me what to do
to those who listen faithfully, even those who are untrue,
to all of those, and to everyone I say

Chorus

Thank you for your time, you make the pleasure mine
you underline the words to every line in every song
I'd be dead wrong if I thought that I could do this on my own
thanks for never leavin' me alone

To all of those in the alley, who gave me an even break
to the man who handed me the only chance I couldn't take
To good coffee in the mornin', when I'm only half awake
to all of those and to everything I say

Chorus

To all of those tonight, who took the time to share
to the drivers and the pilots and all the ones who got me here
To the women who changed my viewpoint, and put up with my
    long hair
to all of those and to everyone I say

Chorus

Tom May copyright 1981 Blue Vignette, ASCAP

WINTERFOLK 32, FEBRUARY 2020 (ELIZABETH CAMPBELL)

For complete discography, tour schedule, details on "River City Folk" radio and Portland's annual "Winterfolk" concert, please visit www.tommayfolk.com

ACKNOWLEDGMENTS

My wife Debbie Dutton, for more than I can possibly express in words alone –

Claire Levine, for forty years of friendship, and hours of patience and work with me on this unruly manuscript –

Bill Howe and Joy Botinelli, for their unwavering support and belief in my artistic and charitable efforts –

To my radio co-producer Clete Baker in Omaha, Nebraska, and recording engineer Dan Rhiger at Medicine Whistle studio in Portland Oregon: who have both made so much of what has been accomplished in these past years possible. Also to Scott Docherty in Astoria, Oregon for his design, photography and website expertise, and shared belief in what this music stands for –

Chris Kennedy, for being the worlds best correspondent and a true pal, musical and otherwise, always –

My son Dylan, who I am so proud of –

The fine work of Masha Shubin and the folks at Inkwater –

Lastly to all the dear companions, rogues and scoundrels, travelers and pickers, and all of you mad musicians-who have made this creative journey anything but dull. I am so very grateful to each and every one of you –

ALSO BY TOM MAY

Promoting Your Music: The Lovin' of the Game
Routledge Publishers, 2007

Paperback 978-0-415-97757-9
Hardback 978-0-415-97756-2

"...funny, instructive stores and recollections gleaned from interviews with veteran players such as Gordon Lightfoot and Eliza Gilkyson, and from his own memory banks, because he's got a story or two from his four decades in the biz. An Old Byrds song taught us how to be Rock n' Roll stars, but until Tom May's new book "Promoting Your Music; The Lovin' of the Game" there have been few how-to guides about making a career writing and playing your own music."

JOHN FOYSTON, FEATURE WRITER, "THE OREGONIAN", PORTLAND, OREGON

JUNE 8TH 2007 LIVING SECTION

Anyone who has ever dreamed of becoming a professional singer/songwriter, but doesnt know how, or perhaps needs a refresher course, can learn something from Promoting Your Music. Folk musicians Tom May and Dick Weissman share with the reader their wealth of experiences and the insights of their peers in a practical way so that the lessons become an indispensible reference for beginning and seasoned performers.

--DIRTY LINEN

"...very informative and well paced; A must have handbook for singer-songwriters of all levels and experience."

Martin Sneyd, singer/songwriter, Dublin, Ireland

"Folk music legends May and Weissman have here a concise, entertaining, and above all an encouraging instructional book for anyone looking for a little recognition, or a little dough! The book is written in the first person, mostly May but often a blend, and frequently uses vivid and often mirthful examples to illustrate its ever-so-practical advice. Greatly enlivening the text are the many contributions by friends such as Eliza Gilkyson and Gordon Lightfoot. Though the author's experiences make the book decidedly "acoustic" the lessons apply to anyone in music and should be required reading. Fortunately, this course is so fun and interesting."

Tom Peterson, Victory Review, Seattle, WA September 2007

"I really enjoyed the book, and thank you for putting it out there. I knew some of the information already, but there's so much more that it would take me years to figure out on my own. Part of me wishes I'd known all this before I started down this musical road. Writing books for musicians isn't exactly the way to make the best seller list. But I think this is an excellent book for any performing writer/artist to own."

Loren Davidson, singer/songwriter, California.
Music with tropical attitude - http://www.lorendavidson.com

www.ingramcontent.com/pod-product-compliance
Lightning Source LLC
Chambersburg PA
CBHW031055080526
44587CB00011B/689